TRAPPED IN TUSCANY
LIBERATED BY THE
BUFFALO SOLDIERS
The True
World War II Story
of
Tullio Bruno Bertini

DANTE UNIVERSITY PRESS
Boston

© Copyright 1998
by Dante University Foundation of America Press

Library of Congress Cataloging-in-Publication Data

Bertini, Tullio, 1930-
      Trapped in Tuscany : the true World War II story of
Tullio Bertini.
               p. cm.
      Includes bibliographical references and index.
      ISBN 0-9378-3235-9 (pbk. : alk. paper)

      1. Bertini, Tullio Bruno, 1930-
      2. World War, 1939-1945--Italy--Tuscany.
      3. World War, 1939-1945--Personal narratives,
               American.
      4. Italian Americans--Italy--Tuscany--Biography.
      5. Tuscany (Italy)--Social life and customs.
      I. Title.
      D802.I82T9219   1998
      940.54'0945--dc21   98-2884
                                                     CIP

DANTE UNIVERSITY OF AMERICA PRESS
17 Station Street
Box 843 Brookline Village
Boston, MA 02147

CONTENTS

1. The Bertini family circa 1900. Grandfather Emilio was in California. Left to right: Fridola, Rosa, grandmother Teresa Bertini, Amelia. Front: Clotilde and eight-year-old Nello Bertini, father of the author.

2. Top: Nello Bertini, U.S. Citizenship photo in 1929.
3. Bottom: Ada Marcucci Bertini, passport photo in 1934.

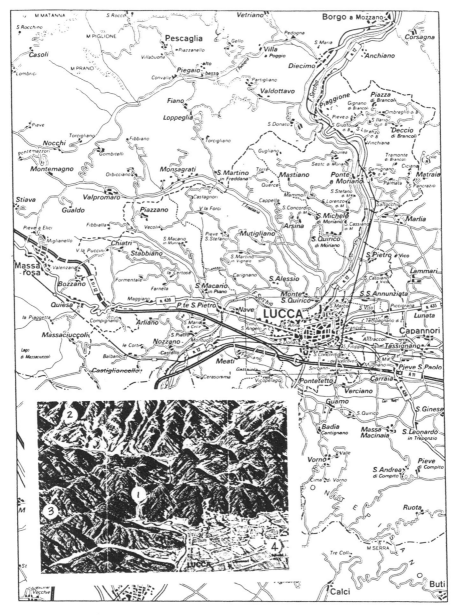

4. Detailed map of Lucca and surroundings. Diecimo is located in the upper right. Convalle is located near Pescaglia, upper left. Pieve di Compito is located at the lower right.

5. Insert: Topographic map shows the mountains around Lucca: 1. Diecimo; 2. Barga; 3. Convalle; 4. Istituto Cavanis, Porcari.

1.
A BOSTON CHILDHOOD

My mother was Ada Marcucci, born in Diecimo, province of Lucca, Italy, on October 23, 1899. She married Nello Bertini in 1920, and, the same year, emigrated to the United States, settling in Boston. My parents moved into an apartment at 9 Shawmut Street, in the Italian section of Boston, and began working. She worked as a seamstress, doing piece work on men's shirts from 1920 to 1930. After I was born, in 1930, she stopped working to stay home with me.

My father, Nello Bertini, was born in Vetriano, near Diecimo, on March 14, 1894. He left Italy in 1908 and at the age of 14, traveled to the United States by himself and began working in restaurants as a dishwasher.

His trip from Genova to Boston was difficult, his contacts being names of people from Diecimo working and living in Boston. On arriving, he located one of them and was given a room in a rooming house for Italian men working in city restaurants. He got a job as a dishwasher and gradually improved his job by learning minor cooking skills, eventually becoming a cook. In 1914, at the age of 20, he returned to Italy to serve in the Italian Army for the duration of World War I. After the war, he remained in Diecimo, married my mother in 1920, and both returned to the United States.

On November 25, 1929, my father became a citizen of the United States in Boston. They moved to 16 Winchester Street, Bay Village, then to 61 Carver Street, Bay Village, in the same building with my father's two sisters, Fridola and Clotilde.

I was born in Boston on July 13, 1930. Within the first year of my life, we moved to Brighton, renting a small house at 35 Cushman Road. In 1934, when I was four years old, after returning from spending the summer in Italy, we moved to 59 Goodenough Street in Brighton, renting the first story flat from Mr. and Mrs. Max Singer.

My earliest memories of my parents are from my early childhood. My mother was a small person, slight, with dark brown hair. She took me out for walks in the neighborhood, letting me play with other children. At first, I did not speak English with the children because I spoke Italian at home. As I began to play in the neighborhood, I learned to speak English and continued to learn more at home. My mother had many sewing skills which she used to make articles of clothing for me. She liked to dress well and enjoyed going into Boston to shop at the Jordan-Marsh department store. Being an only child, I felt she catered to my wishes and perhaps spoiled me a bit. She was always concerned about my health and afraid that I would catch colds. Whenever I left the house, she made certain that I was properly bundled up and well protected from the cold.

My father was a heavy-set man, not very tall, and a hard worker. He seemed to be tired in the evenings after he returned home from work. He enjoyed smoking cigarettes and liked to drink red wine and to socialize with his Italian friends and relatives on Sundays. When we lived on Cushman Road, my parents occasionally asked a couple from Diecimo, Emilio and Lucia Giannotti, to baby sit me while they went out. Emilio and Lucia returned to Diecimo in 1938 and remained in Italy until they died in the 1980's.

On September 21, 1938 we survived the big hurricane that hit the East Coast. Heavy rains with winds of 70 miles per hour struck the New England states causing monumental damages. The Red Cross reported 700 people dead, 1,754 injured and 63,000 people rendered homeless. The

United States Weather Bureau in Washington refused to believe that the storm was going to develop into a full-scale hurricane and did not warn the people in the New England states. The Bureau thought that the storm would eventually dissipate and head out to sea. By 2 p.m. there still were no special warnings for the people, yet Providence, Rhode Island was under water, being flooded by the surging sea. Looters were ransacking department stores and the National Guard was activated. Many did not even read about the hurricane in the newspapers, primarily because much of the news was focused on events in Europe.

The headlines in the papers on the morning of September 22 were about Europe, how, late in the afternoon of September 21, the Czech government capitulated to German forces. Americans did not know about the hurricane; it seemed as if it were kept secret from the public!

I remember the hurricane vividly, especially the high speed winds. I was attending Mary Lyon elementary school in Brighton. When I got home in the afternoon, as usual, I went to the neighborhood park on Faneuil Street to play with my friends. I walked into the wind, and remember how hard it was to walk from our house on Goodenough Street, around the corner and over to the park. Some of the large trees in the park had already fallen to the ground, and the smaller ones with supple trunks were bent by the wind in such a way that the tops would touch the ground. When the wind brought in the heavy rain, I went home because this type of weather was very unusual for Brighton and it seemed unsafe for me to be out and about.

Ours was a two story house with wood shingle siding. The entrance to our level was from the front, after climbing seven or eight steps. The front door was on the left side and led into the living room, followed by a dining room and further back was the kitchen. There was a hallway to the right which led to my bedroom facing the front of the house; my parents' bedroom was to the rear along with the bathroom. There was also a back door leading to the yard and to the basement. The basement contained a wringer type clothes washer and the coal boiler unit which provided the heat during the winter months by circulating hot water into the cast iron heating units in the rooms.

When I arrived home, I saw my mother listening to the radio for news. The newscaster was saying that we were having a full force hurricane and that people should stay in their homes for safety reasons. My father usually arrived home at seven o'clock, commuting from downtown Boston with the subway and then connecting to the local bus or streetcar.

That evening, he arrived late because the electrical power in Boston was shut down, the subway cars were not running, and the electricity to our neighborhood was also interrupted because of fallen power lines affecting the bus schedule in Brighton. My mother and I spent the evening by candle light waiting for my father to come home, listening to the rain and high winds, feeling helpless, and missing my favorite radio programs.

After spending the night listening to the wind and rain and not getting much sleep, we awoke to a somewhat calm day, blue-grayish skies, and no wind. It was raining very slightly, and it seemed safe enough to venture out into the neighborhood. As we walked around the streets, we were surprised to see how many trees had fallen across streets and sidewalks, blocking the flow of automobiles and buses. School is an important aspect of a child's life, but at times it is nice not to have to go to school. I was glad that school was going to be closed for a few days. The electric power remained off for about a day and a half. When it finally returned, we listened to our radio to get the latest news about the storm.

According to radio reports it was calculated that the hurricane toppled enough trees to build 200,000 homes. As the storm unfolded the newspapers and the radio did not fully report the disaster to the rest of the country, so the majority of people in the United States did not know many details about the 1938 hurricane on the East Coast.

In our home, things returned to normal after two or three days. The schools re-opened, cars and buses began to move again, electricity was restored, and my father was able to return to work, commuting from Brighton to downtown Boston by streetcar, bus and the subway.

In 1939 there were two world's fairs in the United States, one in New York City, the other at the Golden Gate Exposition in San Francisco. The New York World's Fair, called the *World of Tomorrow*, offered the public a view of things to come in the future. Germany was the only major nation not participating. The big hit of the fair was the General Motors Futurama exhibit showing what America would be like in the 1960's.

Norman Bel Geddes described in his writings what America would be like in the future and predicted that tall, tanned, vigorous people would spend most of their time having fun. The country would be connected by large super highways, the landscape would be built to bring more automobiles into cities at a faster rate even though there were no apparent provisions for parking.

As a nine year old boy living in Brighton, I was somewhat aware of the New York World's Fair. I neither read the newspapers except for the *funnies* nor listened to radio news programs. I knew about the World's Fair because of the merchandising in the local department and five-and-ten-cent stores of a certain World's Fair item that appealed to me. As a logo for the fair, New York selected a large sphere with a tall obelisk or spike on the side. There were two types of World's Fair rings sold in Brighton which fascinated

me. One was priced at about $10 and the other at about
$1.00. I tried to talk my mother into buying me the expen-
sive ring, but I was not able to convince her to spend the
$10.00. She did buy the $1.00 ring, though.

The ring was made of brass with a gold-like plating and
an expandable overlapping band. The top surface showed
the sphere and spike displayed on an oval face about a half-
inch in diameter. The metal was thin and the design
embossed into the metal from the back, with very sharp
edges on the underside that always left an impression of the
design on my ring finger. The words *New York World's Fair
1939* were also displayed on the ring. I wore it with pride
even though my finger turned green.

I mention the New York World's Fair and the ring
because the Fair and the ring are symbolic to me regarding
a specific time in my life in which events led me to Tuscany
and to the Gothic Line in wartime Italy.

During the Fall of 1938, my father was working as a chef
for Warmuth's Restaurant in Boston, on Devonshire Street
near the business section. He had been working there since
he and my mother arrived in Boston in 1920. He worked his
way up from kitchen helper to cook, to chef, to executive
chef, and was respected by his fellow workers, many of
whom were also Italian immigrants.

Warmuth's was an American restaurant catering to
businessmen by providing quality lunches at reasonable
prices. In January 1932, the *Boston Evening American* did a
feature story on my father with the headline:

**"MAGGIE'S FIGHT IS OFF...BUT JUST FOR TO-
NIGHT!**
Congressmen and diplomats join in feast in Washington
to honor Jiggs."

A large photograph of my father was printed in the paper with the article, with a superimposed picture of the cartoon character Jiggs, indicating that, "Nello Bertini, chef at Warmuth's restaurant, is shown at work preparing the corned beef and cabbage with which he made Jiggs happy." The superimposed picture of Jiggs, holding a bomb, was the insignia of the 11th Bombardment Squadron, U.S. Army.

The reporter who wrote the article made reference to a conversation between Maggie and Jiggs, as follows:

"How about something to eat?"

Jiggs looked up and there, beside him, found none other than Nello Bertini, chef de luxe of Charlie Warmuth's Devonshire Street food emporium.

"How about corn beef and cabbage, Jiggs," the chef queried.

"My boss says you've been trying so hard and so long to get it, you are entitled to it."

Sweet words, unbelievable, but true. Jiggs knew the payment in store but risked the wrath of Maggie and followed the chef down a flight of stairs into a kitchen already permeating with aromas of corn beef and cabbage. Later Jiggs wiped away the ends of cabbage from his lips.

"Say, Bertini, how did you make this? This is great corned beef and cabbage. One of the best plate fulls I've had since Maggie used to make it in the good old days."

"Well, Jiggs, my man, like this the recipe goes:

"You take some corn beef brisket and put it into a pot of boiling water. When it is about half cooked, take off some of the stock, the broth, you know, from the meat and boil the cabbage in this in a separate pot. Let each cook separately. Then serve it with boiled potato and piccalilli and with any other vegetables you like. That's all there is to it."

"Well, it has been a happy celebration for me, my good man," said Jiggs. "You have my blessings."

The reporter stated in the story that the banquet to honor the 11th Bombardment Squadron was held in Washington D.C. on January 25, 1932 and was attended by three cabinet members, 31 senators, 91 representatives and five members of the diplomatic corps as guests of King Features Syndicate celebrating the 20 year anniversary of the comic strip by George McManus. The comic strip featured Jiggs and Maggie and incidents about their married life. Maggie had high-society friends, such as Lord and Lady Bilgewater, while Jiggs was a down-to-earth man, always craving corned beef and cabbage.

I have cherished the newspaper article over the years because it is evidence that my father was well respected.

After recovering from the hurricane and dealing with the snow and cold during the winter months, it seemed as if it would be a good year for me. I was in third grade and really enjoying school.

In 1937 my father purchased a maroon two-door Chevrolet sedan, which he kept in a rented garage down Goodenough Street, right at the top of a slight hill. During the winter, when there was snow on the ground, my friends and I took out our sleds, rode them to the bottom of the hill, and carried them back up the hill over and over again. The hill was steep enough to get a really good sled ride which would carry us all the way down to the main street on which the bus and streetcar ran.

The playground around the corner had a sunken baseball diamond and field. During winter the park staff flooded the baseball field with water, and it became an ice skating pond. I never was brave enough to ice skate, because at the time, I had flat feet and weak ankles, having to wear special support shoes. But it was fun to walk over to the park and watch children and adults ice skating. Usually the streets were covered with snow until the plow trucks came by to clear it, but forming large piles of snow on each side of the street, covering most of the sidewalks and making walking very difficult. When I was allowed to play outside in the snow my friends and I carved out the underside of the snow mounds, then crawled inside pretending we were in igloos.

Winter was difficult to deal with because of the cold weather. My most enjoyable outings, however, took place on Saturday afternoons, when I went to the local movie theater, the Egyptian Theater, for the Saturday movie matinee. I walked to the theater about a mile and a half from our home. Many of the kids also went, walking along as a group. This one time, I walked to the movies with Paul and Vince Sheehan, good friends living around the corner at 109 Parson Street. Paul was my age, about the same height with blond hair. Vincent was a couple of years older with dark hair. My mother usually gave me 15 cents for the afternoon. I spent ten cents for the admission and five cents on candy, usually a package of Walnettos or a Baby Ruth candy bar. The theater generally showed some type of a continuing serial first, then the main feature, usually a western.

Very often on a Sunday afternoon, around 5 p.m., I also went to the Egyptian Theater with my parents. I enjoyed going with them because my father drove and because better movies were shown. Sometimes we also drove to Boston when the weather was nice, to 61 Carver Street to visit my aunts, uncles and cousins.

Giacomo and Fridola Luvisi lived in one flat with their two children, Joe and Teresa. Giacomo worked in Boston at the Hotel Lucerne as a waiter. Fridola was one of my father's older sisters; she was tall and resembled my grandfather Emilio Bertini. Iacopo and Clotilde Pacini lived in another flat with their son Elmo. Iacopo worked with my father as a cook at Warmuth's. Iacopo was born in Casabasciana, near Bagni di Lucca, a few kilometers from Diecimo. Clotilde was the youngest of the Bertini girls and, facially, resembled my father and grandmother Teresa Bertini. My first cousin Elmo was six months older than I, had dark hair, brown eyes and was about my size. I enjoyed the Sunday visits with them, especially being with Elmo. We had similar interests and played well together. Joe and Teresa Luvisi were a few years older and had other interests. We played around the house, went to the roof top and looked at the view of Boston, and also played outside in the dead-end street in front of their house. We usually had a big meal in the early afternoon, then drove back to Brighton before it got dark. We also visited my aunt Rosa DaRu, who lived in Lexington, on Massachusetts Avenue. She was a widow with two sons, Dennis and Emilio. Rosa was my favorite aunt because she catered to me and had a good sense of humor. She always gave me empty milk and soda bottles to return to the grocery store down the block where I used the refunds to buy candy.

Early in the spring of 1939 something happened to my father which drastically altered our lives. One day, he left for work as usual. He took the street car from Brighton early in the morning, transferred to the subway, then reported to work at the restaurant. When he arrived, the son of the former owner, who had taken over after his father's death, told my father that he was fired and for him to clear out his personal belongings and go home.

My father could not believe what was happening. He had been a loyal worker for 19 years and was caught off guard by the predicament. Later he mentioned that he was especially disturbed by the fact that many of the workers were Italian friends from Boston, including my uncle Iacopo, and he felt that they apparently were aware that he was going to be released from his job but did not warn him of what was about to happen. He was absolutely devastated by the turn of events. He was a very dedicated worker for Warmuth's, a respected chef, and now, at age 45, he felt his career collapse! I remember coming home and being surprised to see him there at the table with a glass of wine, talking in a somber way with my mother. I figured that something was wrong, and I asked what happened.

He simply said, "*Mi hanno detto di andare via...*" (They told me to go away...).

At the time, I was eight and a half years old and in the third grade. Our family lifestyle changed immediately because my father became very depressed. I continued to attend school while my mother and father had many discussions trying to figure out what they should do. At first my father decided to start looking for another job as a chef but he was not very successful. He still wanted to stay in Boston but it seemed that there were not any appropriate jobs available. He started to look around the nearby resort regions, such as Cape Cod. We drove to various locations on weekends, stopping by hotels and restaurants. He would go inside and return to the car even more dejected.

During that period, my father had many discussions about Warmuth's, being upset about the method used to fire him, that is, allowing him to come to work, and then firing him in front of all his co-workers. He felt that some of the workers who knew about the firing should have warned him not to go into work on that day. Since my uncle Iacopo was one of the workers at Warmuth's I sensed that the relationship between my father and his sister Clotilde and her husband Iacopo became strained, thus affecting my association with my best friend, my cousin Elmo. We stopped going to Boston on Sundays with Fridola and Clotilde, so I did not get to see much of Elmo during the spring of 1939.

Later in the spring, in May, I overheard discussions between my mother and father regarding the possibility of leaving Boston for California or Italy. My mother's aunt Marianna lived in South San Francisco and would welcome us to stay with her until my father found a job and got us settled into a house of our own. The situation regarding Italy was a bit different.

After my father came to the United States in 1920, he began to save money and was encouraged by his mother and father in Italy to purchase property in Diecimo. His parents then worked the land and did not have to worry about providing food for themselves and for their youngest son, Alceste. My father, against the advice of my mother, began to buy parcels of land in the 1920's and 1930's, including a large house, and a smaller house and barn. According to official records, he bought parcels of land in 1921, 1923, 1925, 1934 and in 1937.

My grandparents moved into the larger house, worked the fields, raised seasonal crops, considering the land and house as their own. If we were to go to Italy, we could either live with my grandparents or fix up the smaller house and barn and make it into a home for ourselves. My father had saved a small amount of money, and, at the time, he seemed to think that we could live on that plus the amount of money that farm crops would generate in Diecimo.

Many European immigrants had similar fixations: come to America, work, save money, and, once they accumulated enough money, return to their native villages, purchase a house with land, and be set for the rest of their lives. It was interesting, in retrospect, that my parents did not seem concerned with the events in Europe, especially what was happening in a Germany becoming more and more Nazi.

In May of 1939 the Wehrmacht leadership had a very low opinion of the Italian military forces. Hitler pressed for a military alliance with Italy and Mussolini was in no hurry to reach an agreement. Count Galeazzo Ciano, Foreign Minister, met with Joachim Ribbentrop in Milano on May 6, 1939, with instructions from Mussolini to emphasize to the Germans that Italy wished to avoid war for at least three years. The Duce, after a discussion of the meeting with Count Ciano, decided that it would be best for Italy to complete a military alliance with Germany, resulting in the *Pact of Steel*, and signed at the Reich Chancellery in Berlin on May 22, 1939. The core of the treaty was Article III:

> If contrary to the wishes and hopes of the High Contracting Parties it should happen that one of them became involved in warlike complications with another Power or Powers, the other High Contracting Party would immediately come to its assistance as an ally and support it with all its military forces on land, sea, and in the air.

Seemingly unaware of these events during the latter part of May, Nello and Ada Bertini decided to return to Italy. Their plans were to leave Boston on July 15 and travel to Italy on the Italian Line's *M/N Vulcania*.

The *Vulcania* was a 24,000 ton *motonave*, part of the Italian fleet crossing the Atlantic Ocean and into the Mediterranean Sea, ending up in Venezia.

When my parents decided to go to Italy, I was in school. I did not realize the implications associated with leaving the United States. We had traveled to Italy during the summer of 1934, on the *Rex*, the premier ship of the Italian Line. We spent the summer in Diecimo, living with my paternal grandparents. I was four years old then, and I remember having had a good time. I also enjoyed the ship and all the activities aboard. The thought of going to Italy again was exciting and I looked forward to the vacation. To be honest, as a nine year old, I do not remember any discussion either with my parents or relatives about Europe. I do not even recall hearing the name of Mussolini, and I don't think that my parents were really aware of the pact between Mussolini and Hitler.

After school ended, around mid-June, we made our final preparations to leave. Our landlords, Mr. and Mrs. Singer, felt sorry we were leaving because we were good friends and good tenants. Max Singer was a policeman in Boston and was also active in the Veterans of Foreign Wars. I have a photograph of Mr. Max Singer shaking hands with President Franklin D. Roosevelt in the White House.

My mother was not really happy about returning to Italy, but she could not do anything about the situation since my father made up his mind to leave Boston. She worked hard preparing our household goods and began to pack items in boxes, trunks and suitcases. For some unknown reason, my parents also decided to take their bedroom set consisting of twin beds, a commode, a chest of drawers, and another chest of drawers with mirror. Only later in life did I realize that they had intended to remain in Italy, because they brought with them their complete bedroom set, which was packaged in large wooden crates by a shipping company.

As mid-July approached, I got nervous about leaving my friends and my neighborhood. I thought about my birthday on July 13, and was upset that because of the July 15 departure I would have to forego my ninth birthday party.

Our house gradually became empty. The shipping company removed the crated bedroom set and trunks. My mother and father gave away other furniture items to neighbors and relatives. My father sold the 1937 Chevrolet to my cousin Dennis DaRu. A couple of days before our departure, we left the house on Goodenough Street with my cousin Dennis, who came to pick us up and take us to my aunt Fridola's for the last two nights in America. I remember my dispirited feeling when I walked out of the empty flat and said good-bye to Mrs. Singer. I thought about my bedroom, the large radio in the living room, my favorite programs, looking out of the living room window in winter and seeing the snow, waiting at the living room window for my father to arrive late at night, and the tap at the window signaling he was home. We broke down our home during the preceding weeks.

Our belongings were gone and I was going to leave my friends and memories of my neighborhood. I said good-bye to Paul and Vincent Sheehan in front of their house and Mrs. Sheehan posed with us for pictures while shaking hands. Later, she sent us copies in Italy. In December 1996 I contacted Paul Sheehan in Florida and spoke with him on the telephone.

On Saturday July 15, 1939 we left my aunt's apartment on Carver Street and took a taxicab to the port of Boston. As we drove across Boston, we followed many familiar streets and passed by some of the landmarks in the city while I was wondering whether I would ever see Boston again. As we reached the port area, I spotted the ship.

The *Vulcania* was a large ship with a single smoke stack. It was designated as a *motonave* or motorized ship and was approximately 180 meters long, more than two football fields. My father purchased Cabin Class tickets and we were going to be located on the A deck with an outside cabin. The dining room was located directly below us on the B deck. First class cabins were above us on the *Ponte Principale* and *Ponte delle Verande*. The *Ponte del Sole* was the top-most deck and had a first class swimming pool. The Cabin Class swimming pool was located on the *Ponte delle Verande* to the rear of the ship. When we arrived at the dock area the taxi driver pulled up very close to the gang plank and unloaded all the suitcases. My father paid the cab driver and shortly after, a porter loaded our luggage on a hand cart and led us to our cabin.

Several relatives and friends came aboard the *Vulcania* to wish us a bon voyage. Old family photographs help me recall those who actually came aboard. A group photograph shows my uncle Giacomo Luvisi and his children Teresa and

Joe. My cousin Emilio DaRu, brother of Dennis, was also present. Elmo was there by himself, having come with Giacomo, while his mother and father remained at home. Mrs. Singer was also present as well as two ladies named Ida and Norma from Goodenough Street. Looking at the old photographs I still observe the look on my father's face in most of the pictures. He was not happy. His face was mournful, his mouth without smiles.

I was dressed in short pants and matching jacket. In most pictures I showed interest in what was taking place, but not looking particularly happy.

The *Vulcania* had come to Boston from New York the day before. In the late afternoon, announcements were made on the public address system for all the visitors to go ashore. We said good-bye to our friends and relatives and watched them descend the gangplank, waving to each other. We watched silently as preparations were made for the tug boats to lead us out to the open waters. As the sun began to set, we started moving out to sea, ready to cross the Atlantic and to begin our voyage to Italy.

I awoke on Sunday morning in this strange place. As the sun came up, the rays of sunlight came through the port hole, hitting me directly on the face. Suddenly, I realized I was not at home, but in a small and confining cabin, without any expectation to go play with my friends or run through my neighborhood. I was assigned to the top bunk and thus had a good view of the ocean from the port hole. While taking care of my morning bathroom needs I realized that the bathroom and shower were also extremely small.

We managed to get dressed and prepared ourselves to go to breakfast in the Cabin Class dining room. We were assigned a table and a waiter for the trip. The menu for the meals was extensive with several choices for each course.

At breakfast I ate cold cereal with milk and hot chocolate. My parents had *caffè e latte* (milk and coffee) with toast. After breakfast I ventured out on my own to explore the ship, discovering several children of my age. Being bilingual, I was able to speak with them in English or in Italian, although I considered English my primary language. I understood Italian, and responded in English whenever my parents spoke to me in Italian. Most of the families on the *Vulcania* seemed to be Italian, so one heard Italian most of the time. While I spoke with other passengers either in Italian or English, my parents spoke Italian between themselves and broken English in public, unless they discovered that the people preferred to speak Italian.

The crew spoke Italian and in the dining room the waiters spoke either Italian or English. Public address announcements were made in both languages, especially the lifeboat drill, directing us to report to a certain location and receive instructions regarding the lifeboats and life jackets.

Our daily routines were typical. We had deck chairs assigned to us and spent time on deck relaxing in the *sdraia*, looking at the immense ocean. My mother read magazines while I sat back watching people walk by. The water was calm and the fresh ocean air refreshing. I don't remember much more except that I made friends with other children, played shuffleboard, watched people swim in the pool, and walked around the decks. After dinner each night in the lounge, the staff set up a horse race with a track layout and large wooden horses each numbered 1 to 6. One then bet on the horses. By rolling dice, the horses advanced according to numbers appearing on the dice. The horse crossing the finish line first won, and those who bet on that horse won cash, depending on the established odds.

We traveled several days without seeing land. We were told that after about six days we would see the Azores Islands off the coast of Portugal. We were scheduled to make a brief stop and drop off a few passengers. I was very excited at the thought of seeing land after being at sea for so long, and fascinated by the action of the tug boats, how they maneuvered the ship toward the dock. On the other side of the ship, a large number of small wooden rowboats assembled in the water, full of young boys in swimming trunks, asking the passengers to throw coins into the water. Several passengers reached into their pockets and began to throw nickels, dimes and quarters. The boys then dove into the water to retrieve them. They were great swimmers and very daring. They followed the coins down several feet. They would catch them and quickly swim to the surface. Because of the clear water, it was possible to follow their progress while reaching for the coins, and it was amazing to see how long they held their breath under water.

After the Azores, the ship headed toward the port of Lisbon, our first official port of call. The voyage was set up by the Italian Line for the two sister ships, the *Vulcania* and the *Saturnia* to complete the 16-day trip. The departure of the two ships was staggered so that while one ship was leaving the United States for Italy, the other left Italy, headed toward the United States. The east-bound ships stopped at Lisbon, went through the straits of Gibraltar, then stopped at Algiers in French Morocco, then to Napoli, and to Palermo in Sicilia then through the Straits of Messina around the heel of the Italian Boot to Patras, Greece, then on to Venezia. People in the United States could book passage for the entire trip, or any portion of it and disembark at any of the ports of call.

In 1958 my wife and I took a trip on the *Saturnia* following the same route, except for a stop in Barcelona, Spain, instead of the one in Algiers.

We arrived in Lisbon at around ten in the morning. When I was in third grade, I studied some geography and was aware of the location of most European countries, especially since I had already traveled to Italy in 1934. In

Boston there were many people of European descent, some of whom spoke Portuguese, very similar to Italian.

The purser of the *Vulcania* announced that passengers could go ashore at any or all of the ports of call. In Lisbon we were scheduled to be in port for about six hours. I watched from the deck as the gangplanks were put in place and people started to disembark. People with suitcases and other assorted packages who were ending their trip in Lisbon started to descend on the gangplank from the Cabin Class deck and left the ship. Thereafter, passengers wanting to visit Lisbon began to disembark.

My father decided that we should leave the ship and take a walk into the city and see the sights. He wore the same suit he wore the day of departure, while my mother and I dressed more casually.

It was very warm. We walked along a tree-lined street which offered some shade. My father had difficulty walking and the heat bothered him. We stopped at an outdoor cafè for refreshments. My mother and I had fruit-based drinks, while my father had a glass of wine and a cigarette.

We remained there only a short time because my father decided to go back to the ship. I don't remember much more about Lisbon, only that the tree-lined streets near the waterfront and the tall buildings reminded me of Italian cities I saw in 1934.

On leaving Lisbon, we toured the Mediterranean as scheduled, stopping in Algiers, Napoli, Palermo, and Patras. For reasons unknown, my father and mother did not want to get off the ship at those ports. The Mediterranean sea was calm and the weather continued to be warm. My father felt very uncomfortable because of the heat. After leaving Patras, we continued up the Adriatic Sea to arrive in Venezia on Tuesday August 1.

We packed before going to bed and placed our suitcases in the hall outside our cabin for the crew to pick up during the night, leaving out clothes to wear the next day for our train trip from Venezia to Lucca.

I had a restless night in my bunk bed, and as soon as I saw daylight through the port hole I responded with relief. Without hesitation, I got up, went to the bathroom, got dressed and went up on deck to view the arrival into Venezia. As the ship made its way into the lagoon, I saw the panorama of the city as we made our way down the Guidecca Canal heading toward the *Stazione Marittima* (Maritime Station or port), being captured by the beauty of the city especially when passing by Piazza San Marco and on down the canal. The houses and buildings jutting onto the water, reflecting themselves into myriad forms truly captured my imagination. Imagine a city without streets, only sidewalks, canals and bridges. I was anxious to leave the ship and see how people traveled about in the city without streets.

We pulled into the *Stazione Marittima*. After the ship was secured, gangplanks were put in place and people started to disembark. The crew unloaded cargo consisting of large trunks which included, of course, our crated bedroom set.

In 1939, when people undertook trans-Atlantic voyages, they packed their personal possessions in steamship trunks and *bauli da cabina* (cabin trunks), which had spaces for hanging clothes on one side and a drawer storage area on the other, placed upright and opening book-like in the cabins. The larger trunks were stored in the cargo area. When unloaded in the ports, the trunks were then routed to follow their owners. We had two trunks, one cabin trunk, three suitcases and, of course, the crated bedroom set. We shipped the trunks and the wooden crates to Lucca, but carried our suitcases on the passenger train. Once we left the ship with our suitcases, we made our way to the *Stazione Ferroviaria* (railroad station), which was nearby, close to the port, across from Piazziale Roma. We walked on narrow sidewalks close to the canal while our suitcases were carried by a *facchino* (porter) on a two-wheeled push cart with handles which he maneuvered through the narrow walkways and steps. I was surprised at the activity on the canals. Many boats moved about transporting people and merchandise. I was completely fascinated by the *gondola*--so sleek and smooth as the oarsman standing on the back pushed on the long pole propelling the *gondola* through the water.

I had been on Italian trains in 1934 while traveling from the port of Genova to Lucca and also on some of the local trains in Toscana to visit areas around Lucca and Montecatini. I was familiar with the process also because I used public transportation in Boston. Therefore, I made comparisons with the streetcars and subway system in Boston and the *Ferrovia Statale* (state railroad) in Italy. We purchased our tickets and got on the train to the city of Prato, located between Firenze and Lucca. We were in a Second Class compartment by ourselves, except for the occasional vendor stopping by to sell drinks and food. We arrived in Prato in around 3 or 4 o'clock in the afternoon. It was hot, and there weren't too many people around.

We waited more than an hour to make the train connection to Lucca, a delay made more boring and uncomfortable due to the heat. There wasn't much to do around the station, so I asked my parents to buy me *caramelle* (candy) and a *gassosa*, a soft drink similar to Seven-up. The *gassosa* was bottled in a clear bottle having a glass cap with a rubber washer fitted to it with a wire sealing system that snapped in place, sealing the *gassosa* in the bottle, much different than the bottle caps used on soft drink bottles in America. The word *gassosa* referred to the carbonated beverage packaged in the clear bottle and was also the brand name for the drink. The empty bottles were returned and re-used by the company producing the soft drinks because of their identity with the *gassosa* company.

Eventually, around 5 p.m., we got on the train bound for Lucca, the uneventful ride lasting about 30 minutes, even though the train stopped in several towns, including Montecatini. After the train wound its way through the maze of railroad tracks into the railway station in Lucca, it stopped at one of the main platforms in the central part of the station. We got off the train, located a porter to carry our suitcases, and walked into the main building to inquire about a train to Diecimo.

The train was part of a smaller train line using steam locomotives to pull the passenger and freight trains up the Serchio River Valley. They also used diesel powered *Littorina* cars for passengers during commute hours. The *Littorina* cars were streamlined vehicles similar in shape to the rapid transit vehicles used in Boston and usually were hooked up in pairs so that the lead car going one way would pull the load and when they would return, the other lead car would pull the load in the opposite direction. The train line went from Lucca to Piazza al Serchio, the end of the line, approximately 40 kilometers long. Our trip to Diecimo was only 16 kilometers and we made a connection with a train pulled by a steam locomotive shortly after we arrived in Lucca. The train wagons had doors on the end of each compartment, opening out to the platform side. We located an empty section and climbed in without much trouble. Since it was warm, most people lowered the windows in each compartment to enjoyed the fresh air as the train moved along the tracks.

We first stopped at San Pietro a Vico, then at Ponte a Moriano, then at Piaggione, and finally at a station with the large letters *DIECIMO-PESCAGLIA* displayed on the wall facing the railroad tracks. We had finally arrived in the village of Diecimo, which, unknown to me, would become our home for the next six years, the village which was to become part of the German Gothic Line of defense.

6. First grade picture of author, Tullio Bertini, Mary Lyons School, Brighton, Massachusetts.
7. Ada with son, Tullio, in Brighton during the winter of 1936-37.

8.   Neighborhood friends in Brighton: Vince and Paul Sheehan
before Tullio's departure in July 1939.

JAN 25, 1932

smen and Diplomats Join in Feast at Washington to

Warmuth's as
es His Own
Dish"

beef and cab-
h?"
rulous, Maggie
er English ac-
to "her man,"
ion of their 20th
not even those
could soften
essing to good-
hes.
man, you won't
o you are."
iggs loved Mag-
years of wed-
t he cared for
abbage more—
plebian food to

O BREAK
a will—
und himself en-
male and fe-
aying him the
anniversary.
what 20 years
for, he mused.
Maggie to hurl
eat corn beef

ething to eat?"
and there be-
none other than
f de luxe of
Devonshire food

beef and cab-
chef queried,
ou've been try-
o long to get
to it."
believable, but

ayment in store
rath of Maggie
chef down a
into a kitchen
permeated with
f and cabbage
away the ends
lips.
did you make
corn beef and
best platefuls
aggie used to
old days."

China J
Stil

Washi
gie" has
all the
can dev
ton gath
night to
most far
The be
annivers
the com
Manus,
bers of
Represer
nent in

And J
shock M
sulting
and oth
friends.
Three
ators, 9
member
will be
dinner,
Syndica
cast ov
from 11
McMa
honor.
years a
lions al
lated in
Messa
nations
happine
after a
married
send
Ludwig,

Nello Bertini, chef at Warmuth's Devonshire st. restaurant, is shown at work preparing the corned beef and cabbage with which he made Jiggs happy. In the circle in the center is the official insignia of the 11th Bombardment Squadron, U. S. Army. (Staff photo.) BOSTON EVENING AMER.

9.   Photo copy of the *Boston Evening American* newspaper article on January 25, 1932, depicting Nello Bertini at Warmuth's

10. Top: Nello, Tullio and Ada Bertini on the M. N. Vulcania, July 1939, before departure from Boston.

11. Bostom: The Bertini family went to Italy during the summer of 1934 for a vacation, traveling on the famous *Rex*, the premiere liner of that time.

2.
LA PROVINCIA DI LUCCA

The region of Italy that includes the province of Lucca and the walled city of Lucca is located in Toscana (Tuscany), one of the northern regions of Italy. The province incorporates approximately 1,800 square kilometers. It borders on the north with the provinces of Massa Carrara, Reggio Emilia, and Modena; on the east with the provinces of Pistoia and Firenze; on the south with the province of Pisa; and on the west with the Mare Tirreno (Tyrrhenian Sea). Currently the population of the city of Lucca is approximately 90,000 and the population of the province is approximately 390,000. Many Italians emigrated from the Lucca Province to the United States and still identify themselves as being from Lucca.

Most of the territory is mountainous, except for the flat areas along the Mare Tirreno and in the Serchio River Valley. The area has a good climate, similar to Northern California, mild along the oceans and beaches, a bit damp and cold along the river valley, with normal rainfall in the mountainous Garfagnana area. The flatlands were gradually built up as the Serchio River meets the Mare Tirreno creating a large delta. According to historical records, the mouth of the Serchio River was once near Ponte a Moriano, a town located approximately 20 kilometers from the present mouth of the river.

The mountains are part of the Apuan Alps and the Appenines that are connected with the mountains from the Pisa area. The height of the Apuan Alps averages 2,000 meters, over 6,000 feet, and the height of the Appenine mountains is similar. The major river is the Serchio River with many tributaries. There are also numerous canals created to bring water to the many paper mills in the region. The flat land is able to produce two crops per year and contains a pattern of small and large canals which bring water to the areas for irrigation. The major natural lake is the Lago di Massaciuccoli, eight square kilometers, located near the town of Torre del Lago, the residence of Giacomo Puccini, the famous opera composer from Lucca.

Because of the configuration of the mountains, there are three sub-regions in the province: La Valle del Serchio, which is composed of Garfagnana, the middle and lower valley of the Serchio River; La Versilia, which is the flat area along the coast of the Mare Tirreno and swings north toward the Carrara marble quarries (this area is populated with tourists during the summer months because of the spectacular beaches); and La Val di Lima, the valley of the Lima River, connecting to the Serchio River near Bagni di Lucca, going in an easterly direction towards Pistoia.

Prior to World War II, the province of Lucca was mainly agricultural, although some areas specialized in unique products such as the Carrara marble industry, the shipyards in Viareggio, the paper mills in the Serchio River valley, the ceramic figurine factories in Garfagnana, and the production of silk. The main agricultural activities included the production of olive oil and wine. Many crops grew on the side of the hills, the terraced land on the mountain sides, established by previous generations.

In ancient times small boats from the Tyrrhenian Sea sailed up the river in order to deliver goods to villages and outposts. The Serchio River was of sufficient depth to allow boats to travel all the way to Ghivizzano. The widest portion of the river was in Diecimo and in later years boats continued upstream by Mozzano passing under the large arch of the Ponte della Maddalena (Maddalena Bridge). This bridge is also known as the Ponte del Diavolo (Devil's Bridge) because the large hump or arch in the bridge structure resembled the humpback of the Devil.

The city of Lucca, completely encircled by ancient walls called Le Mura, is located in the center of a small fertile plain, at the beginning of the Garfagnana region. Lucca is dominated on one side by the Monte Pisano, a mountain which separates Lucca from the coastal plain and the Arno River. On the other side it is topped by the wooded slopes of the Apennini (Appenines) and by Le Alpi Apuane (the Apuane Alps) among which the Serchio River flows. Within its ancient walls, the towers, the church bell towers, the churches and the palaces reflect the history and past glory of Lucca, whose architectural structures are medieval in Romanesque style. From the foundation of the Roman Castrum to the period of the city-state, to the construction of the 16th century walls, a slow and organized development took place in the region, starting with the establishment of the small villages that emerged from the Roman rest stops, such as the village of Diecimo.

One of the main gates leading out through the walls of Lucca was the North Gate that led to the road going to Parma and Piacenza. It was called the Via Claudia or Clodia and led into the Serchio River Valley, following the contours of the river, reaching Sesto di Moriano (Sexto in Latin), continuing towards Domazzano and Valdottavo (Octavo or Vallis Octavii in Latin), reaching Diecimo, and eventually Mozzano. There were also other secondary roads leading to Dezza, Zandori, and following the Serchio River tributary Pedogna up a small valley to Piegaio. At Trebbio, the road split three ways, one of which connected to Montemagno and eventually led to the Tyrrhenian Sea.

To understand a city like Lucca, one must examine the early primitive Roman nucleus, protected by solid walls, later adorned by a theater and amphitheater. Since the domination of the Longobards, from the sixth century on,

Lucca became known as a military center, a road junction and an episcopal seat for the region. During this period, a very prosperous silk weaving industry began. The true greatness of Lucca goes back to the time in which the city-state was a powerful entity in Italy. The political and economic power of Lucca was established in 1118 A.D. when much of the organized construction of houses and public buildings took place. The primitive Roman walls were enlarged and the major churches of San Martino and San Michele built. After the rule of Castruccio Castracani, Lucca fell under the rule of Pisa. During the first thirty years of the fifteenth century, the city was ruled by Paolo Guinigi. Then the small Republic of Lucca, ruled by the Council of Elders, lived an independent and quiet life for four centuries until the Napoleonic conquest.

As for the development of Lucca, the people felt that the most important event was the building of the new protective wall, Le Mura, in the 16th century. The large wall made the city impregnable and contributed to the preservation of the historical center of Lucca. The Provincia di Lucca encompasses a large area, as one can see on the map of the province. People from the areas, *dentro le Mura* (inside the walls) and *fuori le Mura* (outside the walls) say they are from Lucca, which means that they may be from the city or from the Province of Lucca.

Parts of the Province of Lucca were somewhat impenetrable because of the narrow roads and imposing vertical mountain ridges which follow the outline of the Appenine mountains on the coastal side extending as far as the Carrara marble mountains and the Serchio River valley up into the Garfagnana area. Somewhere along the line, the territory must have impressed the German Army commanders in Italy. In 1943 the area became part of line of defense for the retreat of the German troops and Diecimo became part of the Gothic Line which extended from the west to the east coast of Italy.

Diecimo was a Roman outpost or rest stop for the Roman Legions. Located 10 Roman miles from Lucca, it was named Decimo, meaning 10, and later changed to Diecimo. It is located in the Serchio River valley, which leads from Lucca in a north-easterly direction towards Garfagnana; in 1939 the village had a population of approximately 950 people. The valley is very narrow, except where it widens in the Diecimo area. The roads winding up the valley were gravel roads going through the major villages with mule trails joining the road and leading up to smaller hamlets perched on the side of the mountains paralleling the river bed. Transportation into the valley in 1939 was by a single track steam train that went from Lucca, up the valley, passing through Piaggione, Borgo a Mozzano, Bagni di Lucca, Fornaci di Barga, Castelnuovo di Garfagnana, and ending at Piazza al Serchio. There were also buses that serviced the villages on the main road so that people from the mountain villages could walk down, then take the bus to Lucca or to a municipal center, such as the Comune in Borgo a Mozzano. Most of the people living in Diecimo worked as *contadini* (farmers) on small parcels of land that they owned or worked as tenant farmers for landowners. The system was called *mezzadria,* a crop sharing process with the land owner and the *contadino,* or farm worker. Lucca was the site of the provincial government, and the Comune di Borgo a Mozzano was the next sub-level of government which had jurisdiction over the smaller villages called *Frazioni.* Diecimo was a *Frazione* (fraction) of Borgo a Mozzano, in the Provincia di Lucca.

Many names of the locations around Diecimo are derived from Roman roots, such as: Avarano, Lignano, Anchiano, and Dezza which are derived from Latin names of important Roman citizens (Varius, Linius, Ancharianus, Decius).

Excavations in recent years have uncovered relics from the Roman era. One indication regarding the importance of Diecimo during Roman times is the fact the Diecimo was selected as the site for the *Pieve* or the religious center of the area. The first document on the *Pieve* of Diecimo is dated January 761 A.D. In 901 A.D. there are references to Pastino, a location leading into the village of Diecimo where my grandfather Davino Marcucci lived.

The construction of the *Pieve* or church complex with bell tower was started around the end of the XII century and dedicated to the Virgin Mary or *Santa Maria*. In 1728, Diecimo became part of the feudal system of Lucca and there is reference to the "County of Diecimo." Countess Matilde of Lucca was instrumental in recognizing Diecimo as an important center and was partially responsible for developing the official village insignia showing ten mountain peaks underneath a star.

References were made at this time, in writing, that Pastino and the road leading into Diecimo were of strategic importance because they controlled the road leading up the Serchio River Valley. In 1944, the German command forces, planning the retreat of the German Army as the Allied troops advanced up the Italian Peninsula, also thought that Diecimo was in a strategic position to control the valley. The road, continuing north over the Abetone pass on to Modena and eventually to the Brenner Pass, was directly across the Serchio River from Diecimo. Called *Via del Brennero* (Brenner Road), it was connected to the other side of the river by several bridges, *Ponte a Moriano*, *Ponte Pari*, and *Ponte delle Catene* (ponte means bridge in Italian).

3.
THE VILLAGE OF DIECIMO

On August 2, 1939, I awoke to the new sounds of the village. We left our bedroom windows open, but with the shutters closed. The windows of most homes in the village were comprised of wooden framed glass panes on the inside and sliding or push-out shutters on the outside. I was awakened by the *chi-chi-ri-chí* of the rooster in the chicken coop across the street and by the *click-clap* of the wooden clogs that people wore as they walked by in the street below our windows. I also heard people greeting each other with the Italian greeting *buon giorno* (good morning). I looked around our bedroom to assess the situation and wondered if I was dreaming. No, we arrived in Diecimo the evening before and walked from the railroad station to the Bertini home at 82-84 Via del Santo (the main, and only street in Diecimo, named so because of the local saint from the village, San Giovanni Leonardi). My grandparents, Emilio and Teresa Bertini, lived in the house with their son Alceste, his wife Anastasia and three-year-old daughter Teresa. In addition, a teenage girl named Agnese lived with my grandparents; she was an orphan taken in basically as a servant in order to help with the household chores. We had not seen my grandparents since 1934 and when we arrived we were greeted with great affection by everyone. My grandmother was amazed at how much I had grown. We had some refreshments to celebrate our arrival, talked about our voyage from the United States, and went to bed early because we were tired.

The house belonged to my father; he purchased it in 1921 along with several parcels of land, a year after my parents emigrated to the United States. His parents also worked the land and considered the house and the land as their own. I remembered the house from 1934, when I was four years old, because we spent the summer there. The interior was familiar to me, and in fact we used the same bedroom.

The entrance was through the door at number 82 which led directly into the kitchen. The door at number 84, also part of the house, led into a large entry hall leading to a stairway. As one entered the kitchen, there was a large fireplace on the left, then a series of three *fornelli*--charcoal burners with a recessed metal grate built into a brick structure about the height of a stove and used to cook food in pots and pans. The charcoal fire was maintained by using a hand-held fan and moving it back and forth in order to cause an upward flow of air below the burner through a small opening in the front of the configuration. Pieces of charcoal were then added as needed to maintain the proper heat level (very similar in operation to present day barbecues). A large table and several chairs were located in the middle of the kitchen. Against the wall on the right side of the room there was a large wooden cabinet called an *arcile,* also known as a *madia*. The *arcile* was approximately one meter in height and two meters long, and had a lift top that when opened exposed a bread bin or kneading trough. The recessed storage area always contained a small pile of flour in one corner with the starter for the bread which was kept in that location for a week then renewed for the following week. The bread making process took place in the *arcile*. The starter was activated by adding water, new yeast and a small amount of flour. Then enough flour and water was added to make bread for the weekly needs of the family, usually 8 to 10 loaves.

The noon meal, the main meal of the day, was prepared by Agnese and served at the kitchen table. The evening meal was usually served after 7:30 p.m. and was simple: hot milk and a small amount of coffee (known as *caffè e latte*) and bread served in a large bowl called a *ciotola*.

The sink was located to the immediate right of the entry door. It was made from a large slab of stone, rectangular in shape, about 4 to 5 inches thick, with an area carved out by hand, forming a rectangular bowl. Water from the sink ran out through a drain hole in one corner into a pipe system leading to the *gora*, an open waste water ditch across the street. The *gora* usually carried a stream of water which was used to irrigate the agricultural crops in the village and eventually drained into the river.

There was no running water. On the left side of the sink there was a large copper bucket full of water. It was shaped like a standard bucket, without a handle, made of hammered copper with a tin coating on the inside, called a *secchia*. The women usually went for water to the fountain at Zandori or the fountain in the Piazza and returned to the houses carrying the *secchia* full of water on their heads, balanced on a piece of towel rolled up lengthwise, then curled in spiral shape forming a cushion for the *secchia*. The water in the bucket was the main drinking water for the family, and it had a communal copper *ramaiolo* (ladle) with a hook attached to it. So when people were thirsty, they scooped out a ladle full of water and drank it from the ladle; then they replaced the ladle on the side so that the hook on the handle hooked over the top edge of the *secchia* and hung down to drain. The closest water fountain, about 300 meters from the house, was called the *fontana di Zandori* and provided the coolest spring water in the village during the summer months.

The rest of the rooms on the *pian terreno* (first floor), were: a small storage room behind the kitchen; a room which could be considered a dining room to the right of the kitchen, but was not used as such; a large entry hall; and a *latrina* (bathroom). The *latrina* was a small room, about four feet square, consisting of a stone ledge against one wall, with a large hole cut in the stone, covered with a wooden board that was used as a seat, with the proper corresponding hole. The hole was not covered and led directly to the cesspool tank below. There was no such thing as toilet paper. In its place, there was a nail on the wall with small pieces of newspaper stuck on the nail. Much to my disgust I became familiar with newspaper toilet tissue. Near the *latrina*, there were two sets of stairs, one leading down to the *cantina* (basement) and one leading to the upper floors of the house.

The stairs leading up to the second floor brought one to a large *sala* (room). Straight ahead there was a door leading to our bedroom. My father and mother used one large bed and a smaller twin size bed was provided for me. There was a large *banco*, or *armadio* which is a large wooden wardrobe used for clothes in place of the American type of wall closet. There was also a chest of drawers, a commode that contained a *vaso* (chamber pot) for use during the night, and a wash stand. The wash stand was a metal frame structure holding a mirror, a large ceramic wash bowl, and a large ceramic pitcher of water. The wash stand was used in place of a sink and running water. After a few weeks I discovered that the dirty water from the wash bowl was usually disposed of by dumping the water out of bedroom windows onto the street below. It was common practice in the village; therefore, one had to be careful while walking in the streets not to get caught in the unwanted shower of dirty water. Sometimes certain people also dumped their chamber pots down onto the street. Needless to say one had to avoid the chamber pot shower because of the horrible urine smell. It was difficult for me to adapt to the sanitary facilities and customs in the village; it was a cultural shock for me having come from America.

There were two other rooms on the second floor, the first the bedroom used by my grandparents, the other a utility type kitchen with an immense fireplace beside which was the front opening of a large brick oven that was used once a week to bake bread. The brick configuration of the oven extended behind the fireplace wall into another utility room. The entrance to the utility room was through a small door alongside the fireplace. The room was dark, damp and spooky because the rear wall of the room was actually the rough rock of the mountain, chiseled by hand, against which the house was built about 500 years earlier.

The third story had four additional small rooms used as bedrooms, one for my aunt and uncle, one for their daughter Teresa and one for Agnese. The fourth story was a *soffitta*, an area consisting of two large rooms, with open windows, no glass, thus allowing the air to circulate in the room. The *soffitta* was used as a storage area for perishable food, such as fruit, corn, potatoes, and tomatoes. The food crops were spread out on large tables on bamboo slats; during fall and winter the cold air served as a refrigerant and maintained the food for several weeks or months.

In 1939 in the United States most urban families had homes that were equipped with flush toilets, hot and cold running water, coal or fuel oil heating systems, refrigerators, radios, and electricity. The house at 82 Via del Santo, our home for a while, only had electricity. Our stay would certainly be quite an experience as I thought about the lack of conveniences and how we were spoiled in America.

Italian children of the 1939 era did not seem to be informed about family matters nor did they take part in family discussions. I realized after we arrived in Diecimo that my father purchased another house nearby and that the house was being prepared for us and soon would be ready.

The house was adjacent to a barn and the exterior and interior walls were re-plastered and painted with a water based wash. The brick floors on the street level were covered with ceramic tiles which gave a pleasant look to the rooms. The house was located between the *Cappella del Carmine*, a small church dedicated to the Madonna of the Carmine, and a small grocery store and bar. The store belonged to Niccola and Nello Lazzari. Our house was referred as being *alla Cappella* (at the chapel), and was number 81 Via del Santo.

The interior of the church is approximately 20 feet wide and about 40 feet long. The wooden church pews lined the two side walls, two deep, while the altar was in the rear of the church, directly opposite the main entrance. There was a carved wooden statue of the Madonna behind the altar. The church ceiling was about 25 feet high and framed with large, exposed, wooden beams. The floor was made of red bricks which became worn over the years. Church services, such as masses and vespers, were held in the chapel only during church holidays dedicated to the *Madonna del Carmine*. I visited the Cappella in 1995 and found that it was beautifully restored.

A few days after our arrival, the trunks and the bedroom set arrived by train from Venice and were stored in the house at 82 Via del Santo. The house at 81 Via del Santo, which was not quite ready to be inhabited, had three floors: the basement or *cantina*, the first floor at street level, and the second floor. The street level floor had a kitchen, a large room to be used as a dining room, and a small room to be used as a living room adjacent to the kitchen. In contrast to my grandparents' home, the kitchen had a cold water line leading to a faucet high in the wall above the sink. The back of the house had a balcony about three feet wide which ran the width of the house. Access to the balcony was through a door from the main corridor. At the end of the balcony, on the outside of the house, there was a bathroom about three feet square with a flush toilet and tiny sink with a cold water tap. On the second floor there were two large bedrooms, one small bedroom, a smaller room which was designated as a walk-in closet, and a bathroom which was very similar to an American bathroom of that era. It had a toilet with a wall-mounted water reservoir at ceiling level and pull chain for flushing, a claw footed stand-alone bathtub, a pedestal sink, cold running water, and a line for hot water leading to the tub from a stand-up copper water heater with a built in wood burning section below the tank.

On the first floor, between the kitchen wall and Niccola's store there was an outside door and a corridor that led to a barn. The street level portion of the barn was used to store *fieno* (hay), and the lower part of the barn had *stalle* (stalls) for cows. Behind the stable area there was a large room which contained a huge pile of *concime* (manure) from the cow barn. The *concime* unfortunately had a horrible smell which permeated the rear of the house and was especially strong when the *concime* was transferred to a *cesta* (a large, round basket carried on the shoulders by men, or on the head by women) and carried out of the room to fertilize the fields.

Late in the summer, when the house was ready to be occupied, we bought a few things for our new kitchen, such as a table and chairs, kitchen utensils and dishes, a cabinet for storing dishes and food and a wood-burning stove. The kitchen did not have a fireplace as did the other kitchens in the village. Instead, on the basement level, there was a rustic kitchen with a fireplace, *fornelli*, a brick bread oven, and a sink with cold running water. We comissioned Aladino Agostinelli, one of the local cabinetmakers, to make a bed and dresser for me. We planned to move into the house as soon as the construction was finished. My

mother wanted to establish her own home so we did not
have to depend on my grandparents.

Unknown to us, Europe was already at war, and people
in Diecimo began to talk about the possibility of war and to
wonder how Italy might be affected.

As the end of August 1939 approached, German military
chiefs moved ahead with their plans to destroy Poland and
to protect the western Reich just in case other nations
decided to intervene. On August 15, a quarter of a million
German men were called up for the armies of the west with
advanced mobilization orders given to the German railways.
Plans were also made to move Army headquarters to
Zossen, east of Berlin. And on the same day, August 15, the
German Navy reported that the pocket battleships *Graf Spee*
and *Deutschland* and 21 submarines were ready to sail into
the Atlantic. (*The Rise and Fall of the Third Reich* by
William L. Shirer)

Despite these ominous events, as the middle of August
neared in Diecimo, preparations were being made for the
big annual *Festa di Santa Maria*, a feast honoring the Virgin
Mary called the *Assunzione* (Assumption), to be held on
August 15. The event was considered mainly a religious
observance, with several Masses in the morning, the church
choir singing at the 11 o'clock mass, and the afternoon
vespers at 5 p.m., followed by a procession through the
village. It was customary for the residents to drape white
sheets along the exterior walls of all the homes along the
procession route, forming a solid white corridor for the
entire length of the village through which the priest would
carry the Sacred Host in a special gold plated holder,
resembling a sun burst. When houses were built or replaste-
red, metal hooks were imbedded in the exterior wall at a
uniform height so that ropes or wires could be used to tie
a line across each house. The sheets were then attached to
the line with clothes pins. The men of the village who

belonged to the church service group, called *La Misericordia*, dressed in white habits with a navy blue mantle, walked in the procession, taking turns carrying the large wooden statue of the Virgin Mary.

In the afternoon, the women decorated the center portion of the street with flower petals, laying out lovely designs, forming a pathway of flowers where the priest would walk, carrying the Sacred Host. The people participated in the procession, forming two lines, one on each side of the street, walking the distance from the church to the end of the village and back to the church. The *Festa di Santa Maria* brought most members of the families together and much of the celebration actually took place around the dinner tables, where family members ate special food prepared for the *Festa* and drank their best wine in the home.

My maternal grandfather, Davino Marcucci, lived in Pastino with his son Dante, who was married to Massima Sartini. They had two children, Leonello age 6, and Dino age 4. My uncle Dante was a handsome man, 27 years old, tan and strong. We were invited to celebrate Santa Maria with them, as Massima planned one of her great meals.

To reach Pastino, we walked through the village, crossed the bridge over the Pedogna River, and walked down a steep incline in the road to Pastino. From Pastino toward Diecimo, the incline was referred as the *salita* or the ascent to the bridge. I remember that most people riding bicycles would dismount and walk up the *salita* because it was a difficult, steep climb.

I had already developed a friendship with Leonello and Dino even though they were younger than I was. After all, they were my first cousins. Prior to coming to Italy, I had not learned to ride a bicycle, but as any child, I was fascinated by the many bicycles in Diecimo. In 1939 the bicycle was the major means of transportation for the men and the women of the village and many children learned to ride a bike at a very early age. My uncle Dante had two bicycles: one was a man's bike with the horizontal bar connecting the handle bar column to the seat column; the other was a woman's bike without the horizontal bar, but with a tubular support bar which dipped from the seat column down to the lowest point of the frame then back up to the handle bar which allowed women to wear skirts while riding the bicycle. The women's bicycles were the ones usually used by children when they were first learning to ride bicycles because the children were unable to straddle the horizontal bar on men's bikes.

We arrived a bit early for our *pranzo*, which was to take place at 12:30, so I began playing with Leonello and Dino out in front of the house. When the subject of riding a bicycle came up they were surprised that I did not know how to ride, so they offered to teach me to ride Massima's bike, showing me that I would not any have trouble reaching the pedals.

Never having ridden on a two-wheel bike, I was apprehensive, but I managed to get the idea of riding and balancing myself, especially with Leonello holding the seat as I pedaled along. The section of the road in front of their house was a gravel road and the paved section started on the *salita* close to the bridge, so it was a bit more difficult to balance myself and keep going straight because the tires would hit small pieces of gravel and the bike would wander off track. After a few tries with Leonello holding me, Leonello let go of the seat and I managed to maintain my balance and continue to pedal along. Shortly after, I actually was able to start, ride and stop by myself by using the hand brakes on the bike. I really was happy because I wanted to learn how to ride a bicycle in Brighton but no one took the time to teach me. It seemed to me that the bicycle was pretty easy to ride. In Italy, at that time, most bicycles had chain covers which completely enclosed the drive chain so there was no danger of catching your legs in the chain. I was so excited that I told my cousins to go into the house and tell my mother to come out to see what I learned to do. When my mother came out a short while later, I told her that I learned to ride a bicycle and gave her a demonstration. She seemed to be surprised that I learned so fast and said, in Italian:

"*Fa' ammodo*," meaning, "Be careful." She also told me to put the bike away since it was time to come into the house because the meal was going to be served.

My uncle Dante was a *contadino*, which signifies a person working the land as a farmer, usually growing a variety of seasonal crops. The term *contadino* also referred to a person who worked as a tenant farmer or sharecropper for land owners. In Diecimo there were *contadini* who owned their own land and many others who were poor and worked for more wealthy land owners. In 1939 Dante worked the land that my grandfather Davino purchased upon returning to Italy from Half Moon Bay, California. Nonno Davino emigrated to California in 1900, returned to Italy after the 1906 San Francisco earthquake, then went back to California in 1907, and finally returned to Italy in 1912. In California he worked as a ranch hand, saved his money, and when he returned to Diecimo he bought a house and various parcels of land in the village. Dante, his youngest son, was born in 1912 and as he got older worked the land with his father. The middle son, Nello, born in 1907, also worked the land until he decided to become a priest; in 1936 he was assigned a parish in Pieve di Compito, located on the way to Pontedera, past Capannori.

In 1939 my grandfather Davino had bad knees which bowed out, and he could not walk without the help of a cane. In fact he spent much of his time in the afternoons and evenings sitting on a chair in front of the house, by the front door, talking to people as they walked by. Davino's wife, Serafina, my maternal grandmother, lived with my uncle Nello in Pieve di Compito, and did not come to Diecimo very often. In that era it was common for mothers of priests to live with their sons and work as housekeepers.

Most families were *contadini* who worked very hard to raise food for their own use. There were plenty of fruits and vegetables for families, but not very much beef, because the cows were raised to produce milk and were not butchered. The major meat sources at that time for the *contadini* were chickens, rabbits and pigs. Most families managed to plan ahead and serve sumptuous meals for special holidays like *Santa Maria*.

On the day of *Santa Maria*, August 15, 1939, my aunt Massima made *tordelli* (also called *ravioli*), roast chicken and roast rabbit, oven browned potatoes, fried zucchini, string beans, homemade bread and two *torte di riso* (rice torte) for dessert. In Diecimo it was customary for families to serve *tordelli* and *torta di riso* for *Santa Maria*. The *torta* was made with a thin crust with *becchi* around the edges. The excess dough from the crust overhanging the round baking pan was rolled and shaped around the pan in the shape of bird beaks, thus the term *becchi*. The *Santa Maria torta* filling was made with cooked rice, eggs, *bietola* (Swiss chard), olive oil, grated *pecorino* cheese (cheese made from sheep's milk; *pecora* is the Italian word for sheep), and salt and pepper. The crust of the *torta*, once filled with the rice mixture, was then baked in the large family brick oven after the weekly load of bread was baked. When requesting a piece of *torta* for dessert most people would say:

"*Dammi tre becchi*." meaning, "give me a slice three beaks wide of torta."

After the meal it was customary for the children to leave the table and go out and play; the men remained seated, continuing to drink wine and talk, while the women of the house cleared the table and retreated to the kitchen to start washing all the dishes. Often the men took an afternoon nap especially if the weather was hot. I went out in front of the house with Leonello and Dino hoping that I could continue to ride the bike. I was encouraged to do so, using Massima's bike, while Leonello tried to ride his father's bike. We rode up the hill leading to the bridge, going as far as we could, then turned around and coasted down the hill. Even though it was hot, it was a lot of fun.

I thought it might be fun to go all the way up to the bridge and continue on to the Bertini grandparents' house so that I could show them that I learned to ride a bicycle. I told Leonello that I was going to do so. I started pedaling up the *salita* but had to stop about halfway up the hill. I got off the bike, walked the rest of the way to the top of the hill, and remounted the bike when I got to the bridge. The bridge was narrow and usually could accommodate only one automobile or truck at a time. It had a sharp 90 degree turn leading to the main street in Diecimo. I crossed the bridge, made the turn and coasted down hill toward the school and the Pierini house.

The Pierini house was located by the school, next to the monument honoring soldiers who died in World War I. The Pierini family was made up of the father Celestino, the mother Betta (my mother's first cousin), and seven children. As I rode past their house, I was hoping that they would see me so that I could show off my bike riding skills, but no one was around. I continued my ride down *il Piastrone* (a narrow section of the village with homes on both sides of the street) and noticed that people already started to make preparations for the procession that was to take place later in the afternoon. Some families already draped white sheets across their homes. I continued past the *Piazza* (the village square), riding towards the *Cappella* and my grandparent's home. During one of my visits to Diecimo in the late 1980's I drove the exact route and noted that the distance that I traveled by bike on that day was about 1.5 kilometers, equivalent to a mile. When I arrived I leaned the bike against the house, dashed into the kitchen and asked my grandmother, Aunt Anastasia and Agnese to come outside so they could see what I learned to do. They came out and I gave them a demonstration of my bike riding dexterity in front of the house. Agnese and Anastasia were especially thrilled and complimented me on how quickly I learned to ride the bike. My grandmother Teresa did not have much to say. I placed the bike against the house and went back into the kitchen to cool off and to have a *ramaiolo* of cool Zandori water from the *secchia*.

Meanwhile, after my mother and Massima were finished with the kitchen chores they went out front to see what the children were doing. Leonello told my mother that I took Massima's bike, rode it up to the bridge, and did not come back. He told them that I probably went to the Bertini grandparents' house. My mother became very upset, thinking that something might have happened to me because I was an inexperienced bicycle rider. She convinced my father to go after me to see what happened. My father decided to ride Uncle Dante's bike and to search for me. I doubt if he rode the bike all the way up the *salita*, but in any event, he did ride the bike all the way to the home of his parents, at 82 Via Del Santo, a distance of 1.5 kilometers. He walked into the kitchen, hot and exhausted, and saw me sitting with his mother, Anastasia, and Agnese. He was mad at me because I left without telling my mother where I was going and furthermore he thought that it was dangerous for me to ride the bike without supervision. He sat down and asked for a glass of cold water. Agnese gave him a glass of water from the *secchia* and he drank it all in one gulp. Shortly after drinking the water, he suddenly became pale, saying that he did not feel well and that he had a pain in his chest. Anastasia became alarmed and urged my father to go lie down in the bedroom upstairs while someone tried to locate the local doctor. They helped my father climb the stairs while I went to see if I could find my uncle Alceste.

Doctor Lumini, the only doctor in the area, lived in Valdottavo, two miles from Diecimo. An older gentleman, he traveled around the valley on his bicycle. He did not have much hair, shaved his head, never wore a hat, and had the reputation of being a good doctor. When I located Alceste, he immediately got on his bike and rode to Valdottavo to get Doctor Lumini. As Alceste went by Pastino he told my mother about my father, so she came rushing in, upset at what happened, and not very happy with me. When Doctor Lumini arrived with Alceste, he examined my father and determined he had suffered a heart attack. I did not know what it was, except that it appeared serious, and that judging from the way my mother was crying the situation was critical. A single thought kept running through my mind: "Was I responsible for my father's heart attack because I left Pastino and rode the bicycle without permission?" Other thoughts entered my mind as I stared at my father lying in bed. He was only 45 years old. Was he going to die? If so, what were we going to do? If he did not die, would we be able to return to the United States or were we trapped in Diecimo?

12. Top: Panorama of Diecimo taken from across the Serchio River, on the Via Del Brennero. The valley in the background leads to Pescaglia and Convalle.

13. Bottom: The church complex in Diecimo, showing the church, the bell tower, and canonica.

14. Top: The Bertini house at 81 Via Del Santo in Diecimo. The Cappella del Carmine is on the left.

15. Bottom: Summer 1945: Tullio kneeling in front with teenagers in Diecimo.

4.
A NEW LIFE

I don't remember in detail exactly what happened after my father suffered the heart attack. I recall that Doctor Lumini prescribed bed rest, some type of oral medication (pills or *pillole*), and injections to be given twice a day. My father's sister Amelia Barsotti was experienced in giving injections, and she volunteered to help with my father. Amelia was the oldest girl of the Bertini family, the only sister who remained in Diecimo, and was married to Filippo Barsotti, the village *mulinaio* (miller). Amelia had five children: Cesarina, Mena, Giuseppe, Rodolfo and Norma.

She came to the house twice a day, in the morning and the early evening, to give the injections, *punture* in Italian. My mother was not very happy with the situation at the Bertini grandparents' home. Having been in the United States for almost 20 years, she was accustomed to certain everyday amenities, such as having running water, flush toilets, a washing machine, and a gas stove. She was taking care of my father on a 24-hour basis, going up and down the stairs to look in on him, to feed him, to wash him and to give him his medication. It seems that we put up with the situation for a couple of weeks, then made the move into our own house at 81 Via Del Santo, which was nearby, across the street, about 50 meters towards the Cappella.

My father was moved to our new house, carried up the stairs by my uncle and grandfather, and was placed in one of the twin beds that we brought from Boston. I was concerned about my father and could see that my mother was deeply troubled with the situation, especially interacting with the Bertini grandparents.

There was talk about the Fascists and about Mussolini in the village. Early on the evening of August 25, Hitler received a letter from Mussolini. This, along with the news of the signing of the Anglo-Polish alliance, caused him to postpone the attack on Poland scheduled for the next day. Hitler then wrote a curt note to the Duce asking him what implements of war and raw materials he would require and within what time frame, in order for Italy to enter a major European conflict. The letter was telephoned by Ribbentrop personally to the German ambassador in Rome at 7:40 p.m. and handed to the Italian dictator at 9:30 p.m. The next morning in Rome, Mussolini had a meeting with the chiefs of the Italian armed services to draw up a list of his minimum requirements for a war lasting twelve months. It included seven million tons of petroleum, six million tons of coal, two million tons of steel, one million tons of timber and a long list of other items down to 600 tons of molybdenum, 400 tons of titanium, and twenty tons of zirconium. In addition Mussolini included a demand for 150 anti-aircraft batteries to protect the Italian industrial areas in the north, which were a short flying distance from French air bases, a reality of which he reminded Hitler in another letter. This message was telephoned by Ciano to Berlin shortly after noon on August 26 and immediately delivered to Hitler. It contained a hugely swollen list of materials needed. By now the "deflated Fascist leader" was obviously determined to escape from his obligations to the Third Reich, and Hitler, after reading this second letter, could no longer have the slightest doubt of it. (*The Rise And Fall Of The Third Reich* by William L. Shirer)

My schedule in Diecimo during this critical time was typical of most nine-year old children. I was aware of what was going on with my father, and all the work my mother had to do. I was able to develop some friendships with local children my own age. I remember meeting and playing with Dino Cicchi, Umberto Pasquinelli, Piero Paolucci, Lamberto Santini, Luigi Donati, Angelo Catelani, and most of the Pierini children. Dino Cicchi was born in New York and was brought back to Diecimo as a small child. His parents, Napoleone and Eugenia, spoke English and were very friendly with my parents. Napoleone operated the small bank branch of the *Cassa di Risparmio* in Diecimo. Umberto Pasquinelli who lived in the *Piazza* (village square) area was the son of the man called *il fattore* (the land agent who supervised agricultural land for an absentee landowner). Angelo Catelani was the son of Dina and Achille Catelani. He had an older brother named Fausto and an older sister named Miria. Achille resided in the United States, in Healdsburg, California. Once, during the 1930's, he stopped by our house in Brighton and stayed with us for a few days en route to California. I often played with Angelo because he was about my age and I enjoyed his company. Angelo had a lot of chores to perform working in the fields to help out his mother so it was difficult for him to find play time. Our friendship continues to this day.

Angelo and his family came to California in 1946 and settled in Healdsburg with his father. He eventually attended San Francisco State University and became a high school teacher. Angelo lives in Santa Rosa, California, and we see one another often. It is an interesting outcome of events that two children from the small village of Diecimo came to the United States, graduated from the same college, and taught high school in the same state!

Inasmuch as it was the latter part of summer, the kids of land owner families had nothing to do, while those who were *contadini* had their chores to do. I found it fun to associate with the *contadini* and would often accompany them to the fields and hills and help out with their work.

The days were very warm and during the early afternoons I stayed inside the house and rested. In the evenings, after dinner, I walked around the village with some of my friends, going all the way to the bridge, and catch the cool breezes from the Pedogna River Valley.

My Italian language skills were not up to the level of most children because in Brighton I had primarily spoken English. In very short order, however, I switched to Italian. Most of the Italian regions such as Liguria, Veneto, Lombardia, Romagna, have their own dialects. In Toscana, people speak almost the "true Italian" as is taught in school. There are slight variations from village to village, and from city to city. The people in the province of Lucca are descendants of the Ligurians and the Etruscans. In general, they speak *Toscano* (Tuscan), with minor variations and dialects depending on the region. The people in Diecimo speak Italian with a slight dialect variation. The consonant normally *c* has a palatal sound. Before *e* or *i* the *c* is pronounced toward the front of the mouth, *c* is like *ch* in *chill*. In the *Diecimino* dialect the *c* becomes a *sc* before *i* or *e* like the English *sh*. Some pronunciation examples follow: *cena* becomes *scena*; *Diecimo* becomes *Diescimo*; *provincia* becomes *provinscia*; *cominciare* becomes *cominsciare*.

I became acquainted with most of the names of people; they were known by their first names or nicknames, and it was common practice to simply refer to each other by nicknames, some of which were:

Il Poeta - the poet
Il Sarto - the tailor
Tartaglia - the stutterer
Becco Rosso - red nose (from drinking wine)
Zio Fio - Uncle Fig
Il Gatto - the cat
Il Posta - the mailman

Gigione - big Luigi
Ciampa - big foot
Bazza - long chin
Gobbo - hunch back
Mago - wizard

I was known as Tullio, *l'Americano* (the American). My name was not very common and I was the only Tullio in the village. It is also a very unusual name in the United States, but in some areas one hears the name Tullius or Tully, a name that is used in Ireland. According to my mother, Tullio was a derivative of Tullo, the name used by Roman Emperors, such as Tullius Ostilius. According to the Italian dictionary, Tullio comes from Tullo, which derives from the Latin *tollere* to elevate. "A boy named Tullio is destined to achieve great honors."

School in Diecimo began around the end of September. It seemed that because of my father's condition, we were going to remain in Italy for a while. My mother thought about my education, that it might be best for me to have some private lessons in Italian to bring me up to grade level, which, according to my age, would be the third grade.

Dora Ambrogi lived in Piazza with her mother, father, and sisters Maria and Gemma. Her brother Francesco was studying for the priesthood in the seminary near Lucca. Gemma was married to Lorenzo Menesini, who emigrated to England and was working in Scotland making statues from plaster of Paris. The Ambrogi family owned land in Diecimo and its members worked the land by themselves. Dora went to school, became an elementary school teacher, but did not have a teaching assignment. She was a very attractive woman, delicate and kind. My mother asked Dora to tutor me and she said that she would be glad to help me learn Italian.

The tutoring sessions took place in her back yard, in the late afternoons when it was cool, and the lessons consisted of conversation, reading and writing Italian. I don't remember how many sessions I had, but I remember working very hard, and seeing that my Italian improved considerably. I know my mother paid Dora, but I don't recall how much. By the time school started, I felt sure that I would be able to fit right in with the other children of the class of 1930.

Later, after I began teaching high school in California, I taught Italian in evening adult school programs and in high school, and often remembered my experiences with Dora, how I learned the language and how I was able to remember the language as I got older.

In Italy there was always reference to the year in which one was born in connection with the start of school, when one entered the military service, when one made First Communion and when one received Confirmation. For example, my class was of *del trenta*, the 1930 class.

The elementary school in Diecimo was located on the *Viale della Stazione*, the road leading to the railroad station. The school was a large, two-story gray building, with six classrooms. One was the *asilo* or kindergarten, and the other five classrooms were designated for each of the five grades. I remember some of the preparations preceding the first day of school.

The students were required to wear a school uniform, black shirts for the boys and black smocks for the girls, made of cotton, either purchased or handmade in the home, and were large enough to fit over shirts and sweaters, designed to protect clothing from dirt and ink.

Most families bought the fabric and made the shirts and smocks themselves. My mother decided, since she was a seamstress, that she would make the school shirt for me. She took my measurements and sewed the shirt so that it was large enough for me to grow into. The shirt also had an elastic band around the bottom so that the shirt would hang out and fit snugly over the top of my pants. The black shirt was a popular garment during the Fascist regime when the Fascists required that members of their various adult and youth organizations wear black shirts as part of their uniforms. It is questionable whether there was a relationship between the school black shirts and the Fascist black shirts. I think that the color was selected for the school uniforms because the color hid most of the dirt that one picked up around the school. The boys also had to wear a white necktie and the girls had to wear a white collar with their smock. In addition, families had to purchase *matite* (pencils), *quaderni* (notebooks), a *cartella* (briefcase-backpack combination), and the textbooks.

Before the start of school there was a great deal of discussion and speculation among the students in trying to figure out which teacher was assigned to the various grade levels. Former students told stories about specific teachers named *la Silene, la Giunchi* (Silene and Giunchi were last names of the teachers) and *la Gigia*, whose real name was Argia Ambrogi (Gigia was a derivative of Argia). La Giunchi (the article *la* is placed before a first name or last name of a person and is translated as "the") was supposed to be the hardest and the meanest teacher in the school. I hoped not to be assigned to her.

On opening day 1939 I walked to school accompanied by my mother, wearing my new black shirt, short pants, and my *cartella* on my back with my notebooks and pencils inside. On the way, we joined up with many of my friends, all dressed in black shirts or smocks, with the discussion centering around the reputation of the teachers, and trying to guess which teacher was assigned to our grade.

When we arrived, we walked to the main entrance and went into the entry hall to get our assignments. To my pleasure and relief, I found out that I was assigned to *la*

Gigia, the Signora Ambrogi. After saying good-bye to my mother, I went to the third grade classroom located on the first floor. As I entered, I looked around the room and saw that on the left there was a long clothes rack with hooks, and rows of desks for 20 students. In front of the room there was a teacher's desk and large slate blackboard above which there was a large crucifix centered on the wall with a picture of the Duce (Benito Mussolini) on one side and that of the King of Italy, Vittorio Emanuale III, on the other side. To the right, along the wall, there was a large ceramic wood stove. The teacher, *la Gigia*, in the front of the room, told us to sit at our desks, made of wood and having a bench with a separate lift-top writing surface with storage below the lid. Each desk accommodated two students, and each had a recessed glass inkwell. The boys were assigned to one row of desks and the girls to the other row.

La Signora Argia, as we addressed her, was enormous-- wide and tall! Gossip had it that her father, Signor Orselli, emigrated to Brazil, that he married a mulatto woman, and that Argia was the product of that union, bringing Argia back to Diecimo as a child. She went to school in Lucca, became a teacher, and then married Beppe Ambrogi.

As we settled in, and the actual instruction started, la Signora Argia seemed kind, one who treated students with respect, and eloquent in presenting the subject matter, especially in reading Italian stories to the class. I felt that she could have been an actress! My wife and I visited la Signora Argia in 1958 and again I found her to be a very charming person. In turn, she was extremely pleased to see me, and she also was happy to hear that I had continued school in the United States and that I become a high school teacher. She called me her professor, *"il mio professore."*

My school was part of the national school system. After Mussolini came into power, the mandatory minimum school requirement for children was raised from third to fifth grade. My parents had only had three years of school. In 1939, Italian children were expected to complete the fifth grade and prepare themselves to take national standardized exams which could lead them to further education.

The next sequence of schooling was the *Scuola Media* with levels 1, 2, and 3, and was the equivalent of the American junior high school. Before the Fascist regime and the establishment of the *Scuola Media*, there was a different structure: five years of *Ginnasio* classes instead of the three years of *Scuola Media*. At the end of the third year of *Scuola Media* a State exam was taken to proceed to the *Liceo* (similar to high school), and then after the *Liceo*, another exam before being admitted to the University. If a student wanted to pursue a trade he could attend a trade school in Lucca called *Carlo del Prete* and study technical subjects. At the time I attended school, most of the *contadini* students were planning to complete the fifth grade and then remain in the village and work the land with their families. The "richer" students probably continued their studies in the *Scuola Media* and *Liceo* located in Lucca.

The day began at 8:30 and concluded at 12:30, six days a week. I was enthusiastic about attending school and enjoyed meeting new friends. The main subjects taught were Italian, mathematics, history, geography, religion and physical education. I still have a copy of my fifth grade report card showing other topics, such as *canto* (singing), *disegno* (drawing or art), *cultura fascista* (Fascist culture), physical science, hygiene, and manual work.

I was a good student, not a trouble maker in class I always respected the teacher. I attended third grade in 1939-40, fourth grade in 1940-41; and the fifth in 1941-42.

I took the State exam at the end of the fifth grade, passed it, and was eligible to attend the *Scuola Media* in the Fall of 1942.

I have a copy of my report card issued on the 4th of May, 1942. The grades are listed as *Lodevole* which means commendable and *Buono* which means good. In duplicating the list of subjects I translated the course titles into English:

SUBJECT	GRADE
Religion	Buono
Singing	Buono
Drawing/handwriting	Lodevole
Writing/recitation	Buono
Spelling	Buono
Reading/writing Italian	Buono
Arithmetic	Lodevole
Instructions & Fascism	Buono
Geography	Buono
History/Fascist Culture	Lodevole
Physical/natural science/hygiene	Lodevole
Economics	Buono
Physical Educatin	Lodevole
Manual Arts	Lodevole
Conduct	Lodevole
Personal hygiene	Lodevole

The actual report card, called *pagella*, folded in half, about 7 inches by 10 inches, was printed by the National Ministry of Education with Fascist logos on the front and back covers.

The front shows a warlike winged goddess holding a sword and shield sitting on top of a grouping of ships, airplanes and tanks. The main lettering below is *vincere* which means *to win* or *victory*; below that is P.N.F. which means *Partito Nazionale Fascista*, and at the bottom *Gioventù Italiana del Littorio* (G.I.L.).

Each student had an identification number shown on the report card as a G.I.L. number; mine was number 784958.

The back shows a flag with G.I.L., a rifle and a Fascist symbol showing *ANNO XX* which represents the 20th year of Fascism. In retrospect, it is interesting to see how much Fascist brainwashing took place in Italian society starting with school age children.

The lessons in school were also typical. We listened to stories read by the teacher, we read aloud in class, we wrote essays in our notebooks, we did arithmetic problems in our notebooks and on the blackboard, we sang, and we did a bit of physical education outside in the courtyard, weather permitting. The physical education consisted of a few simple exercises led by *signora Argia* followed by informally kicking a soccer ball around.

During winter, it was very cold. To keep the room warm, students were required to bring firewood from home so that we could use the classroom stove to heat the room.

Most of the male students wore short pants, and some of the richer students wore knickers, which were called *calzoni alla zoave* in Italian.

As a child in Brighton, I was provided with good quality clothing and a variety of seasonal shoes. I found out that leather shoes were a luxury in Diecimo because they were very expensive and the people could not afford to buy them. Most people wore wooden clogs called *zoccoli*, made of carved wooden soles with leather or cloth uppers attached to the wood with nails holding the material on to the base. For summer wear, the upper consisted of a cloth or leather strap that went from the large toe of the foot across the top of the foot and over to the small toe of the foot. This type of *zoccolo* resembles Dr. Scholl's wooden clog sold in America. The winter *zoccoli* were different in that they used the same type of wooden sole but the uppers were shaped like boots or shoes and were fastened to the foot with shoe laces. During the summer, people wore *zoccoli* barefoot and most of the *contadini* children walked around barefoot. In the winter adults and children wore the winter *zoccoli* with heavy woolen socks made from the wool of the local sheep. At times pieces of rubber or hob nails were placed on the bottom of the *zoccoli* to reduce the wear of the wood.

I also adapted to the local customs and wore summer style *zoccoli* when it was warm, but I was fortunate to have a pair of leather shoes for winter. As I got older I reached a point where I could wear my father's shoes, again fortunate in that respect, especially as the war progressed, since leather shoes were impossible to purchase.

I mentioned earlier that the Pierini family lived right around the corner from the school. Celestino Pierini married Benedetta Mechetti who was my mother's first cousin. Known as Betta, she and Celestino had seven children: Beppe, Teresina, Dora, Giuliana, Nora, Pier Luigi, and Anna Maria. Child number eight, Pierina, was born during the war.

A mason, Celestino constructed and remodeled many of the homes in Diecimo, and built his own beautiful house--a three-level home large enough to accomodate all of his children. The basement included several rooms and a wood burning bread oven. The street level had a living room, a dining room, a kitchen with an open fireplace and a large storeroom for his construction supplies which faced the street and had an overhead rollup metal door. The third floor had five bedrooms and one bathroom.

Celestino was a true craftsman who took pride in his work, and the quality of the materials that he used in his house reflected this pride. I was attracted to the Pierinis not only because they were relatives, but also because most of the children were close to my age. Being an only child, I sought their company.

The older girls helped around the house with the daily chores and they also worked their parcels of land. The two boys Beppe and Pier Luigi helped their father in the construction business.

My mother always planned lunch or the main meal of the day called *il pranzo* at 12:30, so it was crucial that I go directly home from school. My mother was not a great cook, but she prepared a good *minestrina in brodo* (chicken soup) served at every *pranzo*. My mother had a delicate stomach, consequently the meals were not highly seasoned and at times my father added pepper to the food while making critical remarks.

I especially liked and craved some of the local food such as *polenta, focacciette, necci, ballociori, mondine, tortelli*, and *pasta*. *Polenta* was made from corn meal or chestnut flour; *focacciette* were made similar to tortillas using wheat or corn; *necci* were flat cakes made from chestnut flour; *ballocciori* were boiled chestnuts; *mondine* were roasted chestnuts; *tortelli* were large ravioli. My mother avoided cooking the *contadino* type food.

The Pierini family usually ate their *pranzo* at 1 o'clock when Betta prepared *contadino* type food featuring the local seasonal crops. During the winter months it was common for them to have *necci* almost every day for their noon meal. Necci were served with ricotta cheese, with fried eggs, or dipped in a tomato sauce. I loved plain *necci* because they were naturally sweet since the chestnut flour had a high sugar content. At 12:30 I would dash out of school, run into the Pierini kitchen and help myself to a couple of hot *necci*. I rolled them up, stuck one in my pocket, and rushed out while eating the one that I carried in my hand. By the time I got home I usually finished eating the *necci* and my mother did not know about my illicit snack. Of course the Pierini kids thought that my noon time visit was humorous, seeing me rush in and dash out with hot *necci* in my hands. As I got older I realized that Betta probably did not appreciate my intrusion because I was taking food away from her children, but she never complained. I guess she wanted to keep the American cousin happy.

In the fall, during the chestnut season, I also stopped by the Pierini home on my way home from school, stuffed my pockets with hot boiled chestnuts and proceeded to eat them before I got home. The chestnuts were cooking in a large pot over the open fire in the fireplace and one of the kids scooped them out for me with a ladle, drained the water and gave me a handful. I stuck them in my pocket and continued my walk home eating the chestnuts along the way. I remember to this day that I could barely stand the pain from the heat which transferred from my pocket to my leg! Eventually I confessed to my mother about my snacks at the Pierini house. She told me that I should not continue to stop by because it was impolite to take food from their large family.

In Brighton, my mother had a wringer-type washing machine in the basement and we had hot and cold running water; in Diecimo, clothes washing facilities were very primitive. Most families washed their clothes in the *gora* in a communal wash area (the *gora* was an open waterway that flowed down the valley carrying irrigation water from the Pedogna River to the Serchio River). There was a locally controlled irrigation system so that parcels of land in the valley were assigned water for irrigation during the dry summer months. The *gora* was near the Barsotti *mulino* (mill) and fabricated from natural stones and rocks. Women kneeled on a stone surface, leaned over inclined stones and washed their clothes by dipping them in the running water, soaping them on the stone and working the clothes back and forth. The inclined stones were like washboards.

My mother could not force herself to do that, so at first she had a woman from the village wash our clothes. Later she asked Celestino Pierini if he would construct a wash tub in our basement kitchen. He removed the kitchen sink and put together a two-compartment wash tub so that the hand washing could be done in the house. The other major problem was the water supply; even though we had a water line going into the house, water was not always available, especially during the summer months. The local water system brought in the water from an area called *Colle* and the water flowed in an open trench until it reached a large concrete reservoir, then it was piped into the homes that had water lines and into the three public fountains in the village. Most of the time in the summer we went to the fountain in Piazza to get our water because there was not enough water pressure to carry the water to the houses. The water pressure was based on gravity flow and the small supply of water would not generate enough pressure for the water to reach the homes. One of my daily jobs was to walk to the piazza carrying 2 or 3 bottles in a cloth bag, to get our water supply and to keep our bottles full of water. The fountain in *piazza* had a brass faucet with a manually controlled valve which allowed the water to flow. We used old wine bottles for our water and once they were filled we placed corks in the tops so that the water would not get contaminated. In the summer I went to the fountain at the other end of the village in Zandori at lunch time to get ice cold water for our noon meal. The water came from a different spring than the water in *piazza* and was cool and refreshing. The water from both fountains was not treated with chemicals, it was pure spring water, originating in the local mountains.

As the school year was ending, around the middle of May 1940, I felt that I became a pretty good student and spoke Italian quite well. I survived the school year, earned good grades, and made many new friends. At the beginning of the school year I felt a bit strange because most of the students at the school were from *contadini* families and I was singled out as being from America.

There were several levels of society in the village: the *contadini* who worked for landowners and shared their crops; the *contadini* who owned their own land and worked the fields; and the rich or well-to-do, called *i signori.* At first I felt that our family fit into the last category and that we were considered rich. In Brighton there was no class distinction that I can remember. Fathers worked, the mothers stayed home and raised the children. Everyone was treated the same in our neighborhood. In Diecimo there were subtle layers of class distinction. I felt that my mother liked the role of being the *signora.*

In the Italian language there are two ways of addressing people, the familiar and the polite or formal form. The familiar consisted of *tu,* or *dare del tu*; the polite form of *lei, dare del Lei.* One had to learn which form to use with people, and the preferred form went with the social standing in the village. I used the familiar *tu* with my friends and with the *contadini* adults, and the polite *Lei* with teachers, the priest, and other adults of a higher social standing.

Part of the Fascist reform movement involved changing the Italian language and eliminating the class structure. Mussolini mandated the use of the familar form of the language and forced people to use the term *voi* (plural of the familiar form *tu*). Society was full of nuances that one had to follow in order to establish himself into a certain position in the village. I found the process to be a game, everyone playing it even if it was pointless.

On May 7, 1940, Hitler informed Mussolini by letter that he was attacking Belgium and Holland and that he would keep *il Duce* informed of his progress so that the *Duce* could make his own decisions in time. As soon as the Netherlands and Belgium surrendered, the Anglo-French northern armies defeated, and the surviving British troops began taking to the boats at Dunkirk, Mussolini decided to enter the war.

The Fuehrer asked *il Duce* to postpone his date of entry so that he could first knock out the rest of the French Air Force. Mussolini agreed to enter the war on June 10, 1940. Thirty-two Italian divisions, after a week of fighting, were unable to move a French force of six divisions on the western Alpine region down to the Riviera.

The French forces were also being threatened in the rear by the Germans in the Rhone Valley. Mussolini was upset in that his forces were unable to advance into French territory. On June 17, Mussolini and Count Ciano left Italy by train heading for Munich to confer with Hitler about the armistice with France. Mussolini wanted the Italian army to occupy the Rhone Valley, Toulon, the French naval base, and Marseilles. Of course, Hitler would not consider any of Mussolini's requests and *il Duce* was unable to get Hitler to agree to a joint armistice with France.

For historical purposes, Hitler did not want to share the French victory with the Italians; he wanted full credit for the victory. For the Italian population it was now official: Italy was at war!

I completed my first year of school and was promoted to the fourth grade. School was over around mid-May so that the children would be available to families to help harvest the wheat crops.

16. Top: Don Nello Marcucci Pievano of Pieve di Compito.
17. Bottom: 1958 photo of the author and *Signora* Ambrogi, former elementary school teacher.

5.
LIVING UNDER FASCISM

The *Fascio*, also called *il dopo lavoro*, (after work) was located in the southern corner of the *piazza*, opposite from the public fountain, on Via della Torre. The *Fascio* was a public locale that resembled a cafè or bar, and was part of the Fascist organization in Italy. The word *Fascio* also represented the Fascist symbol, called a *fascio littorio*, which was a bundle of wood, tied in three places with a protruding ax as part of the bundle. The word *fascio* meant bundle, so that if one had a bundle of wood, the Italian term would be *fascio di legna*. To the Fascists, the symbol represented the unification of Italian people fighting for a common cause. Originally the *Fascio* was set up as a meeting place for the Fascists; later the location in Diecimo evolved into a social meeting place for people, providing beverages, tables for playing cards, an outdoor stage, and an outdoor dance floor. Men usually spent the afternoons and evenings playing their favorite Italian card game, *Briscola*, and drinking wine. The wine, red or white, was usually served in 1/4, 1/2 and 1 liter bottles, or could also be purchased by the individual glass. The bottles, which were filled from large containers of wine, had a wide base and a flared top to facilitate the pouring of the wine.

In the early and mid 1930's many Italians were delighted with the works of Benito Mussolini, *Il Duce*, and almost everyone considered him to be a good leader, working hard to improve the social conditions in Italy. Villages were directly affected by the Fascist regime in that there were organized groups for everyone. Young children were in a group called *Figli della Lupa* (*Lupa* refers to the wolf that raised Romulus and Remus). Young boys aged 8 to 14 were in a group called *Balilla,* (nickname of a young boy hero named Perasso who threw a large stone at Austrian soldiers in 1746 initiating the battle which caused the retreat of the Austrians from the Genova area). Young girls were in a similar group called *Piccole Italiane.* When a young boy or girl became a member of the *Balilla* or the *Piccole Italiane* the children had to take the following oath:

Nel nome di Dio e dell'Italia giuro di eseguire gli ordini del Duce e di servire con tutte le mie forze e se necessario col mio sangue la causa della rivoluzione Fascista.

Translated into English: "In the name of God and Italy I swear to follow the orders of the *Duce* (Mussolini) and to serve with all my energy and if necessary spill my blood for the cause of the Fascist revolution."

Older boys, in the 16 to 20 year old range were in a group called *Avanguardisti* and the corresponding women's group was the *Giovani Italiane.* There was also mandatory service in the Italian Army at age 20 for all males in Italy and the men were assigned to different branches of the military, such as the *Fanteria* (Infantry), the *Alpini* (Mountain soldiers), the *Bersaglieri* (Bicycle soldiers), the *Artiglieria* (Artillery) or the *Marina* (Navy). The most avid Fascists would be assigned to the *Milizia* and would be part of the select group of Fascist soldiers called the *Camicie Nere* or black shirts.

There were two popular songs sung by young people in school, at rallies, and often heard on the radio. The *Inno della Patria,* also called *Giovinezza,* was the national anthem of Italy during the Fascist regime; the hymn is now banned in Italy. The other is dedicated to the boy named *Balilla.*

The words to both songs are presented below:

Inno della Patria:
Salve o popolo di eroi,
Salve o Patria immortale,
Son rinati i figli tuoi,
Con la fede dell'ideale.

Il valore dei tuoi guerrieri,
La vision dei pionieri,
La virtù dell'Alighieri,
Oggi brilla in tutti i cuor.

Giovinezza, giovinezza,
Primavera di bellezza,
Il Fascismo è la salvezza,
Della santa libertà.

I poeti e l'artigiani,
I signori e contadini,
Con l'orgoglio d'Italiani,
Giuran fede a Mussolini.

Giovinezza, giovinezza,
Primavera di bellezza,
Il Fascismo è la salvezza,
Della santa libertà.

Nella vita e nell'asprezza,
Il tuo canto squilla e va',
E per Benito Mussolini,
Eia, Eia, Alalà.

Inno di Balilla:
Fischia il sasso, il nome squilla,
Del ragazzo di Portoria,
Che l'intrepido Balilla,

Sta' gigante nella storia.

Era bronzo quel mortaio,
Che nel fango sprofondò,
Ma il ragazzo fù d'acciaio,
Che la madre liberò.

Fiero l'occhio' svelto il passo,
Chiaro il grido del valore,
Ai nemici, in fronte il sasso,
Agli amici tutto il cuor.

According to official records, in 1939 Fascist organizations in Italy were made up of the following numbers of members:

Partito Nazionale Fascista (National Fascist Party)
Combat Fascist units: 2,633,514
University Fascist groups: 105,883
Figli della Lupa: 1,546,389
Balilla: 1,746,560
Piccole Italiane: 1,622,766
Avanguardisti: 906,785
Giovani Italiane: 441,254
Giovani Fascisti: 1,176,798
Giovane Fasciste: 450,995
Fasci Femminili: 774,181
Massaie Rurali: 1,481,321
Operaie e Lavoranti a Domicilio: 501,415

Associazione della Scuola (School Association)
Scuola Elementare: 121,437
Scuola Media: 40,896
Professori Universitari: 3,272
Assistenti Universitari: 2,468

Belle Arti e Biblioteche: 2,500

Associazioni Varie (Various Associations)
Publico Impiego: 294,265
Ferroviari: 137,902
Postatelegrafi: 83,184
Aziende Statali: 120,205
Unione Nazionale Ufficiali in Congedo: 259,865
Opera Nazionale Dopolavoro: 3,832,248
Comitato Olimpico: 809,659
Lega Navale Italiana: 198,522
Reparti d'Arma: 1,309,600

The total number of Italians officially enrolled in Fascist party associations was 20,603,884.

Politically the village of Diecimo seemed to be divided into three distinct factions: (1) the Fascists; (2) the church affiliated people under the guidance of the *Pievano* (priest), Don Udone Diodati; (3) and the Communists (the people who did not feel like working, were trying live off the government and wanted a share of everything). There were also three gathering places in the village called *bars* that seemed to be politically aligned with the three groups. There was *Iride* in *piazza* (2), *Niccola* at the *cappella* (3) and the *Fascio* which I previously described (1). The Italian custom was that only men frequented the bars and the women remained at home. Italy definitely had a male dominated society. The men usually dropped by the bars after lunch, during the warm part of the day, and again at night after dinner to play *Briscola* and drink wine.

Usually the loser of the card game would pay for the wine. The card games generated a lot of noisy talk and often political discussions would ensue regarding Mussolini and what he was trying to do to the Italians. Most of the people seemed to be anti-government, even though they seemed to benefit from some of the Fascist programs.

The store next door to our house which was known as *la bottega di Niccola* (Niccola's store) sold *generi alimentari* (food products). In addition, part of the store was used as a bar which was run by Niccola's husband, Nello Lazzari. The store portion sold food products during the normal operating hours for stores, from 8 a.m. to 1 p.m., then from 4 p.m. to 8 p.m. Grocery stores closed in the afternoon during the noon-time meal hours and the hours of *riposo* (rest time). The bar portion of the store remained open during the *riposo* time and stayed open until late in the evening, usually until around midnight. Nello served wine to the men who came into the bar to play cards and to gossip about the political situation in Italy. The men who frequented the bar seemed to be anti-Fascists, perhaps more aligned with the philosophy of the Communist party.

The store front was made of a wooden frame door with glass windows. There were also windows along each side of the door which allowed light into the store. At closing time the door and windows were covered with a roll-down metal corrugated door called a *saracinesca* which was rolled up at opening time the next day. As one walked into the store one had to walk past several marble-top tables that were used to play cards. In the back, there were two marble-top counters, separated by a walk-through opening for Niccola and Nello. The counter on the right side had two types of scales which were used in the sale of the food products. One of the scales was a counter type scale with a balance arm on which were mounted two large brass plates. Different small brass weights of certain denominations were placed in one plate to make up the required weight. The food product to be sold was placed in the other plate and when the balance arm became horizontal, the weight in both plates was the same. The other scale was affixed to the ceiling by means of a large hook. A large brass dish was secured to one side of a steel balance arm with three pieces of chain. The balance arm had markings on the side and a sliding weight. The product to be weighed was placed in the plate and the weight moved along the metal rod. When the metal weight reached a position of balance, the metal rod was horizontal, then the weight was read off the scale. There was also a stack of yellow, straw based wrapping paper that was used to wrap the food. Later, during the war, when the yellow wrapping paper was not available, pieces of newspapers were used to wrap food. Products were sold according to metric weight, such as a kilogram or fractions of a kilogram. The common unit was the 100 gram unit known as one *etto*. People asked for a certain number of *etti* (plural of *etto*). "*Dammi due etti di salame.*" (Give me 200 grams of salame).

I remember that when we arrived in Diecimo there was a wide variety of food products in the store. I remember seeing displays of canned products on the shelves, along with candy, chocolate, pasta, bread, vegetables, and fruit. The counter on the left was used primarily for the sale of cheese or cold cuts made from pork. One could buy sausage by the link, sliced *salame, prosciutto* and *mortadella*, and chunks of hard *pecorino* or *parmigiano* cheese for grating. During that period of time, the pork products and cheese were not refrigerated because there weren't any refrigerators in the village. The meat products were kept in cool places in stores and homes.

The *contadini* in the village did not have much cash so much of the food that was purchased in stores was bought on credit. Many of the women worked at one of the two factories in the valley. A cotton thread factory was located in Piaggione, the village next to Diecimo, across the river. The other factory, which made ammunition for the military, was located at Fornaci di Barga, further up the valley, about 10 kilometers from Diecimo. Wives and older daughters were employed and brought home money which was used to purchase food and clothing items. The credit system involved keeping the records of the transactions in two set of books. The people came to the store carrying a *libretto* (small notebook). Niccola totaled the expenses and recorded the amount spent in the *libretto* and in her own ledger on the page with the person's name. At the end of the month, when people were paid, they came into the store and paid their entire debt or a portion of the debt. When the people in Diecimo were forced to evacuate in the summer of 1944, the Lazzari family left an empty store. The Germans took the few remaining food products and the people in the village who owed money left without paying and the debts were never paid after the people returned home.

Nello and Niccola worked very hard in their business operation. They lived across the street from the store in a large, three story house with their two children, Sandrino and Fedra; they were both school teachers. Nello's sister Pia was an invalid who lived on the top floor of the house.

At times I visited the bar in the afternoons or evenings and sat around watching the men play cards. The animated conversations around the card tables were about Fascism, the Duce, the war or the game itself, and often the men ended up shouting at each other, often using swear words. There were no bathroom facilities in the store or the bar, so when the men had to urinate, they walked outside and walked a few steps to the *muretto* (small wall), faced the wall with their back to the street and proceeded to urinate against the wall. Due to the fact that my bedroom window faced the street and was almost directly above the door to the bar, at night I found it difficult to sleep because of the noise and the smell of *piscia* (urine).

Children usually were allowed in bars because they were often affiliated with grocery stores and sold food products, such as candy and *gelato* (ice cream). We spent a lot of our time watching the men play cards, learning some of the game techniques, and listening to the village gossip. It was like being in school. The children also played cards, not in the bars, but in their homes at the kitchen table. We also played cards outdoors, typically on front door steps or on sidewalks. *Briscola* was the favorite game, but we also played *scopa, bazzica, tre sette, sette e mezzo* and poker. The Italian deck of cards is different from the American deck of cards; it is a forty card deck, rather than a 52 card deck, thus there are no eights, nines or tens. The Italian card terminology is as follows:

Ace	*Asso*
King	*Re*
Queen	*Regina o La Donna*
Jack	*Fante*
seven	*sette*
six	*sei*
five	*cinque*
four	*quattro*
three	*tre (worth ten points in Briscola)*
two	*due*

The suits:
Hearts	*cuori*
Clubs	*fiori*
Diamonds	*diamanti*
Spades	*picche*

The game of *briscola* could be played by two or four persons with a two player partnership. It was allowable for the partners to signal to each other and show their high card points in *briscola*. In American card games a designated suit in certain games is called the trump suit. *Briscola* means a card suit that can trump other suits. The following signals were used and were standard in Italy:

Ace	wink of an eye
King	raising both eyes to the ceiling
Queen	sticking your tongue out of the center of your mouth
Jack	lifting a shoulder
Three	moving your mouth to the side, like a twitch

Because of the situation at home, with my father still confined to bed most of the time, I did not have much direct supervision, so I did what I wanted to do. During the previous year my mother had bought me a bicycle which I was allowed to ride whenever I wanted, so I had wheels and it gave me some independence. My mother and father purchased a few additional pieces of furniture, such as an inexpensive living room set, a dining room set and a console radio-phonograph. In addition my mother bought a larger bed for my father and he moved into the large bedroom toward the front of the house at the top of the stairs while she remained in the back bedroom. His health was gradually improving, but he was not able to get up and walk to any great extent except to go to the bathroom, and climbing the stairs was out of the question.

After June 10, 1940, when Italy officially entered the war, the American Consulate in Florence communicated with us by mail, pointing out that all American citizens were being asked to return to the United States as soon as possible. Because of the war conditions in Europe, it would not be safe for us to remain in Italy. I remember discussions between my mother and father regarding our possible return to the United States. They decided that it would be impossible for my father to travel since he had not fully recovered from his heart attack. My father and mother decided to remain in Diecimo and take our chances because we did not want to split up the family and leave my father in Italy. They thought that we would be safe in Diecimo during the war. I remember accepting the situation and not worrying about all the consequences that might occur during a war. In fact, I had no idea about war and what it was.

Religion was never a big topic of discussion in our family. I was raised a Catholic in Brighton and received my First Communion in 1938 at the Saint Colombkille Catholic Church in Brighton. My mother and I used to attend Mass on Sunday mornings, but my father did not attend church. My mother was a very religious person, and because my uncle Nello became a priest, the Catholic Church was a very important part of her life. When I arrived in Diecimo I discovered that the church and the *Pievano* (the parish priest) had great influence over the village people. The church, Pieve di Santa Maria Annunziata, was located between Diecimo and the district of Roncato. In order to reach the church, I had to walk about half a mile from our house, though the *piazza*, past the chapel dedicated to San Giovanni Leonardi, and finally on a dirt road to the church complex. The complex included the *chiesa* (church), the *campanile* (bell tower), and the *canonica* (parish house). There were daily masses early in the morning on weekdays, usually attended only by a few women. On Sunday mornings there were masses at 7:00 a.m., 9:00 a.m., and 11:00 a.m. On Sunday afternoons there was a vespers service, at 4:00 p.m. in the winter, and at 5:00 p.m. in the summer. I don't believe that our church in Brighton had a vespers service.

The church was arranged in such a way that the women sat to the rear of the church, while the men sat at the front. The main altar was in the center, and there were two small altars, one on each side, one dedicated to San Giovanni Leonardi and the other dedicated to the Virgin Mary. The main altar had a section directly behind it, hidden from view, which was used by the church choral group (*la corale*) during services that required singing. The church was a twelfth century church, built of stone, with a stone floor, and it was extremely cold and damp during winter.

At the rear of the church there was a large pipe organ mounted high on the wall above large double doors. One could access the keyboard of the organ by climbing a flight of stairs and walking along a narrow balcony that led to the organ. The Sandretti brothers, Giuseppe and Sandrino, were the only two musicians in the village, and they played the organ for special church services. Modern day pipe organs have electric air pumps to generate enough air pressure for their operation. In Diecimo there was a manual pump that was operated by a lever which was located near the keyboard and had to be moved up and down while the organist was playing. In order to keep busy during some of the boring church services I volunteered to operate the pump. I did not mind the work and I enjoyed listening to the organ music and helping my friend Sandrino.

The *Pievano*, Don Udone Diodati and his sister Marzia, came to Diecimo from Marlia, a village near Lucca, in 1928. Don Udone was an influential figure in Diecimo, directing village people, from birth to death, in his own authoritarian way. There were certain unwritten rules established by the *Pievano* for young people in the village: young people were not allowed to attend movies; young people were not allowed to dance; young people had to go to confession every Saturday; young people had to attend mass every Sunday and receive communion; young people had to obey their fathers and mothers; and everyone had to be at Mass on time. It seemed to me that there were a lot more rules to follow in Diecimo than in the United States.

I remember that during the Mass, after the *Pievano* started the service, if he heard people talking outside the church, he left the altar, walked outside, brought back those who were delaying their entrance, and accompanied them to a church pew. His sermons dealt not only with religious topics, but also with the politics of the day, and at times, some of the Fascists in attendance would walk out in protest. The *Pievano* encouraged young boys to become *sacrestani*, or altar boys. The altar boys wore a white vestment with a bright red mantle, and helped the priest during the church services. My mother thought that it would be socially appropriate for me to become involved in the church, so I became a *sacrestano*. My mother sewed my uniform and for a while I participated in many mass and vespers ceremonies. To be very honest, I hated being a *sacrestano* and quit after about six months. Being a shy boy I did not enjoy being in front of people in the church and was fearful that I would not perform my tasks satisfactorily during the religious services.

Children were told that when they encountered a priest in the village they were to say: "*Sia lodato Gesù Cristo*" (Jesus Christ be praised) and the priest would then respond: "*Sempre sia lodato*" (He will always be praised). It seemed to me that the priest demanded too much respect, was in a sense an absolute ruler, and was not at all like the priests I had met in the United States.

There were always religious holidays during the year when special services were held in the main church or in one of the three chapels in the village. There were also the processions through the village on Santa Maria (August 15) and in June for the Corpus Domini holiday. One of the local customs was the annual benediction of the homes in the village by the *Pievano*. This usually took place in the Spring and consisted of the priest visiting each home in the village, examining each room for cleanliness, and, if the rooms were clean, blessing each room of the house with holy water. In order to prepare for the *benedizione*, the women of the village carefully cleaned each room in the house, sweeping, dusting, mopping the floor and making certain that everything was spotless, so that the priest would be able to give the *benedizione* to protect the home from all evil things. I remember that my mother worked hard with the help of a neighbor woman, dusting the furniture, scrubbing the tile floors, and washing the windows in order to make our house presentable. On a regular schedule, traveling from one end of the village to the other, the priest entered the various homes, examined each room, sprinkled holy water in each room, then left to move on to the next house. According to many people, the *Pievano* did not hesitate to tell people if their homes were dirty, and he would not bless them until they were clean.

Within a few days of the birth of a child, it was the local custom that the child be baptized, using the hand carved hexagonal stone baptismal font in the rear of the church. In church historical documents reference is made to a *Pievano* named Iacopo, in Diecimo in the year 979, who helped establish Diecimo as the regional baptismal center utilizing the same hexagonal font. The church in Diecimo was one of five churches to receive a special hand-carved stone font. The other churches were in the villages of Sesto, Mozzano, Barga and Brancoli.

The baptism ceremony usually took place in the afternoon and the Pievano needed to have *sacrestani* present to help him hold the necessary implements. The child who was to be baptized was carried into the church by his *madrina* (godmother) with the help of the *padrino* (godfather), while the parents of the child took a secondary role in the ceremony. As a *sacrestano* I often attended baptisms, helping the Pievano, hoping for a tip of a few *centesimi* from the family of the child for my services. The tiny babies would usually be relatively quiet during the first part of the service, but as soon as the ice cold water hit their heads they would let out a surprised scream which would reverberate throughout the church. On one occasion, in May 1944, I was asked at age 14, to be a *padrino* for my cousin Roberto Marcucci. Over the years I forgot about my role as a godfather until I was reminded by Roberto in 1993 that I forgot to give him birthday gifts for 49 years. It is a custom in Italy for godfathers to give their godchildren a birthday gift each year. I was reminded that I owed him 49 gifts!

The cemetery or *camposanto* was located close to the church, about two hundred meters away, up a slight hill. The *camposanto* was enclosed by stone walls on the back and sides, had a decorative wrought iron fence and gate in the front, and could be reached by walking up one of the two paths leading to the gate from either side of the front entrance. When a person died in Italy, he or she had to be buried within 48 hours because the bodies were not embalmed. If the person died of natural causes at home, usually the female family members cleaned and washed the body. The body was then dressed, using the person's best suit or dress, and the body was placed on a bed in a position of repose, hands crossed on the chest. Usually people came into the home and paid their respects to the deceased by saying a few prayers at the bedside. Some of the family members and friends also took turns remaining with the body until the funeral services. One of the local cabinet makers was commissioned to prepare a wooden casket based on the size of the dead person. Large paper funeral announcements were printed and posted throughout the village to announce the death. The notices, which were bordered in black, showed the name of the dead person, his or her age, and the date and time of the funeral services.

Shortly before the time of the funeral services, the body was placed in the wooden casket and then the casket was nailed shut. During the early 1940's the caskets were transported to the church by horse-drawn carts or by handpulled carts. The casket was then placed on a special stand in the front of the church, in front of the altar, alongside the opening in the communion rail that led to the center of the altar. The funeral ceremony was conducted by the Pievano; the prayers were in Latin, were not understood by the people, but were recited from memory. All of the women mourners attended the funeral dressed in black, and there was also a church rule that the women in the family of the deceased had to wear black for the entire year following the death of a family member. The women of the village followed this rule, while the men wore a black arm band. I noticed that the great majority of the women in the village always wore black, and I often wondered how many people died in their families to justify the constant wearing of the black garments.

At the end of the funeral service, the *Pievano* led the procession of mourners and pallbearers carrying the casket to the cemetery, while the church bells clanged in the background. By that time, the grave was dug in the ground, the pallbearers positioned the casket over the grave and lowered it down by using two ropes. The family members and the *Pievano* recited the final prayers for the repose of the soul of the deceased. When they were finished, a family member tossed a handful of dirt on the coffin, and the gesture was repeated by all those present. Before leaving the *camposanto*, people located the graves of their own deceased family members and relatives and paused to say a few prayers. Current practices in Diecimo still require the burial of a deceased person to take place within 48 hours, but rather than placing the casket directly into the ground, the casket is now placed in a grave dug in the ground, then sealed with bricks and cement. When the cement is dry, the family of the deceased commissions one of the local monument companies to prepare a decorative marble slab or statue to fit over the grave site.

The religious services conducted by our priest were crucial to the people of Diecimo. Most of the people living in Diecimo were born there, lived there and would die there. A few ventured away from their native village, such as those who emigrated to the United States, but most would probably never go further than Borgo a Mozzano, which was three kilometers away. The women seemed to be the most religious and they reinforced the teachings of the *Pievano* by providing good religious practices for their children. The men attended Mass on Sundays and holidays, hoping that their presence in church would be noted by the *Pievano* and would guarantee their entrance into Heaven when they died. The parish priests were powerful political forces in Italy and I feel that they were partially responsible for the fall of Fascism.

In 1968 Pievano Don Udone Diodati died. He spent forty years in Diecimo helping the people of the village, from birth to death. A young man, Nardo Nardi wrote the following tribute to the Pievano, which was published in a local newspaper. I have translated the article from Italian:

Just like that, you take off! (Reference to the death of the Pievano) I see you kneeling on the church steps, by the main entrance, just like it was forty years ago, when you thanked God, moved by the splendid church that He assigned to you.

I see you going off in the distance, along the road, not dusty anymore, like your first days in the parish and I know that in your heart you have such an enormous knot. A knot that will not set anyone free. I address you with the familiar "tu," Don Udone Diodati, Pievano di Diecimo, because one day you told me you gave permission to a privileged few and today I want to be among those privileged ones at all costs. Because today I am speaking to you on behalf of all your parishioners.

We have often "collided" in the brief forty years and the resolution of the issues were not always mutually agreed upon. Very often, for us, you were "high and mighty," Don Udone Diodati, Pievano di Diecimo, and we were mad at the way you treated us. Often many of us would have forcefully carried you to the outskirts of our parish and left you, so that we would not have to see you again because of your free-wheeling comments. At times we would have given our eyesight to see you a bit more calm, to see you smile, Don Udone Diodati, Pievano di Diecimo. You were not with us, Pievano, at certain meetings, where we discussed doing something for you, for example, a celebration just for you.

We were among ourselves, red, whites, blacks, kiss-asses, those that did not give a damn, priest haters. You know what, Pievano? A genuine caring for you was evident among the group. The further they were away from you, the more they cared. The more you mistreated us, the more we cared.

Dear Pievano, you seldom understood from where and from whom you would receive affection; at times you embarrassed your most devoted friend, he who would have done anything for you.

We don't blame you Don Udone Diodati, Pievano di Diecimo, we have also made mistakes in the way that we treated you, don't you take the full blame.

And just like that, you take off!

We were used to you and we feel your absence; in leaving us you are taking something away from us, something indefinable, as if our soul or part of it follows you.

You are taking away forty years of your life, Don Udone Diodati, Pievano di Diecimo. You take with you our best days, the twenty years of my dreams, the passion, the pain, the anxieties, the torment of a full life. You take with you the tears of the penances, the wailing of the sick, the wistful look of the dying, the cry of a just-born at the baptismal font, the emotion of receiving communion, the expression on the faces of the dead. You take with you forty years of life in Diecimo.

Maybe you never saw your church so full of people, moved when you blessed us for the last time, Don Udone Diodati, Pievano di Diecimo, because we love you.

Maybe it will seem strange to you and it will seem strange to everyone that it is I to speak to you in this way. I with whom you have never been indulgent, when we misunderstood each other, and when you also have been hostile with me. It is not important what you think, or what people think. You have been for me and all the others, a man of God, always. The man, Udone Diodati, hurt our feelings, but as a priest, never. Today, we fix our eyes on you as a priest, not as a man.

For this reason, Pievano, we are all around you, emotionally touched. For this reason, Pievano, we fraternally embrace you and we all say "good-bye."

For this reason, Pievano, kneeling in front of you, we request for our children, for our deceased, for ourselves, your last paternal blessing.

On August 31, 1990, the newspaper *La Nazione*, carried an article in the Cronaca di Lucca section honoring the efforts of Don Udone Diodati. The bold face headline was:

GRANDE EROE DELLA LIBERTÀ
(Great Hero of Freedom)

The article following the headline is translated from Italian below:

> Don Udone Diodati, native of Marlia, was able to snatch 300 of his parishioners from the Germans and take them to freedom. On July 16, 1944, while he was Pievano of Diecimo, Don Diodati received a pre-emptive order from the German Command to evacuate the entire village. The destination of the villagers would be the town of Sassuolo, in the Emilia region of Italy, and they would be transported by train and trucks. He assembled the villagers and the climate at the meeting was one of desperation. He did not hesitate to advise the people to disregard the order of the German Command to pack their belongings, to leave Diecimo and head for the valleys and hills nearby, in the areas of Villa Roggio, Colognora, Vetriano and Piegaio, instead of being transported by the Germans to Sassuolo. At Piegaio, on September 23, Don Udone assembled many of his parishioners and during the night, in secret, he courageously guided them toward the Allied Army lines. A column of 300 people made a dangerous journey, and ventured across mine fields, through forests, and artillery fire, and over the mountain. On the morning of September 24, the people, led by Don Udone, reached San Martino in Freddana where they encountered an American patrol and reached freedom.

I'll never forget Don Udone Diodati. He did his very best for the people, his mission was to provide the spiritual leadership for the community. He went beyond that and tried to influence the personal lives of many by being forceful in his demands. He appeared to be a dictator, but under that brusque exterior there was a sensitive and caring man.

6.
VILLAGE LIFE

During school, the afternoons were essentially free time for most of the children in Diecimo. The girls my age went to Delia's or Beppina's to learn how to sew, so they were busy all afternoon. The boys hung around in piazza, by the water fountain, some with their bicycles. If the weather was nice, we stayed outside; if it was cold, we found a warm place for our shelter. Because of this procedure I became well-acquainted with much of the craft work going on in the village, and this is possibly why, as I got older, I became interested in working with my hands and becoming a craftsman. After I graduated from high school and went to college I became an Industrial Arts teacher. I developed manipulative skills in drafting and working with metals and wood, and taught those skills to my students.

One of my prized Christmas presents in 1938, before we left Boston, was a Red Ryder B-B rifle. My parents gave me the rifle because many of the neighborhood children in Brighton had them. My father liked to hunt and at the same time thought that the B-B gun was an appropriate gift for a young boy. I liked the rifle and actually had a pretty good eye. When we left Boston I bought several packages of B-B's to take along to Italy.

The air rifle was a novelty among my friends and I remember sharing my rifle with them when we were trying to shoot small *lucertole* (lizards) off exterior walls where they were sleeping in the mid-day sun. I was a good shot and usually hit the lizards in the head. Unfortunately I ran out of American B-B's and had to use the Italian version.

They were lead pellets which fit the Red Ryder rifles; they were shaped like a small lead bullet, hollowed out in the rear, so that the air could propel the pellet. They became difficult to locate because of the war, and with no ammunition available we had to give up hunting lizards.

Diecimo had four cabinetmaking shops. The cabinetmakers in the village were: Aladino Agostinelli, Pietro Malerbi, Remo Nardi and Medoro Frugoli. They were skilled woodworkers who also hired other *falegnami* (cabinetmakers), trained young apprentices or at times worked by themselves. Medoro had a small shop, so he primarily worked on small jobs, as did Remo Nardi. Aladino Agostinelli and Pietro Malerbi always had several of the local boys working for them as apprentices. All of the young men eventually became excellent craftsmen. Pietro Malerbi had Beppe Sandretti as an apprentice, and Aladino Agostinelli had Aldo Giambastiani as an apprentice.

I often went into the shops and watched the workers construct furniture for people in the valley. They specialized in making fine wood furniture of chestnut and oak. They typically made tables, chairs, bedroom sets, armoires, chests of drawers and china cabinets. I was fascinated while watching the workers use the large saws and machines to cut and shape the wood. Some of the machines were driven by water power and others were powered by electricity. The water flowed in the small water races, called the *gora*, that brought the water to a large water wheel at the Malerbi shop and turned the wheel so that the rotary motion turned a series of shafts and pulleys which powered the machines inside the building. The shops which were not located near the *gora* used electrical power for the operation of the machines. The line voltage in Italy was, and still is, 50 cycle alternating current and rated at 240 volts.

The *falegnami* made sketches of the pieces of furniture they were going to construct, with all the necessary measurements, and planned which kind of wood they were going to use. Chestnut wood was used for the majority of the furniture since it was plentiful and easy to cut and shape on the machines. The large chestnut tree trunks were cut on the local mountains, brought in, cut lengthwise on huge band saws, then planed into boards and eventually assembled into beautiful pieces of furniture. Occasionally Aldo or Beppe would hand me several pieces of scrap wood with a few hand tools, such as a plane or hammer and chisel and encourage me to produce something with the wood. I kept busy for hours making my own creations and I also remember volunteering to help with the finishing process. In those days the finish for the wood consisted of several coats of a French polish shellac-based finish. The process involved soaking a rag pad in shellac and rubbing the wood in circular motions until the surfaces became smooth and shiny. In order to achieve the high luster finish used on furniture, several coats of shellac were applied. The final polishing was accomplished with an alcohol soaked pad made of linen. I enjoyed being in the cabinet-making shops very much, smelling the wood, being around the machines and using the hand tools. I marveled at the beauty of the finished furniture products. When one entered homes in the village it was a pleasure to see the many beautiful pieces of furniture designed and constructed by the cabinetmakers in Diecimo. I really appreciated the shelter and warmth provided by the cabinet-making shops during the rainy season and during the cold weather. The owners of the shops did not mind having one or two kids hanging around watching them work, because occasionally some of the observers were recruited to be apprentices and eventually became an asset to the owner of the business.

The tailor shop in piazza was operated by Mario Mechetti who specialized in making men's suits, jackets, trousers and overcoats. The shop was called *Sartoria Mechetti (sarto* means tailor, thus *sartoria*). It was a small shop and Mario employed a few of the local men to work for him as *sarti*. I remember Cecchino, Aldo Paolucci, and Aldo *Il Simi* sitting in the room basting and assembling the garments by hand, then sewing them on the pedal driven sewing machines and ironing the clothes with the charcoal heated iron. It was always warm in the *sartoria*, probably because of the heat generated by the hot coal container which kept the charcoal lit for use in the large iron which was used to press the finished garments. The iron was about 16 inches long, four inches wide, five inches high and had a wooden handle connected to the top lid. One lifted the lid, placed the hot, glowing pieces of charcoal in the iron, closed the lid, and then waited for the heat to transfer to the sole plate of the iron. Mario was a very tall man, probably 6 feet, 4 inches tall, so he was the perfect height to do the ironing on the high cutting table. In order to test the iron to see if it was at the proper temperature, he spit on his finger tips, then touched the sole plate of the iron, and if it sizzled the proper way, the iron was ready for use.

Before the war started there was plenty of fabric available in clothing stores, especially woolen fabrics from England and Scotland. Most men in Diecimo owned one good suit which was worn only to Mass on Sundays and holidays. Ready-made suits were not available in stores, so when a man decided to buy a suit, Mario measured the person and made a paper pattern from which the suit was made. The type and quality of the material determined the price of the suit. After the war started, fabric became scarce, and was sold at inflated prices. The tailor shop was generally busy not only with the sewing of new suits but also with alterations. Old suits and overcoats were carefully taken apart by removing old stitches, and then the fabric was cut into patterns for the smaller members of the family. During some of the slow periods, when I went into the shop I tried to copy some of the procedures that the tailors were using. I was given pieces of scrap materials, needle and thread, and I pretended that I was sewing articles of clothing by hand. I learned to baste pieces together before sewing on the machine. I learned to make button holes, and I learned how to make simple cuffs on trousers. Sometimes Aldo or Cecchino actually let me use the sewing machines to assemble my creations. It is interesting that I still can remember some of the techniques that I learned at that time and use them to do minor sewing jobs at home. The best thing about being in the tailor shop was that we were able to listen to all the village gossip and keep warm at the same time. Some of the men from the village, including my father, came into the shop, sat around and talked about the war and the political situation in Italy.

There were two other locations where one could learn how to sew. One was at Beppa Luvisi's home and the other was at Delia Menesini's home. I preferred Delia's home because it was close to my house and the girls attending her sessions were cute, especially her cousin Ione, who came to Diecimo during the summer months. When I visited Delia I sat around with the girls, preferably next to Ione, and observed what they were doing. In many instances they were practicing various hand sewing techniques. At times I was given a needle and thread and participated in the exercises, such as making button holes, hems, assembling parts of garments and actually I completed the tasks with some satisfaction. The sessions, normally held in the afternoons, usually became social gatherings where we were able to pick up a lot of village gossip. I primarily attended the sewing sessions so that I could associate with some of the girls who were my age. I did not think that my presence and partici-pation in the sewing excercises was unmanly, it was an excuse to flirt with the girls and at the same time learn a few skills.

Giacomino Derni was an orphan, a few years older than I was, who lived with his sister in the *Piastrone* area. Giacomino was a hard working boy, always doing something mechanical, especially with bicycles. During the war years bicycles were a great asset to people because they were the only method of transportation available and it was prudent to keep the bicycles in good running condition. Because of this, Giacomino opened a bicycle repair shop in the street level room of his sister's house so that he could work and earn some money. The large room did not have any fancy equipment, but was roomy enough to accommodate a workbench and several bicycles at a time. Giacomino designed and made a few fixtures to hold the bicycles off the ground while he repaired them. The bicycle shop became a hangout for some of my friends and me because we all rode bicycles and at times Giacomo made minor service adjustments on our bikes. I spent hours in the shop watching Giacomo disassemble and repair bikes. I was fascinated by his ability to diagnose the trouble and make the repairs. By watching Giacomo, I learned how to maintain and repair bicycles and took care of the all the bicycles in our family.

Rubber was a scarce commodity during the war because most of the rubber in Italy was being used to manufacture tires and inner tubes for military vehicles. As a result, new bicycle tires were hard to find, and people had to be creative in order to keep the old tires in good running condition. Giacomo devised a system to repair worn bicycle tires that extended their life for a while. He removed the worn tire from the bike, used a grinding wheel to remove a portion of the rubber around the worn area without damaging the tire casing. He then cut out rubber patches from thick old automobile inner tubes and glued the patches in place to cover the hole. Once the adhesive was dry, he again used the grinder to smooth and feather out the rough edges of the inner tube patch so that it blended in with the original tire tread. If done properly, the patch lasted a long time and gave a fairly smooth ride. The patches were made from old, red or black heavy duty automobile or truck inner tubes. When the red inner tubes were used to patch the tires the patchwork made an interesting pattern against the black bicycle tire casing. While observing all this work I became proficient in removing tires from bicycle wheels and learned how to patch inner tubes. The experiences helped me in later life in maintaining and repairing bicycles for my children and for myself. After the war Giacomo continued along a mechanical career. He became an automobile mechanic, married Elvira Malerbi, and operated a gas station and auto repair shop in Diecimo. Giacomo is now 70 years old and is retired from work, but he still loves bicycles and rides his racing bike around the valley once a week.

During the war, shoes and leather products were difficult to procure, either from normal sources such as stores, or on the black market. People living in Diecimo and the surrounding villages wore *zoccoli* instead of leather shoes. As I mentioned previously, the *zoccoli* were made up of a wooden base sculptured by hand to the shape of the sole of the human foot by using large draw knives. Once the wooden platform was made, then the top portion of the *zoccolo* was cut out of leather or canvas in the shape of a boot with holes for laces, and it was fastened to the base with nails. There were several families in the village who made the wooden bases for *zoccoli* by hand and they were custom made as people requested them. Michele, the local shoemaker, made leather shoes, re-soled shoes, and made the leather tops for the *zoccoli*. His place of business was located near the piazza, in a very narrow room, about eight feet wide and about twenty feet long. The entry door was made of wood with glass windows so that one could see the interior of the shop from the street. The walls of the shop were lined with paper shoe top patterns and wooden shoe forms hanging from nails. Michele was a very short man, about five feet tall, who always sat on a small child-sized stool, behind his cobbler's bench, facing the street. He always wore a dirty apron that was covered with pitch and shoe polish stains. One of his rituals was the preparation of the thread for stitching the leather together while assembling shoes or when he replaced worn leather soles. He first determined the length of thread that he needed for the hand sewing operation. For example, if he was going to sew the leather sole of a shoe to the welt of the shoe, he needed a piece of thread that was long enough to go completely around the shoe. The material that he used for the thread appeared to be a hemp string or twine. He then attached the ends of the string to a length of a single horse tail bristle, pulling and undoing the string so that the ends tapered to the diameter of the horse tail bristle. He then coated the string with pitch in order to waterproof the string and to seal the horse tail bristle to the string. In order to ensure that the string was coated properly he would run it back and forth with his hand across his leg which was covered by his apron, pulling it back and forth across a larger piece of pitch. The process used to sew the leather involved punching a hole in the layers of leather with an awl, next feeding the horse bristle from each end of the string through the hole from both sides, then pulling the strings through, and finally pulling the two ends of the string tight against the leather. In this way he had the stitch on both sides of the leather. In order for the stitch to be recessed on the sole of the shoe, he scored the leather around the perimeter of the sole with a knife before starting, and as he pulled the stitches tight, the stitches disappeared into the cut groove, hidden from view, and protected from wear.

As the war continued Michele became more involved in repairing shoes, rather than making new shoes, because of the shortage of leather and rubber. As leather for soles became more difficult to obtain, Michele used parts of old automobile tires to replace worn soles of shoes. I often went in to visit Michele and observed what he was doing. In the wintertime the shop was fairly warm, because Michele always had a *scaldino* on the floor near his legs. A *scaldino* was a ceramic or metal container with a handle, shaped like a small basket. During the winter months it was common for people to place the *scaldino* by their feet when they were working or sitting down. The *scaldino* was filled with charcoal pieces which were taken from a fireplace and kept burning by natural air flow, adding additional charcoal as needed to keep the fire going. The *scaldino* generated enough heat to keep the person's feet and legs warm and also kept people warm who were sitting nearby.

Sometimes when I walked by the shop, if there was no one with Michele, I stopped by and sat alongside him at the workbench in order to observe the various techniques used in assembling and repairing shoes. Occasionally Michele kept me busy by assigning me some simple tasks. Once a piece of new leather was cut to size and readied to fit the bottom of a shoe, the leather was pounded flat with a hammer and hardened while the leather rested on a small platen, such as a clothes iron with a handle. It was a boring job, not very difficult to do, and at times he would ask me prepare the leather. I placed the iron handle between my legs, and gently hammered the entire piece of leather with a small flat hammer on the surface of the iron until the leather was compressed and hard. The leather started out about 1/4 of an inch in thickness and was compressed to about 3/16 of an inch. I did not mind doing the various chores, because I found the work interesting and it involved the use of my hands.

I remember later on during the war, in the winter of 1943, that my feet had grown, and I needed a new pair of boots for the winter. My father had a pair of American hunting boots, made of leather, which laced up to a point just below the knee. While discussing the possibility of having Michele make a pair of boots for me, he told my father that if he cut the leather off the top part of the boots, from the ankle to the top of the boot, that the upper leather portion of the boot could be used to make me a pair of boots. My father liked the idea, so Michele cut the boots and made a paper shoe pattern to fit my foot. The next problem was to find leather for the soles before he could actually make the boots. It was preferable to have leather soles on the boots and hobnails on the soles to prevent wear. It took Michele several months to find the leather for the soles, but eventually he did finish the boots. Unfortunately too much time elapsed since he made the pattern for the boots, and by the time they were ready, my feet grew so much that the boots were too tight. I then gave them to my father, who at that time had a smaller foot!

On the same side of the street as the shoe repair shop, but closer to my house, a boy named Lulu lived with his widowed mother in a three story house. Lulu was three years older than I and was working as an apprentice *stagnino* with a man named Piria from the next village, Borgo a Mozzano. The job title *stagnino* comes from the word *stagno* which means solder. A *stagnino* performed tasks that required forming metal of different types, such as tin plate, galvanized iron, copper and brass into various shapes and bending the metal into functional objects. The homes facing the main street, Via del Santo, in most sections of the village were attached to each other. The homes had tile roofs and all had copper gutters on the street side of the house emptying into copper downspouts that brought the rain water to the street and eventually into the *fosso* or *gora*.

The gutters and downspouts were made from pre-formed copper which came in certain lengths. They were then cut to size, assembled and soldered by the *stagnino*.

Most families used copper kitchen utensils and cookware which was plated with tin on the inside. Some of the kitchen ware was also made from tin plate and assembled with solder. The actual fabrication and repair of the pots and pans was done by *stagnini*. There were also minor jobs involving plumbing, usually not the water supply lines, because most homes did not have running water, but with the installation and maintenance of pipes distributing the waste water to the *fosso* and the pipes leading from the toilets to the cesspools.

At first Lulu was out in the field working with Piria, learning his trade. Then Piria decided that it would be advantageous to have Lulu establish a small shop in the street level room of his home. Signor Piria eventually organized the shop for Lulu, and I occasionally went to keep Lulu company and to see what he was doing. The work in the shop involved the assembly and repair of smaller items such as pots and pans, and making vent pipes for some of the wood stoves that people used to heat their homes. I remember being fascinated with Lulu's ability to start out with a flat piece of metal, and using only hand tools, shaping it into a meaningful form. In 1950, when I attended San Jose State College, I was enrolled in a sheet metal development course taught by Mr. Van Arsdale. While doing assignments, I recalled some of the metalworking processes in Lulu's shop and how the experience in Diecimo motivated me to major in metals and to eventually teach sheet metal and art metal courses in high school.

I continued to be fascinated by mechanical devices and felt fortunate that I had access to the water-power-driven flour mill that my uncle Filippo Barsotti and his two sons Rodolfo and Giuseppe owned. The milling stones were operated by water power that was captured through a series of water races bringing the water to a large wooden water wheel set up in the pathway of the *gora*, which flowed towards the village near the communal clothes washing area. The waterway started up in the mountains and came down to Diecimo through the village of Dezza and the Roncato district. The Barsotti mill had three large milling bins which were set up during the year to mill grain, corn and dried chestnuts. The people in the village brought these seasonal items to the mill in cloth sacks, leaving them for a few days until they were milled into flour. The Barsotti family also picked up sacks of crops to be milled from neighboring villages, such as Borgo a Mozzano, and Anchiano. Filippo Barsotti and his sons retained a percentage of the milled flour as payment for their work and then sold it.

I often dropped by the *mulino* to spend some time with my cousins Rodolfo and Beppe. I watched the operation of the mill and helped out by lifting sacks and loading the flour on the mule drawn delivery cart called a *barroccio*.

The stone milling wheels were huge, about four to five feet in diameter, about 10 inches thick, and very heavy. They were lifted into place with pulleys and adjusted manually according to the type of product being milled and according to the final type of flour desired. As the grinding surfaces of the wheels became worn, the wheels were removed from the mill and placed outside to await resurfacing which was done by a traveling stone cutter. I remember seeing Rodolfo, Beppe and my uncle Filippo at work in the mill with wheat flour flying through the air forming a white veil on their hair and clothing. Whenever I saw them walking around the village during the day, I always saw the white flour dust on their clothes and hair.

My big adventure was helping Rodolfo with the weekly delivery of the flour to the nearby village of Borgo a Mozzano and the village of Anchiano which was across the

Serchio River. The cart was pulled by their mule and in order to have the cart pulled correctly, without straining the mule, the cart was balanced perfectly. Therefore the sacks were loaded on the cart in a precise way. We usually left in the afternoon, when it was cool, to start our delivery route. When we reached Borgo a Mozzano we always stopped at the bakery and Rodolfo bought me a sweet roll shaped like a brioche called a *colombina* which was my pay for helping him. The best part of the ride was the return trip, on the dusty gravel road between Borgo a Mozzano and Diecimo. Since the cart was empty, Rodolfo stood up on the front, with the reins in one hand and the leather whip in the other, and while I balanced the back portion he cracked the whip motivating the mule to run as fast as he could. The ride back to Diecimo was a fast, exciting, and bouncy ride, since the road was full of rut holes. As we went along we left a wake of dust behind us, similar to the wake left by a boat on a lake. The ride home was the most enjoyable part of the day for me.

If one followed the waterway from my uncle's *mulino* toward Roncato, one found another water-driven flour mill and an olive oil producing business called a *frantoio*, operated by a man named Piccinini. Roncato was a section of Diecimo which was on the way to the next village called Dezza. *Frantoio* means a location where olives are ground, pressed and converted to olive oil. The olive harvest in Diecimo was not noteworthy, as the crop was just large enough to produce olive oil for local use. World War II caused problems for the people of Italy in that many of the familiar products that Italians considered essential parts of their diet, such as bread, pasta, and olive oil, were confiscated by the government and used to feed the troops. It was not worthwhile for agricultural communities to publicize the size of their crops, so the olive harvest and the quantity of olive oil produced was kept a secret. Olive oil was usually sold in stores by the liter; however, during the war olive oil was rationed and not available on the open market, so at times people could purchase small amounts of oil at a time from neighbors, such as 1/4 liter or 1/2 liter. Olive oil was also available on the black market at inflated prices and could be traded for other unavailable goods, such as wheat, clothing, or shoes.

Olives were harvested in the fall, during the latter part of November and early December, followed by the olive pressing. Since we only had one *frantoio* for Diecimo and the other small villages nearby, people were scheduled to press their olives in groups, like a co-operative operation.

The olive pressing process first required the grinding of olives in a special hand operated machine which consisted of two stone wheels. The wheels meshed at a point so that olives fed into the wheels were crushed, along with the olive pits, into small particles resembling a paste. The ground mixture was collected and placed in large containers made of hemp that can be best described as being shaped like unmounted automobile tires. The ground olive mixture was placed on the inner part of the *tire* and filled to capacity. The hemp *tires*, full of crushed olives, were then stacked on top of each other in a press. When there was a sufficient quantity, a flat piece of hard wood capped off the stack and gentle pressure was applied to make sure that the stacks were aligned. At this point, gravity would cause the oil from the ground olives to start to drip and to collect at the bottom of the press. This olive oil was considered to be the best in flavor even though it was not clear oil at this time, but had a certain amount of sediment in it. The oil, collected in bottles and kept apart from the other oil, was called *olio vergine*.

The center portion of the oil press had a long, large screw which ran from the bottom of the press to the top, with a T handle affixed to a large nut at the top of the screw. Once the top piece of wood was in place, two men, one on each side, would gradually turn the handle forcing the nut to progressively go down, thus compressing the olives in the hemp *tires*. This pressing action would force the oil down and out of the bottom; the first oil coming down would be considered the second best and would also be separated from the rest. As the olives were further pressed more sediment was forced down with the oil. This oil was considered to be of a lesser quality and was also separated from the rest. Since the pressing was a cooperative process, the people would keep track by weight of the amounts of olives used in the pressing and divide the oil according to the percentage due to each one, based on the initial weight of the olives. Signor Piccinini held out a percentage of the olive oil for himself, as payment for the use of his facilities.

The flavor of freshly pressed olive oil cannot be described very well in writing; the oil has to be tasted. In order to assess the flavor of the oil, the workers dipped pieces of bread into the new oil and as they ate the bread made comments regarding the flavor of the oil. In addition, it was common to prepare food which combined well with olive oil and filled the stomachs of the workers at the *frantoio*.

A food that was often prepared at the oil pressing was *farinata* which was made from corn meal and a vegetable soup stock. Women started by chopping onions, garlic, parsley, celery and basil into fine pieces, and then they sautéed the mixture in olive oil until lightly browned. Next they added water, and other chopped seasonal vegetables, such as beans, potatoes, carrots, celery, black cauliflower leaves, and tomatoes or tomato sauce conserved from the summer. The vegetable soup combination was simmered until the vegetables were done, then coarsely ground corn meal was gradually added and stirred constantly for about 45 minutes. The consistency would be similar to that of cream of wheat cereal or soft *polenta*. The *farinata* was served in large soup dishes and topped off with new olive oil and grated *parmegiano* or *pecorino* cheese. As everyone ate the *farinata* the flavor of the olive oil was evaluated and comments made about its quality.

After the oil pressing, the oil was divided, decanted into two or five liter *fiaschi* (glass containers encased in straw), and stored in the cool, dark basements of people's homes. The oil was later transferred to smaller containers as the sediment sank to the bottom of the *fiaschi*.

I remember that during the winters of 1943 and 1944 the olive crops were not abundant in Diecimo, and we did not have enough olive oil for our own use. Often my mother and I bicycled to Pieve di Compito (about 26 kilometers) to pick up olive oil from my uncle Nello who was the parish priest and always had plenty of olive oil. I remember that he stored the oil in a large metal barrel similar in size to the American 50 gallon barrels. The barrel was painted red and had a lid mounted on a hinge which was lifted to get to the oil. I remember dipping a ladle into the golden oil and filling the green one liter bottles we brought along.

In 1943-44 the German soldiers in the region always stopped people traveling on roads to check their documents and to ask what they were doing. The soldiers also confiscated any food products that were found and kept the food for their own use. At times men and teenage boys were picked up by the German troops and sent to northern Italy or Germany as slave laborers. The process was called a *rastrellamento* (a raking up of people); therefore one had to be very careful while traveling to avoid contact with the German patrols. The bicycle trip to Pieve di Compito with my mother was slow; because of her small size she could not pedal as fast as I could. We went along the gravel road to Ponte a Moriano, then on to the *Stradone di Marlia*, (a long, straight road through the town of Marlia), over to Capannori, and along the back roads to Pieve di Compito. Fortunately the back roads were not traveled very much by the German soldiers and we did not have to worry about being stopped. My uncle Nello and my grandmother Serafina lived in the *canonica*, the house adjoining the church which was built for the parish priest. The church and *canonica* were built on a small hill and had an imposing view of the valley leading to Pontedera, a large industrial city nearby. I always enjoyed going to Pieve di Compito because I was able to explore the large house and the church, and was also able to climb to the top of the church bell tower to get a better view of the valley. In addition, my grandmother always spoiled me by making my favorite food, potatoes fried in olive oil. The next day I was able to fit four liters of olive oil in my back pack, and then my mother and I bicycled back to Diecimo, using the back roads, trying to avoid the German soldiers. I was an oil smuggler!

The seasonal crops in the Serchio River Valley were varied, but the major crop was wheat, which was harvested in June.

In 1928 the Fascist Government initiated a propaganda campaign called *La battaglia del grano,* (the battle of the wheat). Benito Mussolini's objective was to encourage the Italian people to produce enough wheat in Italy in order to guarantee each Italian his proper portion of daily bread and not have to rely on imported wheat. One of the photographs used by the press to publicize the campaign was a picture of *il Duce* working on a *trebbiatrice* (thresher) feeding bundles of wheat into the machine. The photograph, along with color posters which showed *contadini* carrying bundles of wheat from the fields, promoted a national contest rewarding *contadini* with monetary prizes for increasing their production of wheat.

In Diecimo the wheat fields were intermingled among the various parcels of land in the valley and occasionally on the lower terraced areas on the nearby mountains. During the month of June the wheat fields turned a golden color signifying that it was time to harvest the crop. The golden fields mixed in with the bright green of the *prati* set aside for alfalfa crops provided a colorful green and gold patch-work pattern throughout the valley. The parcels of land were bordered with vertical fences made of grape vines to separate the parcels according to the ownership of the land. Wooden poles, about eight feet in length, were placed in the ground, spaced about ten feet apart, and tied together with strands of *filo di ferro* (steel wire). The grape vines were tied to the wire and trained to grow in a vertical direction, thus providing a natural fence around the property.

When the golden shafts of wheat were ripe and ready to be harvested, the *contadini* families, including children and grandparents, worked to gather up the wheat from the fields. The wheat was cut by hand using a *falce* or *falcetto* (sickle), a curved cutting instrument with a wooden handle, shaped like the letter "C," with the cutting angle on the "inside of the C." The cutting process was hard work and consisted of one reaching down with his left hand, grabbing the amount of wheat that could be grasped with the hand, then reaching in with the *falce* and in a sweeping motion, cutting the stems as close to the ground as possible. The cut shafts of wheat were placed in an orderly fashion on the ground, behind the cutter, and later gathered up and formed into *fasci* (bundles). The *fasci* were temporarily stored in vertical stacks, with the grain facing up, in tee-pee fashion, to dry out, until the wheat was ready for threshing.

Next, the wheat kernels were removed from the glumes and this was done by hand or by machine. The machine was a *trebbiatrice* (thresher) which was a large gasoline or diesel powered device about the size of a large pickup truck that was pulled from village to village by a tractor. The *trebbia-trice* was placed in several central locations in Diecimo that were accessible from the wheat fields. I remember that one of the locations was in front of the Pierini house where every year I spent some time observing the threshing, even climbing on top of the machine to watch the action. The process of threshing the wheat involved the cooperation of several people. There was the operator of the thresher who controlled the machine and kept it running smoothly. The owners of the wheat that was being processed worked on top, feeding the bundles of wheat into the mechanical portion of the machine. The machine then "beat" the wheat, separating the kernels from the straw. As the wheat kernels were separated, they were directed toward a raceway leading to a spout which was fitted with a burlap sack. When each sack was full, it was tied, then a new one placed under the spout. The straw from the wheat was ejected, collected and bundled for future use. The men stationed on top of the *trebbiatrice* were subjected to clouds of dust and chaff. They always had *fiaschi* of wine and water in the work area to quench their thirst.

When people were finished with the threshing of their own wheat they carried the grain to their homes and the bundles of straw to their barns. The straw was used primarily as bedding for cows, pigs and mules. Placed on the floor around the animals in the barns, straw absorbed the urine and excrement from the animals. When the stalls were cleaned, the smelly wet straw was collected and stacked into piles of *concime* (fertilizer) in a room in the barn next to the animals. The *concime* was like a compost pile generating considerable heat and emitting a horrible smell. When the *contadini* needed to fertilize the fields they loaded up the *concime* into a *cesta* and carried the mixture into the fields. The piles of fertilizer were then spread evenly over the entire field by hand using large rakes.

Families who produced a smaller quantity of wheat often elected to thresh their own wheat by hand. This was done in a clean outdoor courtyard which had a brick or tile ground cover. The location was called an *"aia."* The Italian term *battere il grano sull'aia* (beating the wheat on the aia) was used to describe the process. A hand operated device called a *trebbia* was used to beat the kernels out of the wheat. The *trebbia* was made from two pieces of round wood, similar in length and in diameter to a baseball bat, but without the taper for the bat handle. The two pieces of wood were hooked together with two steel rings embedded in the ends of the wood and connected with a steel ring so that the two pieces were free to bend and rotate. One of the pieces was grabbed with both hands and the flexible piece of wood was brought down with a descending blow to the wheat bundles on the ground. The action caused the kernels of grain to fall out onto the floor along with small particles of *pula* (chaff). Later, when there was a sufficient quantity of wheat kernels they were swept up with a broom and formed into piles on the floor. The grain was later separated from the particles of chaff by using a large hand held wooden device, shaped like a large dust pan, called an *arbuolo*, which was rocked back and forth causing the light particles of chaff to go to the front and eventually onto the floor while the kernels of grain settled at the deep end of the "dust pan." Threshing the wheat by hand was a labor intensive process which took a long time and was shared by everyone in the family. The machine threshing was faster and was more practical if people had large quantities of wheat. Although it generated a lot of noise and dust, it was exciting for the children to witness the activities around the *trebbiatrice* because although it was work, it was also a social gathering for the people of the village.

After the wheat harvest the fields were prepared for the corn crop which was harvested in late September. The chestnuts in the hills were harvested around mid-October, followed by the olive crop in November. Some of the hills on the gentler slopes of the mountains were terraced so that the olive and chestnut trees had a place to drop their fruit on a somewhat flat surface to facilitate the gathering of the crops. Of course there was the *vendemmia* or harvesting of the grapes in September which led to the wine making process. In addition, people planted seasonal vegetables in the fall, winter, spring and summer months. In an agricultural community, there was normally a variety of crops which provided enough food to feed the local people. However, during the initial war years, things changed because the Fascist officials came in and took the major portion of the crops, such as wheat, potatoes and corn, without compensating the people. Thereafter there was a shortage of food and at times people did not have enough food to feed their own families. So it became convenient not to publicize the size of the crops, but to lie and tell the officials that the results were less than expected.

During the seasonal harvesting of the crops there were many learning experiences for me involving the processing or preparation of the food products. When chestnuts were harvested, a small percentage were set aside and boiled in water, seasoned with salt and bay leaves, and served as part of a meal. It was best to peel the boiled chestnuts, *ballociori*, and eat them while warm, although some people ate them cold. The boiled chestnuts were quite tasty, had a soft texture and were very sweet. Chestnuts which were roasted on open fires were called *mondine*. They were usually prepared in the evening and served as a snack.

However, most of the chestnut crop was dried in *metati* or drying shacks. The *metato* was a small shed, detached from the house, usually built of bricks, with a tile roof. It had an entry door at the lower level, and on the second level there was a flooring made of thin wooden slats spaced approximately the width of a chestnut. One had access to the top level via a window which was situated above the door. A ladder was propped up against the window and after the chestnuts were picked in the hills and brought home, the men carried the sacks of chestnuts up the ladder, and then dumped them onto the wooden slats. When the chestnuts were all picked, and the upper level was full, a wood fire was started on the floor at the lower level and allowed to burn slowly for about two weeks. The heat produced by the continuous, slow burning fire dried out the chestnuts. Once they were dry, the skins were easily removed by hand tumbling and the chestnuts then were ready for grinding into chestnut flour at the Barsotti mill.

The chestnut flour was preserved without refrigeration. Families stored the flour in wooden barrels, compressing it by hand using a piece of wood with a handgrip and tamping the flour into place. One of the problems with the flour was that sometimes little insects liked to eat it, and often people found the flour to be contaminated. They felt that compressing flour kept it fresh longer and minimized the invasion by the insects. Since the flour was sweet, children liked to remove small chunks of the compressed flour from the barrels and eat it like pieces of candy. While preparing chestnut flour-based food products, such as *necci* (flat pancakes cooked between two metal plates on an open fire), *polenta* (porridge made of water and chestnut flour), *vinata* (porridge made of red wine and chestnut flour), and *castagnaccio* (baked flat torte made of water, chestnut flour, olive oil, walnuts, rosemary and orange peel), the women broke up the chunks by hand and then sifted the flour in a *staccio* (sieve) before using it. The dried chestnuts were also used to make *tullore,* which were boiled, dried chestnuts. The chestnuts were first soaked in water, then placed in a pot over a fire and boiled until they became soft. The result was a sweet syrupy liquid, and the softened chestnuts were delicious and filling.

The agricultural crops in Diecimo were rotated in order to utilize all of the land in the village. The flat parcels of land spread out in the valley were small, belonging to many different families. After the wheat was harvested in June, the fields were spaded by the *contadino* with his *vanga* (specially shaped spade) in preparation for planting corn. The corn was the type that was used for food and was an essential element in the diet. Although some of the corn was eaten fresh, most of it was dried and ground into corn meal. After the corn was converted into corn meal it was cooked in the form of *focacciette* (corn tortillas), *polenta, farinata* (corn meal cooked in vegetable soup without pasta) and occasionally corn bread. When the corn was ripe, usually sometime in late September, everyone in the family went to the fields to pick the corn. The ears of corn were removed and stacked in large *ceste* (baskets made from flexible branches of certain trees in the area, such as the fruitless mulberry tree). The baskets were about three to four feet in diameter, and about 18 inches high. The baskets were carried on the head or on the shoulders The *ceste* were also used to carry cut grass from the fields for rabbits.

I remember helping out during the corn harvesting period. I often went with the Giambastiani family, our *contadini*, and worked with their children, Aldo and Francesca, picking corn. The corn was carried home and temporarily stored in a large, ground floor room, at 84 Via del Santo, the house in which the Bertini grandparents lived in 1939, which was now occupied by the Giambastiani family. As the crop was picked and brought into the home, the mound of corn grew larger and larger, eventually taking up about half of the room and forming a pile about six feet high. When all the corn crop was picked, the next step was to shuck the corn, removing the husks. This activity usually took place at night and was in the form of a gathering, or as the people said, *a veglia* at someone's house.

The evening of work started by having all the people attending sit on top of the pile of corn, spread out along the length of the pile. Then the shucking of the corn began. In Italian the term was *scartocciare*. The greenish yellow corn husks were pulled-back, exposing the golden corn. At that point, the person shucking the ear of corn made a decision based on what the corn looked like. If the ear of corn was perfect, that is full of corn kernels, the pulled back husks were left on the ear of corn. The ear of corn was then thrown in a separate corner of the room, on the floor. Later, five or six ears of corn were grouped together, the husks gathered and tied, to form a cluster of beautiful ears of corn. These clusters were later hung in *soffita* (the open top floor of the house), to dry out. Once dry, the kernels of corn were removed from the cob by hand, using a stationary V-shaped metal tool through which the ear of corn was pulled by the husks thus removing the individual kernels of corn. The corn was then placed in sacks, taken to the *mulino* and ground into corn meal. When shucking the ears of corn if one discovered an imperfect ear of corn, then all of the husks were ripped off, and the ear of corn, without husks, was thrown into a separate pile and generally used as feed for chickens or hogs.

As the evening began we found ourselves sitting on top of the pile of corn, being able to reach up with our hands and touch the ceiling of the room. Then we gradually lowered ourselves as we shucked the corn so that eventually we ended up sitting on the bricks of the floor. The children were kept entertained by the adults who told stories and passed the wine bottle around. Sometime during the evening the homeowner also made large pans of *mondine* (roasted chestnuts) which were always enjoyed by the young people. By the end of the evening my hands were red and sore from shucking all of the ears of corn. Yet, because of the socializing, the task did not really seem like work.

Most people in Diecimo ate a variety of food based on the availability of seasonal crops in the village. The *conta-*

dini were lucky of they had meat one day a week, usually on Sundays; the most common types of meat available were chicken, rabbit, and pork. Cows were used primarily to provide milk and to pull carts to and from the fields. Butchering of local cows for beef was very uncommon, and beef was expensive. Italians were given ration stamps to buy beef, but it was very seldom available at the butcher shop because the meat was used to feed the Italian army. Rabbits were easy to raise in cages or hutches and were fed grass cut daily from the fields. Since rabbits reproduced quickly, they were plentiful. I did not like rabbit meat even though it was prepared much like chicken, that is, fried or cooked in a tomato based sauce and served with polenta. I felt sorry for the animals, especially after seeing how the farmers killed them and cut them up for the various dishes.

The men were usually delegated to kill and skin the rabbits and it was done in such a way that probably was the same in all farming communities. The rabbit was held by the hind legs in one hand, then the side of the other hand was used to deliver a chopping blow to the neck of the rabbit, breaking the neck. In order to remove the rabbit skin and fur, incisions were made with a knife around the legs, above the paws; the skin was then cut away from the legs, pulled up to the neck, then trimmed away from the head. The rabbit skin was hung up to dry, and when dry, the rabbit fur was used to line jackets and hats for warmth in the winter. To this day, I cannot eat rabbit, though it is considered an Italian delicacy. I feel sorry for bunnies!

Chickens were raised primarily to produce eggs. People kept chickens in small coops or kept them in confined areas near their houses, often only 4 to 6 chickens at a time, and they gathered in the eggs every day. When the chickens stopped producing eggs, they were killed and served roasted or boiled. Chickens were killed in the usual way: one grasped the neck of the chicken with both hands and twisted, breaking the neck. In the United States, farmers chopped off the head with a hatchet or large knife rather than breaking the neck. The entire chicken was used for food, including the head and the feet. The liver, heart and gizzard were usually chopped up and used in the preparation of spaghetti sauce.

Pigs or hogs were also raised by the *contadini*. The pigs were kept in a *stallina* which is a word derived from *stalla*, which means a stable. The *stallina* usually housed one or two pigs at a time and very often was part of a barn that was attached to a house. The pigs were fed very few leftovers, because there weren't any. They were fed some of the inferior corn, sour milk, whey (a milk liquid left over from making cheese), and *crusca*, the outer skin of wheat which was left over when the locally milled flour was sifted for making bread. I saw pigs around the village and of course heard them, but had never seen one killed or butchered.

The people who owned the store next door to our house, Niccola and Nello Lazzari, raised a pig and prepared to have it killed and butchered sometime during the winter of 1943. The killing process involved securing a permit from the Comune di Borgo a Mozzano, the municipal government office. When the permit was issued, a special guard was sent out to the house to kill the pig. The man wore a uniform and carried with him a weapon that looked like a large pistol. I was able to observe the episode because the pig was let loose in an enclosed area in a yard below the street level, which offered a full view of the killing. The uniformed man, called *guardia di finanza*, had an ear of corn in his left hand and was trying to get the attention of the pig. The pig smelled the corn, made a move toward the guard and reached for the corn with his mouth. As the pig raised his head to grab the corn, the guard placed the weapon with his right hand on the forehead of the pig and released the trigger. A loud noise, like a shot, rang out and a large spike, about 6 inches long, embedded itself into the forehead of the pig. This happened so suddenly that it caught me by surprise, I did not expect the pig to be killed by a spike. The pig collapsed, rolled over, the legs kicked, and it appeared to die quickly. A man then came out carrying a large kettle of boiling water and proceeded to clean the skin with a coarse brush.

The next step involved bringing the slain pig into the Lazzari house and preparing it for butchering. The pig, weighing probably 300 pounds or more, was carried up from the yard into the house across the street from us. Preparations were made to use the dining room at the street level as the butchering shop. I noticed before that there were two large hooks in the main wooden beams which supported the second story floor. Now the hooks were used to lift the pig into place so that it could be split open. A rope was tied to each of the rear hoofs and placed over each hook while two men pulled on the rope, lifting the hind quarters up to the ceiling. When the hoofs were at the hook location, the rope was tied in place holding the pig vertically with its head dangling down just above ground level and the hind legs spread apart. One of the men secured a large knife and as he slit the pig from rear to front, along the center of the belly, all the entrails fell out dangling to the floor. A large metal pan was placed directly below to catch all the blood that was dripping from the pig. The small and large intestines were cut and removed, as well as the stomach and the bladder. The intestines, bladder and stomach were taken into the kitchen and the excrement removed from the body parts with running water. The pig remained hanging, dripping blood, until the next day.

I got up early the next morning because I wanted to go back to the Lazzari house to see how the pig was going to be butchered and made into the various pork products that were part of the Italian diet. I knew that *salame, salsiccia, pancetta*, and *biroldo* were made from pork, but I did not know how the products were made. When I arrived at the Lazzari house three men, each wearing an apron, were already at work. The dining room table was set up as a cutting table, with a large hand-cranked meat grinder attached to one edge. The men were working on the carcass of the pig, cutting off certain pieces of meat and placing them on the table. They began a sorting process, cutting off skin, lean meat, fat, bones, liver and other organs, and placing the pieces in different stacks.

The *biroldo* (blood sausage) was made mostly of parts from the head of the pig, such as the ears, the snout, and the cheeks. Once the assorted pieces of meat were chopped into small pieces they were placed in a large pot along with the blood from the pig. Certain spices were added as well as salt and pepper and the whole mixture was cooked. I also believe that an amount of corn meal was added to the blood to serve as a thickener. When the mixture was done, it was cooled and set aside. Some of the larger pieces of intestines were then selected to form a casing for the mixture. The intestines, which were washed and cleaned the day before, were attached to a wide funnel with a large spout so that the intestines slipped over the spout. One end of the intestine was tied, then the *biroldo* mixture was fed through the funnel and into the intestine which became the casing for the *biroldo*. When the *biroldo* reached a length of about 8 or 10 inches, it was tied off with a piece of string and another one started. The *biroldo* was then hung on hooks in the house to dry out before it was ready to eat. As I mentioned before, the *biroldo* was a type of blood sausage, so when it was sliced, it was red in color and one could see all the small irregular pieces of the head and other by-products of the pig. I never did like *biroldo,* not only because I did not like the taste of the sausage, but also I did not like eating parts of the head.

The salame and the sausage were made by using better cuts of meat with certain percentages of lean meat and fat. The meat was cut up, and then ground into small pieces and mixed with pieces of fat, salt, pepper and *salnitro* (saltpeter, potassium nitrate). When the mixture had the right texture it was ready for processing into the salame or sausage shapes. The whole process of cutting up the pig and making various products was called *insaccare*, which means to stuff into something. The smallest intestines were used for making sausage. The clean intestines were carefully pushed on a long tubular extension on the front of the meat grinder. As one fed the ground meat mixture through the grinder, turning the handle by hand, the meat was forced into the intestine, thus pushing the casing out and away from the grinder. As the length of the sausage was formed, one of the men tied off the sausage into links with a continuous piece of string. When the sausage was finished, the links were cut into approximately 6 to 8 foot lengths and hung up to dry in the kitchen area of the home. I remember that the sausages had to cure and dry out for a certain period of time before they could be eaten by the family. Sausage meat was a bit on the fatty side, and sometimes people ate the sausage raw, like salame, with bread. Most of the time, though, the sausage was cooked and served in a tomato based sauce with polenta.

The salame was made in a similar fashion, except that the meat was leaner, but considerable fat was added to the mixture. *Salame Toscano* is made with large chunks of fat, approximately 1/2 inch in diameter or larger. The fat is mixed with the lean meat so that when the *salame* is sliced, you see the red meat dotted with large pieces of fat. The salame was made using intestines that had a larger diameter than the sausage and was prepared in longer lengths. The salame had a different flavor than the sausage but also had to dry out to cure for a period of time.

The rear portion of the pig, the hind leg area, was used to make *prosciutto*, a salt cured, uncooked ham, which is a popular delicacy in Italy. The two legs were trimmed and cut to size, with the bone left in the center. The meat was placed in a wooden barrel and covered with salt. The salt in Italy was sold at the *appalti,* a state monopoly store, and was not a refined salt like the salt that was common in households in the United States. Instead it was coarse, like rock salt and had to be crushed into smaller pieces by using a mortar and pestle. Italian families did not use salt and pepper shakers, they used small glass dishes for the salt and pepper. When one wanted to add salt at the dinner table to the food on the plate, the salt was scooped up from the small dish with the tip of the knife and drizzled over the food. The *prosciutto* was left in the salt until the meat no longer absorbed salt. At that time, the leg was removed from the barrel and was squeezed under a press until all the salty fluid ran out. When the liquid was completely removed from the *prosciutto* it was hung up to dry out for several weeks. When dry and properly aged the prosciutto was sliced very thin and eaten with bread. Prosciutto has become an Italian delicacy in the United States and typically is served with melon or other fruit as an appetizer. Prosciutto is also used in cooking to flavor other types of meat, such as veal, when making *saltimbocca alla Romana*. Another cut of meat, from the shoulder and neck area of the pig is used to make *coppa* or *capo di collo* which is similar in flavor to prosciutto, except the *coppa* is smaller in diameter. The shoulder meat is de-boned, then rolled up and salted. When cured, it is sliced thin and served with bread.

There were two other pork products which were not familiar to Americans. One was *mezzina* or *pancetta* made from the belly of the pig. This is similar in appearance to

American bacon, except that it is seasoned with salt and pepper, rolled, and tied with a string. When properly cured, the roll is thinly sliced and the meat is used to flavor certain dishes or it can be eaten raw with bread. The back part of the pig next to the skin, which is all fat, was cut up into small slabs, covered with salt and allowed to cure. Slices of *lardo*, as this fat was called, were used to flavor other food or it was eaten raw with bread. Finally all of the scrap pieces of fat were collected, placed in a large pot over the fire and the fat was allowed to render. When melted, the liquid fat was poured into containers, such as the bladder, the stomach, or terra cotta jars, and then allowed to solidify. The product was called *strutto* (the English term is lard) and was used for cooking and frying. If stored in a cool place the *strutto* kept for a long period of time.

By the end of the day all of the pig was gone, cut up, chopped up, and packaged into the various shapes and products which would last a family most of the year. It was a luxury to have a pig which was *insaccato* because the meat items could be eaten or traded for essential clothing or other types of food. As the war progressed, the government took away all visible livestock for military consumption. Some of the *contadini* still managed to hide their pigs and butcher them sight unseen for their own families.

Milk was an important part of the Italian diet. In Diecimo the *contadini* who had milk-producing cows milked them twice a day, keeping a portion of the milk for themselves, and selling the rest to Nelda and Tono Tonelli, the local *lattaio* (milkman). The *contadini* brought the milk to Nelda in buckets; she transferred it to a measuring container, and then deposited it in large metal storage tanks. The amount of milk delivered was recorded in a ledger and at the end of the month people were paid a certain amount of money for the milk their cows produced. Tono delivered milk to nearby villages by means of a mule-drawn wagon.

People boiled the milk to sterilize it and then placed it in a a cool area so that it would not spoil. After the milk was boiled and cooled, the cream in the milk rose to the surface and formed a thick scum. The scum was carefully removed and saved to be used later to make butter. Hot milk was poured over hard pieces of bread and served to family members for breakfast and for dinner. A small amount of coffee was sometimes added to make *caffè e latte*.

Cow's milk was also used to make cheese which was cured and firm enough to slice and serve with bread or polenta. The Italian word for cheese is *formaggio* but another word was used to describe cheese, the word is *cacio*. The flavor of cheese made from cow's milk was very mild and not as pungent as cheese made from sheep's milk.

An activity evident to all was one that generated a smell which permeated the entire valley. During the time that I lived in Diecimo the sanitary facilities were very primitive according to our present day standards. Human waste was collected in cesspools, or storage tanks, which were generally located to the rear of the house, underground, and made of brick and cement. The opening to the tank consisted of a large hole, approximately two feet in diameter, covered with a large stone lid. The toilets in most homes were not flush toilets, they were simply large holes that carried the waste undiluted by water directly into the *fogna* (cesspool tank) from the toilet area, via large terra cotta pipes.

The storage tanks full of human waste were emptied, and in Italy, as well as other European countries, the waste was used to fertilize the fields and crops of the area. The process was very orderly, and one could tell when it occurred because of the smell all over the village. A wagon with a large wooden tank mounted horizontally between the four wheels was used to transport the liquid waste to the fields, pulled by either a donkey, a cow, or by several people. The wagon was positioned on the street near the house while the liquid waste was scooped out of the tanks with a wooden bucket attached to a long wooden pole, then emptied into wooden barrels, which were then carried to the wagon on the street. For some reason, unknown to me, the smelly liquid was referred to as *Perugino* or *Perugina* by the *contadini* (*Perugina* is the name of a major Italian chocolate company). I often wondered how many times over the centuries this process was repeated, and how food products were grown in the village, fertilized by human waste, and recycled into the ground in the valley. I also wondered about the sanitary conditions, and how the use of human waste as fertilizer affected the people's health.

The various agricultural activities and seasonal crops were like time lines in my life, they occurred each year, in precisely the same way. The winter months in Diecimo were very depressing because of the position of the village in the valley. The mountains blocked out the sun for most of the day, so the village was dark and cold. The only public transportation during the later war years was the train coming from Lucca which stopped in Diecimo and then continued up the valley to Piazza al Serchio. Darkness usually set in fairly early, between four and five p.m. After dark, most kids went home to await the evening meal. The evening meals took place at different times, depending on the families. We still followed the American schedule and ate our evening meal fairly early, around seven p.m. After dinner, families stayed at home, huddled around the fireplace in the kitchen, trying to keep warm. Sometimes people visited other families in the evening, which was described as *andare a veglia*, literally translated as staying up or having an evening party. Most of the time I went *a veglia* by myself, spending time with the families of my friends. I often went across the street to the Luchi house because my friend Renzo Orsi lived there with his grandfather. He came from the town of Torcigliano, near Camaiore, and was about my age. Renzo was a nice friend, but worked hard in the fields to help the family. Rather than calling him by his first name, Renzo, most of the other kids called him *Torcigliano*. After the war he returned to his native village and had a successful career as an officer in the *Carabinieri* (a branch of the army, similar to a police force).

Whether at home or *a veglia* the families sat around the large fireplaces, in a large semi-circle, facing the heat, while their backsides faced the cold kitchen. The men occasionally lit up small cigars, known as *Toscanelli*, which were smelly and extremely strong. They lit the cigars by taking a small piece of burning wood from the fireplace and holding it to the cigar tip while they puffed on the cigar. The men drank wine during the evening which kept them warm and facilitated the story telling. The women of the family always kept busy, doing *ricami* or embroidery work, spinning yarn from sheep's wool, knitting socks and sweaters. Many of the homes in Diecimo did not have electricity, so the only light in the room was the light emanating from the fireplace. In addition, during the occupation of the country by the Germans and the Allied soldiers, the electrical generating plants at Pian della Rocca and Gallicano, utilizing the hydroelectric power of the Lima River and the Serchio River, were inoperative and the villages were without electricity for long periods of time. When candles were available, they were used to light the home in the evening. People also used special lanterns operated by *carburo*, flammable carbide gas generated by placing water on pieces of calcium carbide inside the sealed steel container at the bottom of the lantern. The gas flowed upward into the top chamber, through a small metal tube, which then could be lit and the bluish flame provided light. The *carburo* lamps were used by men working underground digging the hydro-electric and train tunnels in the mountains.

When going to the various homes for the *veglia* one always expected to hear the patriarch of the family, called *nonno* or grandfather, telling stories about times past. The stories probably were partially true, based on past family experiences, or at times they were embellished to make the stories scary for the young people present. Because of the lack of electricity and the shadows created by the burning fire, the children were afraid to venture into the dark rooms of the house and remained with the group sharing the warmth of the fireplace. During chestnut season there would always be a large pan of *mondine* cooking. *Mondine* were made by roasting chestnuts in a special steel pan, shaped like a deep sided frying pan with holes in the bottom. The chestnuts were *castrate* (castrated) by making a small incision on the side, removing a small portion of the skin so the chestnuts would not explode, and then placing them in the pan. The pan had a long handle, about three feet long, and was held over the open fire in the fireplace. As the skins on the chestnuts on the bottom became burned, the chestnuts were flipped over allowing the ones on top to become cooked. The process continued until all of the skins were crisp and practically burned off. The chestnuts were dumped on a table and rolled by hand on the hard surface until the skin was removed. At that point, we had roasted chestnuts, golden brown and crisp. These were *mondine* and were ready to eat accompanied by a nice glass of red wine.

Later in the winter, after the chestnuts were harvested and made into chestnut flour, the families made *vinata*. *Vinata* was made by heating a large pan of red wine, and then placing chestnut flour in the wine and stirring the mixture until the flour was cooked. The *vinata* was dark red in appearance and contained quite a bit of alcohol, so when one ate a bowl of it, the warm combination of chestnut flour and wine would heat up your entire body. Usually one ate the *vinata* just before going to bed so that the ice cold sheets would not seem as bad as they were.

People delayed going to bed as long as possible, not wanting to leave the warmth of the kitchen. Eventually, when people could no longer keep their eyes open, they discussed the order in which the family should go to bed. Usually the children and older people went first, and the mother and father of the family last. As a result of burning a fire in the fireplace all evening, by bedtime there was a huge accumulation of embers in the fireplace. The hot, glowing embers were then placed in a ceramic *scaldino*, a container which was shaped like a basket with a handle. The *scaldino*, very hot from the glowing charcoal inside, was then placed in a *trabicco* which was a wooden structure made of slats and shaped like a half sphere about three feet in diameter. The *scaldino* was suspended on the inside of the frame, on a metal hook, and was then placed on the center of the bed, under the sheets and blankets. Once in place, the *scaldino* heated the sheets and blankets on the bed. The heating device was placed in the bed for about five minutes, and then moved to the next bed in the sequence of the going-to-bed routine. Because of the humidity in the cold rooms of the stone houses, once the *trabicco* was in place and heating the bed, the damp sheets and blankets gave off columns of steam which went straight up to the ceiling. This was a strange sight, because at first it looked like the bedding was on fire, but at a closer examination, one could tell that the columns were made of steam and not smoke. When I went to bed, after the *scaldino* was removed, I would really enjoy the warmth in the bed, knowing that it would become ice cold in a short time, and hoping that by that time I would be asleep.

I was a typical child who enjoyed the new experience of living in an Italian village, especially playing games with my friends whose games which were new to me. While living in

Brighton, I played marbles with some of my friends. In Diecimo there was a game similar to marbles which was called *palline*. The *palline* were small terra cotta balls which were baked and painted different colors, similar in size to the American marbles. The major difference was that the *palline* were not exactly round, as if formed by hand. In addition, they were brittle and occasionally broke apart. When rolling the *palline* on the ground it was difficult to keep them on a straight line because of their surface irregularities. There were two variations of the game. If playing against one person, each of us placed a certain number of *palline* in our hands and then combined them together. If I was allowed to play first, I dropped the handful of *palline* to the ground and as they hit the dirt surface, they scattered in all directions. The objective of the game was to indicate which ones you were going to shoot by drawing a line on the ground with a finger between the two *palline*, then snap your index finger to propel one ball. The ball then advanced toward the other ball and if it struck the other one you picked up both balls. If you missed, then your opponent played, repeating the process until he missed. The objective was to capture or hit as many balls as possible.

Another game involved placing a certain number of balls in a common pool, for example 6 balls apiece, arranged in a single file, spaced about two inches apart. At a preset distance from the line, like ten feet away, we each rolled one towards the row of balls. The person farthest from the row shot his marble first, using the same technique of snapping the index finger to propel the ball. If your ball hit a ball in the row, you could claim all the balls. If you missed, your opponent shot next. The shooting continued until all balls were hit and claimed.

There was another game which involved the use of dried peach pits. One of the joys of summer was eating the fresh, sweet peaches which were grown in the area. After eating the peaches people saved the pits for different reasons. Children used the pits for playing a game, while the adults saved the pits so that when they were dry, they could crack them open and use the bitter almond for baking. The basic peach pit game was called *giocare a castelli* (playing castles). The players put a certain number of peach pits in a common pool. Then a small *castle* was assembled by placing three pits together and topping the three with another pit. The balance of the pits in the common pool were then arranged in a large circle around the castle. The players then backed off a certain distance and pitched a *shooter* peach pit along the ground. The person furthest away from the castle was first to shoot his peach pit. The same process as used in the marble game was used. A person shot the peach pit by snapping the index finger to propel the peach pit. You could only claim the peach pits that you hit. One had to hit the peach pits in the circle first, the castle was saved for last. The *shooter* peach pit was the largest one could find and was filed flat by rubbing it on a stone surface so that it had a smooth top and bottom surface in order to slide easily on the surface of a sidewalk and hold its line.

The transistion from Brighton to Diecimo was an unsual experience for me. I was able to cope with the situation and as I became part of the village life I learned new things which gave me a different perspective of life. I discovered that the people in Italy were very resourceful in their lifestyle and relied on cooperative efforts to get along. There was a feeling of belonging to the village which was very different from the neighborhood in Brighton.

7.
COLLEGIO CAVANIS

By the end of the summer of 1942, Adolf Hitler seemed to be on top of the world. German U-boats were sinking 700,000 tons of British-American shipping a month in the Atlantic Ocean, more than could be replaced in the shipyards of the United States, Canada and Scotland. Though Hitler strapped his forces in the West by siphoning off most of the troops, tanks and airplanes in order to focus his efforts on the Russian front, there was no sign in the summer of 1942 that the British and the Americans were strong enough to make any kind of troop landing from across the English Channel. The Allies did not risk attempting to occupy the French-held Northwest Africa, though the weakened French, of divided loyalties, had nothing much with which to stop them even if they made the attempt, and the Germans had nothing at all, except a few submarines and planes based in Italy and Tripoli.

On the map the totality of Hitler's conquests by September 1942 was appalling. The Mediterranean was dominated by the Axis (thanks to small groups of Italian frogmen who sank over 30 Allied navy units), with Germany and Italy holding most of the northern shore from Spain to Turkey and the southern shore from Tunisia to within 60 miles of the Nile River. In fact, German troops covered the region from the Norwegian North Cape on the Arctic Ocean to Egypt, and from the Atlantic Ocean to the southern end of the Volga River on the border of Central Asia. (William L. Shirer, *The Rise And Fall Of The Third Reich*)

People in Diecimo were concerned about the war and the effect it would have on them. Reports in the newspapers and the radio were not very encouraging. We were already experiencing food shortages and the adults constantly talked about the Fascists and the Nazis. After I passed the examination at the conclusion of the fifth grade in May 1942, I was qualified to continue school and to attend the first year of *Scuola Media*. The only *Scuola Media* program for the region was located in Lucca. Children from the Serchio River Valley took the train to Lucca and then walked into the city from the railroad station which was located outside the walls. My parents wanted me to continue with school, even though the war was expanding in Europe and their financial resources were being depleted by everyday expenses. My father, before leaving the United States, had set up an annuity program with the John Hancock Insurance Company in Boston so that he would receive a certain amount of money each month, and in the event that he died, my mother would continue to receive the annuity. The money, around $130.00 per month, was to come directly to him while in Italy; at that time it seemed like quite a bit of money, but it was his only source of income. Around 1942 or 1943, after the United States entered the war against the Axis, the money stopped coming; after that time, we had no income except for money generated from selling our crops.

I was surprised when my parents decided to send me to a Jesuit boarding school, Istituto Cavanis, in Porcari instead of the *Scuola Media* in Lucca. Porcari was located near Capannori, off the road called the *Via Pesciatina* leading from Lucca to Pescia. The first *Istituto Cavanis*, established in the Veneto region of Italy, north of Venice, was a very successful school, and the campus in Porcari was the second such school established in Italy. At the time I did not know much about the school, except that the *Istituto Cavanis* was a boarding school, called a *collegio*, and that meant that I would have to live at the school, away from my family and friends in Diecimo. I was not aware of the cost of attending the school, but I realized that because of our family's financial situation, my mother and father probably could not afford to send me there. Even now, as I write this story, I cannot imagine why they decided to enroll me in the school. I wonder if the decision had something to do with their social standing in the village. They felt they had to impress the people by enrolling their son in a prestigious school rather than the ordinary public school in Lucca.

School was scheduled to start around the end of September. During the latter part of August, my mother began to assemble my wardrobe by altering certain articles of clothing so that they would be roomy enough for me to grow into during the year; she also bought me new underwear, socks, shirts and sweaters even though it was difficult to find articles of clothing in the local stores. I also needed to have two pairs of shoes for school. We decided that I should take a pair of my father's shoes, and that we would try to locate a second pair of shoes on the black market that would fit me. After some searching, we were able to find a pair of shoes on the black market and traded a certain quantity of wheat for the shoes. On every clothing item that I was going take to the school, my mother carefully sewed, by hand, little strips of white cloth tape with the red number 110, which was my student identification number.

I was to report to the *Istituto Cavanis* around the last week of September, on a Sunday, which was the day before the start of school. My mother hired a man from Diecimo, called *Il Lungo* (the tall one) who owned a horse and provided carriage service in the area to transport me to Porcari. *Il Lungo* came to our house with his horse and carriage called a *calessino*. The *calessino* is a two-wheeled horse drawn vehicle, usually covered, with seating space along each side directly above each wheel. After loading up my luggage, my mother, father and I climbed in and settled on the seats for our ride to Porcari. The ride took about an hour and a half because we had to travel slowly, bumping along the unpaved dusty gravel roads. As we entered Porcari we made our way to the campus of the *Istituto Cavanis*, a five story structure, which could be seen from a distance. I noticed that Porcari was a large village; it had a much larger railroad station than Diecimo, several brick factories, and a milk processing plant. The school was located on the outskirts of the village, just past the parish church. The main building was rectangular in shape with an adjoining area enclosed by a wall on the front; at the rear there was a chapel with another lower building to the left. On the right hand side of the main building and parallel to it there was a full-size soccer field, with patches of grass on the turf and wooden goal posts. On the inside of the wall on the left side of the building there was a courtyard with an outdoor basketball court. The rest of the area was covered with fine gravel, except for a cemented walkway leading from the main building, past the chapel to the bathrooms.

After we pulled up to the main entrance of the school and assessed the situation, *Il Lungo* parked the *calessino* near the stairs that led up to the main door above which was located a large painted sign with the words *ISTITUTO CAVANIS*. My mother, father and I climbed the stairs while *Il Lungo* remained by the carriage with the luggage. We entered the door which led to a reception area and were greeted by a priest dressed in a long black gown. He checked a list, found my name, then welcomed me to the school and arranged for a tour of the campus for me and my parents. We told the priest that my suitcases were with a man in the horse carriage at the bottom of the stairs. He said he would make arrangements to have them sent to the dormitory. The tour was conducted by an older student and was very brief. We walked along the second story hall, saw several of the classrooms, then walked up a flight of stairs to the top floor of the building to see the dormitory and the personal washing area. We came back down the stairs to ground level into the courtyard, into the chapel, to the bathrooms, then across the courtyard to the main entrance.

I was apprehensive about leaving home and being away from my parents and friends. I did not know what to expect at the *Istituto Cavanis,* especially knowing that the school was run by priests who appeared to be pretty serious. After the tour my parents decided to leave and return to Diecimo. I said good-bye reluctantly as my father showed no emotion, but my mother, I thought, was shedding a few tears. As the *calessino* pulled away, I cried as I continued watching the carriage make its way down the street. I remained at the front of the building, wiping away my tears, hoping that no one saw me cry, then walked slowly into the courtyard.

As I walked into the courtyard I looked around and saw a familiar face from Diecimo among the students. His name was Luigi Donati, the son of the village veterinarian, Dottore Donati. I often played with Luigi, but I did not know that he was planning to attend Porcari. He was away for most of the summer at their vacation home near the ocean, and we lost contact for a few months. I was pleased to see Luigi and after our initial greeting we stayed in the courtyard where he introduced me to his cousin Vittorio who came from Lammari (a village near Marlia).

We were told to remain in the courtyard until we were instructed to report to the church for our orientation session. It is difficult to remember, after fifty-two years, the exact time frame in which everything happened, but I seem to recall that around five or five-thirty we were asked to go into the church and sit down. The interior of the church was small, more like a chapel than a full sized church. There was a main altar, a communion railing, an elevated pulpit, several rows of pews, and small organ to the rear of the church. As we made our way into the church, Luigi, Vittorio and I sat together in one of the pews and watched as the rest of the students entered. There were students of different ages, some our age and some older; the age range appeared to be from twelve for the first year *Media* students up to sixteen or seventeen for the third year *Media* students. After the church was filled, an older priest climbed the steps to the pulpit and introduced himself as Padre Giuseppe, President of the College. He introduced the other priests by name and by the subjects they taught, including Padre Cesare, who was in charge of discipline.

We were told that the students at the school were to be divided into squads according to grade level. There were approximately 20 students in each squad with a squad leader assigned to watch over them. The squad leaders were selected from older, former students who were still attending school, such the *Liceo* (high school) or the University, who studied on their own at Porcari and were able to keep up with their outside school work. Their room and board was free, and they received tutoring from the teachers at the college. The *Prima Media* class was divided into two squads, number six and number seven. Luigi and I were assigned to squad number 6 and Vittorio to squad number 7. We were assigned a squad leader studying to become a priest in a nearby seminary. His name was Francesco, and he always wore a black gown similar to the ones that priests wore.

The daily schedule was explained next. The schedule really seemed complicated to me, and it looked as if we were going to be pretty busy. The Monday through Saturday schedule was as follows:

6:00   A.M.   Rise, wash, get dressed

6:30   A.M.   Walk down the stairs as a squad, go to the bathroom on the way to the 6:30 daily Mass.

7:00	A.M.	Study hall
7:30	A.M.	Breakfast in the cafeteria
8:00	A.M.	Playtime in the courtyard
8:30	A.M.	Classes start
10:30	A.M.	Half hour break for *spuntino* (snack), bathrooms, and playtime
11:00	A.M.	Classes resume
12:30	P.M.	Bathroom and play time until lunch
1:00	P.M.	*Pranzo* (dinner) in the cafeteria, then play in the courtyard until 2:00
2:00	P.M.	Study hall
3:00	P.M.	Playtime in the courtyard or the soccer field
5:30	P.M.	Study hall
6:30	P.M.	Evening church service, the Rosary
7:00	P.M.	Supper
8:00	P.M.	Study hall or courtyard for play
9:00	P.M.	Bathroom visit and preparation for bed
9:30	P.M.	Lights out

My dormitory located on the top floor of the building, had beds to accommodate squads 6 and 7, about 40 students. The two squad leaders had separate bedrooms just outside the dormitory door. There were also washing facilities next to the dormitories, about 8 wash basins with mirrors and a large shower room with four shower heads. We were required to shower once a week, usually Saturday afternoons. There were no toilets in the dormitory area; the only toilets were located at ground level, past the church, at the far end of the courtyard. If one needed to use the bathroom during the night he had to get permission from the squad leader before descending the stairs. The bathrooms were very rustic, a long open trough urinal, and about 8 enclosed stalls, with doors, and *footprint* type waste receptacles. One positioned his feet on the *footprints*, lowered his pants, squatted, and relieved himself. Regular toilet tissue was not used, but there were nails on the wall with pieces of newspaper affixed to the nails. After listening to all the rules and regulations and reviewing the daily schedule, I had a feeling that I was not going to like the formal structure of the school activities!

The schedule for the first night was simplified and turned out to be another orientation session. Since we were in the church, we participated in the evening religious service, which consisted of saying the Rosary and receiving a benediction. The Rosary was recited in Latin and the students were required to respond in Latin to the second half of the prayers, five Our Father's and fifty Hail Mary's. We were then instructed to go to the cafeteria and sit with our squad leader at the table which was identified by our squad number, and that once seated we would receive further instructions about the meals and the procedures to follow in the cafeteria.

As I entered the cafeteria I spotted the table for squad number 6 and Luigi and I walked over and sat down waiting for the next sequence of events. As we sat there, other students began to sit at our table. Our squad leader, Francesco, was standing and moving around the table introducing himself to students. We introduced ourselves to the students sitting near us. The tables were numbered 1 through 7 and each table had room for about 20 students. There was also a special table set up for the faculty of the school and most of the priests were already seated at their table. About half way down, along one wall of the cafeteria, there was an elevated platform, about two feet above the floor level, with a table and one chair. When most of the students were seated, Padre Cesare, our disciplinarian, stepped onto the platform and began to speak in a low, booming voice:

"Students, you will be in the dining room four times a day, for breakfast, for *spuntino* (snack time), for *pranzo* (noon time meal) and for *cena* (supper). We have certain rules that you must follow while you are in the dining room eating your meals. At breakfast and *spuntino* you may talk among yourselves in a quiet, orderly way. At *pranzo* and at *cena* there will be no talking. At those meals, one of the proctors (squad leaders) will sit at this table (he pointed to the table on the platform) and will read to you from a classic novel while you are eating. (The only novel that I remember being read was *Don Quixote De La Mancha* by Miguel de Cervantes Saavedra).

"Since Italy is at war, food is scarce, so you will be expected not to waste food and to eat everything that is put on your plate. This evening you will be allowed to speak to each other at the tables in the hope that you will get to know the other members of your squad. The meal will be served shortly, so please follow the directions of your squad leader."

The meal was served by women who worked in the kitchen and lived in Porcari. I don't remember the food served at our first meal, because I was more interested in meeting the rest of the students from our squad. I remember names, such as Pieretti, Galletto, Agresti, Quilici, Biagi, Donati, Marsili, and as I look at a picture of my squad, taken before the end of the term in the Spring of 1943, I vividly remember the faces and the students, but I cannot remember all of their names. After the meal we walked out into the courtyard talking among ourselves and with our leader, Francesco. We went to the bathrooms, then walked up the four flights of stairs to our dormitories to put away our clothes and get ready for bed.

We were each assigned a bed with our student identification number affixed to it and a small storage chest at the foot of the bed. The dormitory was a large room with rows of beds; along the outside wall there were about 4 windows that opened out, overlooking the soccer field. The windows were open to allow some air to circulate in the warm room. Beyond the soccer field, there was a view of a large brick factory, and one could see the hundreds of red bricks that were laid out to dry before baking. We were told to unpack our suitcases, and place our clothing in the storage chest. We were shown the containers in the washroom areas for dirty clothes. The dirty clothes were going to be washed by the women working at the school and would later be returned to our bed, according to the student identification numbers affixed to the articles of clothing. We were reminded about the time schedule for the following day, and that lights would go out at 9:30 p.m. this evening and every evening. Most of us unpacked, placed our clothing in the storage chests and fooled around a lot that first evening. We did not have pajamas to wear, but went to bed wearing our undershirts and shorts. I did not feel embarrassed disrobing in front of others. Often in Diecimo, many of my friends and I would go swimming in the river Serchio without wearing any clothes; it was a common practice at that time for boys to swim without a bathing suit in secluded areas along the river. As I settled in my bed, watching all the activity in the room, waiting for *lights out*, I felt a bit betrayed by my parents and I was not quite sure that I would like the *Istituto Cavanis!*

Rather than trying to recall every incident or event that happened during the school year, I'm going to describe certain happenings that I still remember and that I feel influenced me while I was in Porcari. The experiences were typical of boarding schools of the time.

In general the food that was served in the cafeteria was not too bad. There was sufficient bread at meals, small amounts of meat, a lot of pasta, vegetables and fruit. The *spuntini* were not highly structured; if students wanted a snack, they went into the cafeteria, picked up the snack, then went out into the courtyard carrying the food with them and joined the rest of the students. The snacks were prepared with seasonal food products such as chestnut flour in the late fall and winter. Every day during that period of time we were served *castagnaccio*, which is a type of pie, made with water, chestnut flour, olive oil and rosemary. When the castagnaccio was baked it became quite solid, so that one could pick up the pieces and carry them out into the courtyard. There was another snack, served in the early spring, made of *zucca* (pumpkin), served by the slice and even though I did not like vegetables, I liked the pumpkin snack very much because it was sweet.

The breakfast meal was simple, typical of Italian breakfasts of that era: *caffè e latte* (milk and coffee) and bread. The *caffè e latte* was made by boiling the milk, adding a small amount of coffee, then placing the mixture in *ciotole* (bowls) which were located on the tables. Slices of bread were placed on the tables next to the bowls and we then broke the bread into small pieces, placed them into the bowl to soak in the milk, and then ate the milk-soaked bread. If sugar was available, we sweetened the mixture to make it more appetizing. I remember a disgusting thing that happened at breakfast time during the first week of school. There were lots of flies around the school, especially in the dining room. One day, as we came into the dining room for breakfast, I noticed that many of the bowls of milk had flies floating on top of the scum formed on the surface. When I sat down by my bowl, I saw about six flies floating in my milk, trapped by the scum, unable to fly away. I asked one of the serving women if I could have another bowl of milk. She laughed, and said:

"Pick the flies off the milk by yourself; we don't have time and we can't waste food. The flies won't kill you!"

From that day on, my daily ritual when I came into the breakfast room was to check my bowl; if it had flies floating in the milk I would try to exchange the bowl with one nearby that did not have flies. If the exchange could not be accomplished, I would lift out the flies with my teaspoon, flick them onto the floor, and proceed with my breakfast!

The church services began to get boring after a few Rosaries and Masses. We attended Mass every day, receive communion every day, go to confession every Friday, and go to the evening services every day. (I could never figure out why we went confession every week because under our strict schedule, we did not have time to commit any sins). The headmaster delivered his daily sermon at the Rosary and tried to influence our behavior with familiar parables.

Sundays were designated as visitation days for the parents of the students. When parents came to visit their sons, the boys could leave the school grounds and walk into Porcari. If one did not have visitors, the afternoon schedule was unstructured, so students could play in the courtyard or on the soccer field, sleep in the dormitory, or use the study halls. After eight weeks of school my mother and father had not yet come to visit me. Even though I wrote home once a week, and received letters from my mother, I missed seeing my parents. Finally, frustrated at being abandoned by my parents, I wrote a letter to my mother pointing out to her, in no uncertain terms, that I was really mad at her and hated her for not coming to see me. I also said that it was not right for a mother to abandon a child by sending him off to *collegio* and never coming to see him.

To my horror, at a church service, as part of the sermon, the headmaster made reference to a letter that a student wrote to his mother. He said that the student said horrible things in the letter and showed complete disrespect for his mother. He then read the letter to all the students of the school. As soon as he started to read, I knew that he was reading my letter. As he read, I sat motionless, hoping that he would not give the name of the student who wrote the letter, because it would have been very embarrassing for me. At that moment I also realized that I had better be careful when writing letters home, because all of our letters were being read by the priests!

The letter did reach my mother and accomplished its purpose: my mother and my uncle Dante came to see me. They rode their bicycles from Diecimo to Porcari on the subsequent Sunday and brought me some *biscotti*, a few pairs of socks, and some underwear. We were able to leave campus, walk into Porcari, and sit at a bar where we enjoyed some ice cream. I apologized to my mother for writing the letter. She understood and said that my father was not feeling well, that she had to stay at home to take care of him. I really enjoyed seeing my mother and my uncle and hearing about Diecimo and all my friends. Home did not seem that far away...

Even though I was homesick, missing my family and friends, I tried my best to do well studying the various school subjects. The subjects taught at the Istituto were typical of the first year of *Scuola Media*; some were taught on a daily basis, others on alternate days. Classes were in session six days a week, Monday through Saturday, and the school day was from 8:30 to 12:30. I remember having classes in Religion, Latin, Italian, Geography, History, Mathematics, Science, Art and Physical Education (some of the physical education classes were held in a small gymnasium or *palestra*). Each day we were assigned homework in the classical subjects which was to be completed during the study hall sessions. In all Italian schools, both public and private, it was the responsibility of the students to purchase the necessary materials for each class, such as books, notebooks, pencils and pens. The school had a small bookstore which was open in the evenings, and we were allowed to go there from our study halls to purchase items that we needed in school.

I would occasionally go to the bookstore to purchase materials for my classes and found the process enjoyable, since I liked to browse around and look at some of the nice books that they had for sale. Students did not need cash for the transactions; there was a charging system in place so that when students purchased items, they signed a slip of paper and then the parents paid that amount along with the monthly school fee. I usually did not abuse the charging system because I knew that my parents did not have too much money, but I did purchase something once that turned out to be bad judgment on my part.

The bookstore had a copy of the book *Gulliver's Travels* (*I Viaggi di Gulliver*) by Jonathan Swift. The book was large, in Italian of course, with a beautiful illustration on the cover and many drawings inside. The cover showed Gulliver tied to the ground with tiny men from Lilliput climbing all over him. I was fascinated by the premise of the story that a normal sized person could be taken prisoner by a large group of small men, so it seemed to me that *Gulliver's Travels* might be an interesting book to read. I decided to purchase the book, and followed the procedure for charging the book to my parents' account. I took the book to my desk in the study hall, and as soon as I was finished with my homework, I began to read the story and to look at the pictures. Since the study hall time was almost over, I wrote my name in the book, and left the book in my study hall desk, along with my other books.

The next evening, when I finished my homework, I took out Gulliver's Travels and began to read. The study hall supervisor for the evening was Padre Cesare, and as usual he walked around the room, keeping an eye out for misbehavior, and occasionally stopping by desks to talk to students. Padre Cesare stopped by my desk and asked what I was reading. I showed him the cover and said in Italian: "*I Viaggi di Gulliver.*"

Padre Cesare looked at the book and said: "I must take that book, because it is not a suitable book for children to read. There are many situations described in the book that are contrary to Italy's political policies."

I replied: "Padre Cesare, I just bought the book at the school bookstore and my parents are paying for it. If the book is not suitable for me, why did the school sell it?"

Padre Cesare ended the conversation by saying: "Tullio, be quiet, give me the book, and return to your homework."

Padre Cesare took my book, and that was the last time I saw *Gulliver's Travels*, though my parents paid for the book.

In 1994, my son Robert gave me a Christmas present, a copy of *Gulliver's Travels* in English, with the inscription "Dad, I hope that you have better luck reading this the second time!"

In spite of everything school progressed well; I felt that I was successful in my classes. My behavior was good and, other than the *Gulliver's Travels* incident, I did not get into any trouble. I got along well with my squad members, and I especially enjoyed playing soccer and other sports activities. Some of the students seemed to come from wealthy families and had much nicer wardrobes than I had. I did not have a great selection of clothes; some were old; others were sewn by my mother or made from garments belonging to my father. My hand-knitted woolen socks shrunk so much that they would no longer fit me, because at the school they washed everything in hot water. I had a very large foot, so when my socks shrunk, I gave them to other students with smaller feet.

There was one major interruption during the school year: the school closed because of a shortage of heating fuel. We went home for a long Christmas vacation in mid-December and returned to school after the worst of the cold weather was over, around mid-February. It was nice to be back home, to be able to sleep in my old bed, to enjoy my mother's cooking and to see all my friends.

When I arrived back home in Diecimo, I noticed some changes, especially in the two grocery stores in the village. There wasn't anything available for the people to buy. Ration stamps were required for the basics, such as bread, pasta, sugar, olive oil and meat, but even though people had the stamps for their monthly allotment, very often there wasn't anything available. People seemed even more concerned about the war and much of the talk revolved around the lack of food and clothing and what was happening on the Russian front.

There were 16 men from Diecimo who were in the *Alpini* division of the Italian Eighth Army. The *Alpini* were soldiers trained to fight in the mountains and the name was derived from the Alps which are the mountains bordering Italy in the north with France, Switzerland and Austria. There were four divisions of *Alpini* on the Don River front, the *Tridentina*, the *Julia*, the *Cunese*, and the *Vicenza*. The men from Diecimo were mostly in the *Julia* division. According to historical accounts, on November 19, 1942, the Russian Army began a counter-offensive which surprised the German Army. The *Alpini* were along the Don River, south of Korotojak and along the river to Ivanowka. On the morning of December 17, the Soviet Army broke through the Italian Eighth Army farther up the Don at Boguchar and by evening opened up a gap 27 miles deep. Within three days the hole was 90 miles wide, the Italians were fleeing in panic, and the Romanian Third Army to the south was disintegrating. The survivors of the Italian Eighth Army on the Don were running for their lives. The four *Alpini* corps fell back. Without food, they walked to Germany wearing only the clothing they had on their backs. They went past Postojell, Limarev, Schellakino, Romachowa, Arnautovo, Nikolajewka, Nowj-Oskoi, Morosova Balka, Bessarab, Shebekino, toward Belgrade and the Donez river.

According to news reports, the Italians, retreating from the Don River, were abandoned by the Germans and left to fend for themselves. It was extremely cold, and the Italian army suffered the loss of most of their divisions. Some of the men were able to walk all the way back to the German border, struggling for survival, seeking food from Russian people stranded in small villages, removing clothing and shoes from dead soldiers. Many Italian soldiers died.

There were a few survivors of this ordeal, one of whom was Giulio Luchi from Diecimo, who eventually became the village butcher. He still remembers his escape and considers himself lucky that he was able to return home. He often recounts stories about his ordeal. In 1990 a Russian man wrote a book recalling his experiences as a small boy during the winter of 1942-43 and how his family befriended and helped an Italian soldier named Luchi from the Lucca area. Giulio and the author were able to meet in Italy and talk about some of their experiences during that difficult winter. The man also had in his possession a photograph taken in 1942 of his family with Giulio Luchi standing next to him. There was an article in one of the Italian national newspapers describing the reunion.

The remaining 15 men from Diecimo who were in Russia fighting on the Don River never returned home. In fact the Soviet government never acknowledged their presence in Russia and never reported their deaths. To this day the families of the soldiers have never heard what happened to them. (It wasn't until many years later, that the Italian government presumed that all the men had died and started to give the survivors the same financial benefits given to families of soldiers who were officially reported dead during the war). Even though I was home enjoying Christmas vacation, playing with my friends, and spending time with my family, I really felt sorry for Paula and Licia Tonelli, two girls who lived a few doors away from me. Their father, Biagio, was in Russia, and his wife Iva and mother Nelda were very concerned about him and hoped that he would survive the ordeal. Biagio never returned, and the family never found out what happened to him.

After I returned home from Porcari I decided to try to put together a large *presepe* (manger scene) for the Christmas holidays. According to Italian history, the tradition of the *presepe* goes back to the year 1200 when Saint Francis of Assisi recreated the Nativity with statues that represented Mary, Joseph, Jesus, and the shepherds. The autobiography of Saint Francis indicates that on Christmas Eve, 1223, Saint Francis asked a friend to help him construct a replica of the manger in Bethlehem so that he would be able to celebrate a Mass in front of a live baby representing baby Jesus. From that time on, manger scenes or *presepe* were constructed, first in the churches, then on a smaller scale in the homes. The *presepe* was symbolic of the religious nature of Christmas and still continues to be popular in Italian homes along with the Christmas tree. (However, Christmas trees were not set up in Italian homes until well after World War II).

I planned to make my *presepe* on a small table which was placed in my bedroom against one of the walls. I first looked around the fields for large rocks and brought them home. I used the rocks to construct a small mountain and cave which was to include the manger. Then I went up the mountain, near the chestnut tree groves and searched out areas where moss was growing. I carefully lifted off large pieces of moss and brought the moss home to cover the rocks and table top. A nearby town, Bagni di Lucca, was the center for the manufacturing of plaster of Paris statues and statuettes, so there were many statues for sale in stores and at the weekly open air markets. I purchased several statues representing Joseph, Mary, baby Jesus, angels, the three kings, shepherds and sheep. I placed the statues on my *presepe* in the proper places, and I was really pleased with the outcome. I placed a small light bulb at the rear of my cave to shed a small amount of light on the manger. My mother and father thought that I did a good job and said they were proud of my work.

Christmas was primarily a religious holiday in Italy, commemorating the birth of Christ. Children did not receive gifts on Christmas day as is done in the United States. Gifts were given to children on the sixth of January, which is the day of Epiphany (when the Three Wise Men visited baby Jesus), when the *Befana* (an old woman) came around during the night and left presents for the children. Christmas Day was a day of religious celebration which involved attending Mass and spending time with family and friends at a big *pranzo*. I remember looking forward to January 6 and the day that the *Befana* came around to the houses to deliver the presents to the children. Even though I was old enough not to believe in the *Befana* my mother provided me with a few treats such as caramelle, oranges, and *befanotti* (cookies shaped in the form of a *Befana*).

A traditional midnight Mass was held on Christmas Eve in the main church and the town choir participated in the services by singing Christmas hymns. December in Diecimo was very cold and at times there was also snow on the ground. The interior of the church was freezing cold because it was not heated. I remember attending the midnight Mass, sitting in a pew and watching the warm breath vapor trails being emitted by everyone in the church. Many children attended the midnight Mass because it was exciting to be out and about during the middle of the night without parental supervision. One of the customs in the church was to place a full-sized statue of baby Jesus on the top of the altar covered with a cloth. At the proper time, during the Mass, when symbolically Christ was born, someone from the rear of the altar would reach up and remove the cloth, exposing baby Jesus, thus representing the actual birth. The children were fascinated by the process and always looked up to see when this would happen, thinking that the cloth was removed by a miracle.

School started again around mid February and this time I was able to return to Porcari by train. It was nice to see all the members of my squad and to hear about their experiences. There were several boys from Florence who told us stories about the food shortages that they were experiencing in the city and that their homes were without heat because of a lack of fuel. I felt pretty lucky having been in Diecimo; village life was simple, but we still had wood for the fireplace and stove and there was always some type of seasonal food available. We gradually got back into the school routine, resumed our classes, played in the courtyard, ate our meals in the cafeteria, and attended Mass. The two month layoff caused me to forget much of what I learned during the fall, and I found it difficult to resume studying.

It was interesting to observe the interaction between students in the school courtyard. The older students took over the better half of the courtyard which had access to the outdoor basketball court. The younger students were segregated at the other end of the yard and had only a gravel covered surface on which to play soccer. At first there were a few small rubber soccer balls to kick around, but as they became worn and leaked air, we resorted to making our own balls by rolling up paper and tying the paper into a ball. We kicked the balls with our every-day shoes and as the year progressed our shoes became worn, so at times, during the warm weather we played barefoot. Behind the bathroom building and near the gym there was a small alley way that was accessible to students, and since it was somewhat hidden, students sometimes sneaked into the area to smoke cigarettes. Even though I was raised in a family in which my father smoked, at age 12, I did not have the desire to smoke. Many students smoked and somehow managed to sneak cigarettes into the school. Once in a while Padre Cesare would catch someone smoking and the student would be disciplined by having to spend his play time in the study hall.

At the end of the school year, in mid May, I was promoted to the *Seconda Media*, but to be very honest I was not anxious to return to the *Istituto Cavanis*. Some time during midsummer I was delighted to hear that the school would not re-open in the fall because of the war. In fact, all schools in Italy were closed in the fall of 1943. I don't know how my experiences in Porcari at the *Istituto Cavanis* have affected my personal life today, but in looking back I feel that it was not an enjoyable experience. The organization of the school was too regimented for me and I felt that the priests on the staff were not at all compassionate to the needs of the students. I resented the fact that my parents sent me away from home, and in spite of friends and many activities, I felt very lonely at school.

18. Top: A photo copy of the cover of the report card issued at the completion of hte fifth grade to Tullio.
19. Bottom: The *Prima Media* Squad # 6, Istituto Cavanis in Porcari, taken in 1942-43. Tullio is in the second row, third from left.

20. Tullio on the left, Beppe Pierini in the center, Giancarlo Piacentini to the right. Winter 1939-40. The Bertini grandparents' house in the rear.

8.
THE NAZIS ARRIVE
IN DIECIMO

By the end of May 1943, when the Allied forces defeated the Axis army in North Africa, it was evident to Mussolini that the Anglo-American armies would next turn on Italy. Mussolini was ill, disillusioned and fearful of what was going to happen to the nation. On July 10, 1943, the Anglo-American forces landed in Sicily. The Italians did not want to fight and therefore the Italian army was in a state of collapse. On July 19, at Feltre, in northern Italy, Hitler met with Mussolini insisting that they must continue to fight on all fronts; Sicily and Italy could be held if the Italians fought. At that same time there was a heavy daylight air attack on Rome. Shortly after, when *Il Duce* returned to Rome he faced a revolt from some of his closest friends in the Fascist Party. On July 24-25, 1943, the Fascist Grand Council, by a vote of 19 to 8 passed a resolution demanding the restoration of a constitutional monarchy with a democratic Parliament. It called for the full command of the armed forces to be restored to the King of Italy. On the evening of July 25, Mussolini was summoned to the Royal Palace by the King, who dismissed him from office and had him arrested. He was transported under guard to the police station in an ambulance.

So fell, ignominiously, the modern Roman Caesar,
a bellicose-sounding man of the 20th century, who had
known how to profit from its confusion and despair,

but who underneath the gaudy facade was made largely of sawdust. As a person he was not unintelligent. He had read widely in history and thought he understood its lessons. But as dictator he had made the fatal mistake of seeking to make a martial, imperial Great Power of a country which lacked the industrial resources to become one and whose people, unlike the Germans, were too civilized, too sophisticated, too down-to-earth to be attracted by such false ambitions. The Italian people, at heart, had never, like the Germans, embraced Fascism. They had merely suffered it, knowing that it was a passing phase, and Mussolini toward the end seems to have realized this. But like all dictators he was carried away by power, which, as it inevitably must, corrupted him, corroding his mind and poisoning his judgment. This led him to his second fatal mistake of tying his fortunes and those of Italy to the Third Reich. When the bell began to toll for Hitler's Germany it began to toll for Mussolini's Italy, and as the summer of 1943 came the Italian leader heard it. But there was nothing he could do to escape his fate. By now he was a prisoner of Hitler. (*The Rise And Fall Of The Third Reich* by William Shirer)

After the fall of Mussolini, the Italians became even more fearful of the threatening situation in their country. They already had made sacrifices in their life style: food was scarce, their sons fighting in far away lands, schools closed, and public transportation curtailed. Many villages in Italy were fortunate enough to have a railroad station with train service to and from their villages. In the past the railroad provided a means of escape for many Italians from their villages to unknown lands. Men, women and children were eager to emigrate to the New World in the hope of finding their fortunes and returning to their native villages with enough money to buy land and homes. The railroad was the link to the major ports of Genova and Napoli, delivering passengers to the trans-Atlantic ships that transported many Italians to the United States. During the time of the Fascist government, Benito Mussolini improved the *Ferrovia Statale* (National Railway System); *Il Duce* took great pride in proclaiming that the trains always ran on time!

In Diecimo, however, the railroad station was a simple two story building painted in the Ferrovia Statale colors, orange and yellow. The ground floor included an office with a ticket window opening into a small entry room. A door led from the entry room to the waiting room which was furnished with stark wooden benches and a wood stove. The room had a ceramic tile floor and a very high ceiling. There were two large wood frame doors with glass windows leading to the train platform so that one could view the tracks from the waiting area. The second story of the building provided the living quarters for the *Capo Stazione* (Station Master) and his family. The train station office included a desk, cabinets, a telephone, a telegraph line, and a large clock. The large manual track switching levers outside the office were used to switch the track so that a train could be placed on a siding while another train passed through on the single track mainline.

During the Fascist years, most train stations had famous quotations from Mussolini's speeches displayed in large letters on the exterior walls. Our station had large bold letters facing the train tracks that spelled out DIECIMO-PESCAGLIA. The name Pescaglia was placed there to indicate that in order to go to Pescaglia one had to get off the train in Diecimo, then make a bus connection for Pescaglia or walk the distance of about eight kilometers, up the hill. The double name was confusing to people, and still is to this day. When one mentions to someone from Lucca that he is from Diecimo, the Lucchese says:

"I know, that is Diecimo-Pescaglia, the next stop from Piaggione."

In addition to the railroad station, the *Capo Stazione*, also had other railroad buildings under his jurisdiction. There was a large building close to the track siding that was used to store freight. In addition there were two *caselli* nearby. The term *casello* means a small house or structure. One *casello,* located by the steel railroad bridge that traversed the Pedogna River, was manned by a man named Coli. His duty was to guard the bridge, to make sure that the trains could cross safely, and to check that there was no damage to the tracks. He was also responsible for controlling the rail siding levers that placed the Piazza al Serchio bound trains on the siding. The other *casello* was located at the Zandori entrance to the village and the man stationed there had to lower the road barriers to block automobile traffic for ten minutes before a train was scheduled to pass.

One of the reasons why I mention the railroad station is that while I was in Diecimo the station was a distraction from normal life and a source of information for me and the other children in the village. During the winter months the waiting room was usually nice and warm because the station master would light the wood burning stove in the morning. This made the waiting room a comfortable gathering place for teenagers. Many of my friends and I bicycled to the station to meet the late afternoon trains. We were curious about who was arriving and wanted to see if there were any new girls coming to the village.

During the summer of 1943, the Allied Air Forces started to bomb some of the coastal cities, such as Livorno, Pisa, La Spezia, Genova and others. The bombing caused many people to leave the cities and seek shelter in some of the remote villages away from the coastline. People packed as many personal items as they could carry, boarded a train, and headed for unknown areas further inland. These people were called *sfollati* (evacuees). When coastal bombings took place we heard the noise of the explosions and saw fiery reflections in the sky over the tops of the mountains which divided our valley from the coastal area.

After the bombings started, the trains heading up the Serchio River Valley gradually became more crowded with *sfollati*. The trains stopped as usual in Diecimo and each day several families got off the train carrying suitcases and bundles of possessions. The *Capo Stazione* tried to help them locate a home in which they could live, and in general most families found a place to stay. Sometimes the father of the family returned to the city in order to continue working.

A family named Cuomo came from Livorno and stayed in the home of Michele, the shoemaker. The Cuomo family had two sons and two daughters. I made friends with their son Mauro, my age, and enjoyed spending time with him. His older brother, Luciano, was a singer with theatrical experience in Rome. Mauro left Diecimo after the war and his family moved to Florence. He ended up working at a gas station in Florence and I was able to locate him and spend an evening with him during the summer of 1958.

In 1941 or 1942 I remember the departure from the train station of a young man, Egidio Luciani, who was in the military service. He was an *Alpino*, and when I saw him at the station he was dressed in his *grigio verde* uniform, wearing his *alpino* hat and carrying his rifle, bayonet and cartridge belt. Egidio was home on furlough and went to the station accompanied by his parents and his girlfriend in order to catch the train that would take him back to his unit. As the train pulled into the station he began to cry like a child saying that he did not want to return to his unit and did not want to leave home.

He screamed: *"Non voglio andare..."* (I don't want to go...)

His father walked across the waiting room, placed an arm around his son and said: *"Devi andare.""* (You must go.)

The train stopped and Egidio and his family walked out on the platform. He hugged his parents, kissed his mother and girlfriend.

He then said: *"Non ritornerò."* (I will not return...)

Egidio was sent to Russia to fight on the Don River front, fighting with the Italian *Alpini* divisions. Egidio never returned to Diecimo, his family never found out when or where he died, and he was one of the many thousands of Italians brutally lost in Russia. I'll never forget the scene at the railroad station as long as I live. I can never forget Egidio's hopelessness and how he resigned himself to return to his unit and fight for his country.

After World War II, as things got back to normal, the monument dedicated to those who gave their lives in World War I was restored. The bronze sculpture of a World War I soldier had been removed by the Fascists, melted down and the bronze used for making artillery shell casings. The residents of Diecimo erected a carved stone obelisk with the following seventeen names engraved into the stone:

> Frugoli, Lio
> Paoli, Rolando
> Maggenti, Ivo
> Piacentini, Paolo
> Tonelli, Biagio
> Tucci, Tullio
> Barsotti, Luciano
> Biondi, Olinto
> Cortopassi, Ferdinando
> Cortopassi, Giuseppe
> Luciani, Egidio
> Marchi, Mansueto
> Motroni, Giuseppe

Piacentini, Arturo
Polidori, Pietro
Romani, Mario
Simonetti, Guelfo

Fifteen of the above soldiers were lost in Russia and never came back to Diecimo.

People went about their business in the village, working the land, trying to raise enough food for their families. News about the war circulated among the people. Sometimes a newspaper surfaced, and people listened to the Italian radio broadcasts. On September 3, 1943, Allied Forces landed in southern Italy, and on September 8 a public announcement was made declaring an armistice between Italy and the Western Powers. Field Marshal Kesserling, headquartered in Frascati, near Rome, put in motion plans for the German army to disarm the Italian army and occupy the country. For several days the situation of the German forces in southern Italy was critical, because they were concerned with the Allied troops as well as the Italian troops. The Italian divisions eventually surrendered to the Germans and were disarmed. Also on September 8 the Allies landed troops at Salerno. The code name was Avalanche, and the purpose was to capture the Germans and clear the entire Italian Peninsula of Axis troops. Unfortunately Gestapo intelligence discovered the preparations for the landing and the Germans were ready for General Mark Clark's Fifth Army. On September 10, Hitler told Goebbels that southern Italy was lost and that a new line would have to be established north of Rome on the Apennines. This was to be the Gothic Line.

Mussolini was imprisoned by the monarchy and his whereabouts kept secret. In early September he was moved to a hotel on top of a mountain, the Gran Sasso d'Italia, in the Abruzzi region of Italy. The area was secured by Italian troops and was accessible only by funicular railway. In spite of these precautions, on September 13 the Germans, led by Otto Skorzeny, landed glider troops on the Gran Sasso and, without firing a shot, rescued Benito Mussolini and flew him to Rome in a tiny Fiesiler-Storch airplane.

On September 15, Mussolini created the new Italian Social Republic, establishing his headquarters in Northern Italy at Rocca delle Caminate, near Gargana, on the shores of Lake Garda. As all these events took place, the news reached the people of Diecimo by radio and in the local newspaper. There weren't many radios in the village, but we had one, so my father listened to the news and relayed the information to others. In addition, during the night my father listened to the BBC news broadcast in English, and notified the people in Diecimo about the war situation in other parts of Europe. When people found out about the surrender of Italy to the Anglo-American Forces, the occupation of Italy by the Germans, the Allied landings in southern Italy, the imprisonment of Mussolini, his rescue by the Germans and the formation of a new Fascist government, they began to speculate about their fate, especially since the Germans announced that they would establish a line of defense further north in the Apennine mountains.

After the September 8 surrender of Italy to the Anglo-American Forces, the soldiers in the Italian Army disbanded and tried to reach their homes using whatever means possible. The soldiers who were able to reach their villages or towns remained hidden in their homes hoping they would not be captured by the Fascists or German troops. If they were unable to reach their home areas, they hid in the mountains and became partisans, living off the land and being assisted by non-Fascist people in the area. After Mussolini formed his new government, some of the strong Fascist leaders in our village took control and tried to impose their rules and regulations on the people, causing a lot of conflict as the situation got more tense.

The northern line of defense planned by the Germans was named the *Gothic Line*. The term is of German origin, probably derived from a defense line established by the Goths who were opposing the Byzantines in the same zone of Italy in the 6th century B.C. Around the middle of June, 1944, the German command changed the name Gothic Line to the term *Grune Linie* or Green Line (in Italian, *Linea Verde*). The Gothic Line, as devised by the German Command forces in Italy, was to be a complex of fortifications about 170 miles long, extending eastward from Pisa on the western Ligurian coast across Versilia to the Serchio River Valley and on to Rimini on the Adriatic coast.

To fully understand the Apennines as they relate to the Gothic Line, one must view them as a series of continuous mountain ranges slanting and zig-zagging southeasterly from Genova. As a war front, the Gothic Line presented a tortuous configuration of peaks, ridges, and sheer rock faces up to 3,000 meters in height, crisscrossed by many rivers carving out deep ravines and low-lying valleys. This would be the defense line upon which the Germans would attempt, as a final effort, to slow the Allied Army advance, until the line ultimately gave way to the advancing American troops in April 1945. Two major mountains came into play, to the west *La Brugiane* and to the east, *Il Belvedere*.

At the end of the summer of 1943, as the Germans prepared to set up the Gothic Line of defense, a group of TODT workers and German soldiers came into Diecimo and took over the railroad station complex. The TODT organization, named for Dr. Fritz Todt, a German engineer who was involved in Nazi politics and was the designer of many German autobahns, was used by the German Army to construct military facilities in Italy in preparation for major battles. The German command placed many of the workers and soldiers in homes in the village. The work force was made up mostly of older German soldiers, Polish prisoners of war, and older Italian men. Other similar units were placed further up the valley in the villages of Borgo a Mozzano, Gallicano, Barga and Bagni di Lucca. They were identified by the letters O.T. (Organization Todt).

As one came up the Serchio River Valley from Lucca, the entrance to the valley was very narrow, practically just the width of the river, plus the width of a road on each side of the river. As one got to Piaggione, the village before Diecimo, the valley began to open up and in Diecimo was at its widest point. Here the valley was approximately 600 meters wide, with a mountain on each side that climbed up almost vertically from each road. The valley narrowed down again at Borgo a Mozzano, by the *Ponte del Diavolo*, to a width of about 40 meters.

Most people thought that the TODT workers planned to block the entry to the valley so that the Allied troops would not be able to advance towards Modena and Florence. As one continued up the valley, past Borgo a Mozzano, there was a wye in the valley, where the smaller river Lima, coming down from Bagni di Lucca to the east joined the Serchio. The road going up the Lima valley led to Pistoia, then Florence. Another road led more directly north to Abetone, a ski area at an elevation of 2000 meters, then on to Modena in Northern Italy. This road was known as the *Via del Brennero* and was the main road leading to the Brenner Pass into Austria. The Serchio River Valley went to the west and continued to Gallicano, Barga, Castelnuovo di Garfagnana, Piazza al Serchio and eventually led back to the coast near Carrara. The mountains at Piazza al Serchio are the backside of the famous Carrara marble quarries.

The German TODT workers did not discuss their plans with the people in Diecimo, but we could see what they were trying to do. At first they started to work on the mountains that had a commanding view of the valley. They dug tunnels and prepared emplacements for machine guns and artillery units. The gun emplacements were connected to tunnels dug in the rock which were to house the soldiers and to store ammunition. As no trains were running, some of the railroad tunnels between Diecimo and Borgo a Mozzano were prepared for the storage of arms and ammunition. The next series of constructions involved the use of the Pedogna River bed and the area where the Pedogna joined the Serchio River. The Pedogna did not have much water in it during the summer; in fact it was dry most of the time and in the winter the flow of water was based on the amount of rainfall in the area. A winding narrow road followed the Pedogna as it came down from a small valley, from Piegaio to Diecimo. Entering the Diecimo area, the roadway paralleled the Pedogna and the steep road construction provided a natural barrier, about 20 feet above the river bed. The Germans planned to use the natural terrain of the Pedogna Valley to their advantage by constructing concrete bunkers along the east bank of the river so it would be like a continuous wall from one side of the valley to the other up the Pedogna river.

There were two bridges crossing the Pedogna River, one on the main road leading into Diecimo, which was built of stone and bricks, probably two or three hundred years old; the other was a steel railroad bridge, which was located near the railroad station. As part of their preparations the Germans worked on the support columns of both bridges, drilling large holes to accept dynamite sticks so they could blow up the bridges when the Allies entered the valley.

South of the bridges, there was a large flat area near the Serchio River bed called *La Macchia* that ran the width of the valley. The Germans planned to fill up the *Macchia* area with land mines which would make the valley inaccessible to military vehicles and foot soldiers. The work started around mid-September 1943 and continued until the summer of 1944. The people of Diecimo reluctantly accepted the German workers and did not have any trouble with them. On the other hand the villagers were very cautious about their activities when the Nazi soldiers were around. There were two groups of soldiers, one group was part of the corps of engineers who worked with the TODT organization and the other group were SS troops. The SS troops, known as Schutzstaffel, wore black uniforms similar to the Fascists, with the SS insignia which looked like small lightning bolts worn on their shirt collar. At that time my friends and I had no idea of the reputation of the SS soldiers, but we were afraid of them and tried to keep out of their way, sensing that they were not very friendly.

People continued raising their seasonal crops, often exchanging some of the fresh fruits and vegetables for bread and meat that the Germans had. Most of the young men from the village were in the armed services, so the population of the village was made up of old men, women, girls, and boys under the age of 16 or 17. The Germans imposed a curfew on all the people and thus we were confined to our homes from 6 p.m. to 6 a.m. The SS soldiers patrolled the village during the night in order to keep people in their homes so that there would not be any interference with the German construction work.

By now my father was feeling pretty well healthwise and he became interested in working with the Italian Red Cross. In conjunction with the Red Cross organization in Lucca, he opened up a small office in our living room and placed a Red Cross sign on the outside of our house designating it as an official Red Cross zone. My father was supposed to help individuals who were trying to correspond by mail with relatives in countries that were at war with Italy. The Red Cross helped to facilitate the movement of mail from Italy to other countries, such as the United States, England and

Brazil. Since my father spoke English he was also able to translate letters for the people of the village and from the surrounding area. The Red Cross sign probably gave us a certain amount of protection from the Germans, and we certainly did not publicize the fact that we were American!

The wine supply was critical to Diecimo, not only for the residents, but also for the German workers in the village. Therefore, in the latter part of September 1943, when the grapes were ripe, the harvesting of the grapes, *la vendemmia*, took place just as it had in past years, even though the Germans were in town. Grapes were grown all over the village, on flat areas as well as on terraced hillsides. Because many of the parcels of land on the flat part of the valley were owned by different people, grape vines were planted to grow to a height of about 6 to 8 feet to act as fences between the various properties. In order to harvest the grapes the members of the families not only had to pick in the flat areas but also had to be healthy enough to climb the hills and pick grapes on the terraced parcels of land.

The process was to bring a two-wheeled cart, pulled by a cow, a donkey, or people, and to place it as near as possible to the location of the grape vines. The old men, women and children went along the vines with a small knife, cut off the grape cluster and deposited the grapes in a basket. The baskets, when full, were dumped into a *bigongia* (an oval shaped wooden barrel). When the *bigongia* was full, some of the stronger women placed the barrel on their heads, on a rolled up towel, and carried the load to the cart. The men also carried the barrels using a gunny sack which was folded in such a way that the corner of the gunny sack fit over the head, and the barrel nestled into the other corner of the sack, which was rolled up and placed on the shoulder. I helped both of our tenant farmers and their families by picking grapes and carrying some of the barrels to the cart.

Even though it was hard work, it was fun being out in the fields with the other kids.

Part of our house extended under the church next door, the *Cappella del Carmine*, and was used as a *tinaio*, or a place where wine was made. The *tinaio* was a rustic room with a packed dirt floor, ventilated by open windows with iron bars. Lined up around the walls were *tini*, large wooden vats, and *botte*, large wine barrels. The wine making process was simple and was a method probably used by Italians for centuries. As the grapes were brought into the *tinaio* they were placed in a hand-cranked crusher whose handle was turned by the stronger men. The juice, skins and stems of the grapes were collected in barrels below the crusher, then dumped into a large *tino*. The *tino*, about 6 feet tall and about 6 feet in diameter, was made of wooden slats, held together with bands of steel. The various vats were designated mostly for red grapes; if certain areas produced white grapes, they were separated from the red before crushing. The crushing continued until all the grapes were harvested and the vats were about 3/4 full of the grape mixture. The liquid settled on the bottom, along with some of the skins, and the stems floated to the top. The mixture was left to ferment for a certain number of days (it seems to me that the time period was about two weeks) until the alcohol level reached a certain percentage. Every few days, Angelo Giambastiani, our *contadino*, went to the *tinaio*, removed his shoes and socks, rolled up his pants, climbed into each *tino* and stomped the mixture, thus forcing the stems and skins to go down into the liquid so that they could aid the fermenting process.

At the beginning of the fermenting process, the juice from the grapes was sweet, but as time went by and the alcohol content increased, the liquid lost its sweetness and started to become wine. When the wine was ready, the liquid was removed from the *tino* and placed in a *botte*, which, as I mentioned, was a large wine barrel. The process was called *il tempo di imbottigliare il vino* (literally translated as the time to place the wine in barrels). Usually the process took an entire day and extended well into the evening. Plans usually were made to provide food for the workers and for visitors who came to sample the new wine. When the wine was ready for tasting, a wooden spout with a valve control was driven into the plug hole at the bottom of the *tino* with a hammer. The wine flowed into a small container, was sampled by all those present, and comments were made regarding the taste. If it was satisfactory, then the wine was collected in *bigongie* (a type of wine barrel) and poured into the large *botte*. The *botte*, made of wooden slats held together with steel bands, were about 3 to 4 feet in diameter, and approximately 4 feet tall. The *botti* were sealed at each end, and stored on their sides. The wine was poured in from the top and when the container was full, a wooden plug was placed in the top hole, sealing the barrel.

As the liquid poured out of the *tino*, the fermented stems and skins settled to the bottom. When all the liquid in the *tino* was gone, the reddish mixture of stems and skins were removed and placed in a hand operated wine press to squeeze out the remaining precious wine. The mixture or pulp, was called *vinaccia*, and when squeezed produced a cloudy liquid which was kept in a separate barrel from the first pressing. Eventually the cloudy sediment settled to the bottom and the result was a satisfactory wine that was used for everyday meals. When the *vinaccia* was squeezed dry, it was dumped back into the *tino*, covered with water and allowed to ferment again for several days. This process produced a reddish-pink beverage called *picciuolo,* which was also used as an everyday table wine. It was not very strong, but had a mild taste similar to wine, and looked a lot like the *Rosè* wines marketed today in the United States. After the *picciuolo* was made, the *vinaccia* was still saved and used for the production of *grappa*, a drink that was almost pure alcohol made by a distillation process which will be explained later.

The property owner was responsible for providing the food for the workers on the day that the wine was transferred to the *botte* and, depending on the availability of food, great meals were prepared by the women of the house. Nearby families came by to sample the new wine and also to share in the meal. Homemade pasta was served with tomato sauce; corn meal *polenta* was also prepared and served with *baccalà* (dried cod fish, prepared in tomato sauce). There would also be bread and cheese, and at times homemade salame. I did not care for wine very much, but I did enjoy some of the new wine because it was a bit on the sweet side, similar to grape juice. Umberto Pasquinelli and I drank a bit too much new wine on that day in 1943, and we did not realize the impact of the alcohol in the wine on our young bodies. As we were feeling giddy and talkative, we were able to steal a couple of small Toscanelli cigars from one of the men, and ventured out behind the *Cappella*, with the cigars and a bottle of the new wine. We were both only 13 years old, but by drinking and smoking we thought we were acting like adults. We lit up the cigars and continued to drink and smoke, but suddenly I felt terribly sick to my stomach; for the first time in my life I vomited, and the contents of my stomach flew all over the grassy area on which we were sitting. As the reddish liquid squirted out of my mouth, I was in so much pain that I thought I was going to die. I dumped the wine from the bottle, threw the cigar away in the field, and vowed to myself that I would never smoke or drink wine again!

The wine making process was slow, even after the wine was placed in the large wooden barrels. The wine had to age for a period of time and also the sediment had to settle to the bottom of the barrels. When the wine was ready and free of sediment, it was removed from the barrel and transferred by a mouth-operated suction hose to 50 liter *damigiana* or demijohns (large glass bottle-shaped containers, with a woven basket supporting the lower portion). The secret was to keep air from the wine so that it would not turn to vinegar and this was accomplished by placing a small amount of olive oil on the top surface of the wine. The oil was removed from the top of the bottle with a piece of *stoppa* (shredded hemp, looking like a cotton ball) before pouring the wine in glasses. The first glasses of wine usually had drops of olive oil floating on top.

Grappa is a traditional Italian drink made from *vinaccia* or from wine by a distillation process using an *alambicco* or "still." It dates back to the year 1100 when Italian monks discovered how to make alcohol. It was illegal for the *contadini* to make *grappa* because the local *comune* wanted to collect taxes on the production, but many people went ahead and secretly made enough for their own consumption.

Distillation was accomplished by placing *vinaccia*, that was not fully squeezed but containing some liquid, into a large copper kettle which was then sealed with a tight fitting lid. Connected to the top of the lid was a small-diameter copper tubing which was coiled like a spring. When the contents of the copper kettle were boiled over a fire in the fireplace, the alcohol in the *vinaccia* turned to vapor and began to collect in the copper coils. As it cooled, it returned to liquid form and dripped down into a bottle. The actual distillation took place at unusual times and in locations such as basements and barns, because the process was kept a secret. The resulting *grappa* was a clear liquid with a high alcohol content, probably 70 or 80 percent, with a hint of vinaccia flavor. Grappa was drunk by men during the winter, especially on cold days. Now, *grappa* is served as an after-dinner drink, sometimes added to *espresso* coffee, and the best *grappa* is produced in northern Italy. In Diecimo during the war, the *grappa* was used by families and also sold or traded for food. The German soldiers stationed and working in Diecimo liked to drink the local wine and grappa. In the evenings, after dinner, they would go to the bars and drink, even though there was a curfew in the village.

During the winter of 1943-44 there was a shortage of food and fuel, and very often we were without electricity. We could hear airplane bombardments along the coast and we also saw large formations of American bombers heading toward Northern Italy and Germany. Most people were concerned about their village and their lives. The children could not attend schools because they were closed, so we tried to stay out of trouble, to be as helpful as we could with our families and to stay out of the way of the Germans.

Some time in the spring, around mid-May, a group of my friends and I decided to clear off a field near the river, in the middle of the valley and make it into a soccer field. The grass covered field was full of a variety of sizes of river rocks which we had to lift and carry one by one to the nearby river bank. After much work and sweat we were able to prepare a fairly level field on which we could kick a soccer ball. We were able to find a few pieces of lumber, constructed two goal posts for the field, and placed them into the ground, one at each end of the playing area. Someone in our group was able to find an old soccer ball which still held air, even though the leather on the outside was pretty worn. We coated the leather with a bit of *lardo* (pork fat) which waterproofed the ball and made the leather softer. After we completed the field, we met in the afternoons and played soccer among ourselves. Sometimes we had enough players so that we had seven players on each side; at times we only had three or five players on each side. We enjoyed kicking the ball around even though most of us played barefoot because we did not have soccer shoes; we had fun pretending we were famous Italian soccer players.

One afternoon in May 1944, the German soldiers were working on the bridge, preparing it for future demolition. They were drilling large holes into the bridge structural supports for the placement of *tritolo* (dynamite), so that the bridge could be blown up when the Allied troops were approaching. On that particular afternoon a group of us were playing soccer on our new field. Often while playing soccer on our field, which was located directly in the center of the valley, we observed military airplanes flying overhead, at high altitudes, heading north. The planes, American bombers flying in formation, were often greeted by German anti-aircraft fire exploding directly above us and sending black puffs of smoke into the sky.

On this day in particular while we were playing soccer, I suddenly heard a loud roar coming from the western end of our valley. We all stopped playing, looked in the direction of the noise and saw two fighter planes zooming down to a very low altitude, heading for the bridge, coming toward us. When the planes got to Pastino, they opened fire on the bridge with their machine guns. They continued firing until they were past the railroad station, then continued up the valley, directly above us and started to climb rapidly toward Borgo a Mozzano, regaining the altitude necessary to fly over the mountains. As the planes went over us I could see the pilots very clearly since the planes were only about twenty feet above ground level. They were British fighter planes painted with camouflage paint and with the round British bullseye insignia on the fuselage. My first reaction was to throw myself to the ground, cover my head with my arms and hope that they would not fire on us. After the planes went by, I watched them continue along the valley and as they started to fly over the mountains I got up and started to run, full speed, toward the village. As I ran toward my house, weaving in and out of the fields, panting, my heart pounding, I was hoping that the planes would not come back and attack the village.

I arrived home gasping for air, ran into the house, wanting to tell my parents what had happened. My parents listened to my story and said that they already knew what had happened because people in the street also saw the airplanes and heard the machine gun fire. We did not know exactly what happened at the bridge, but because we were fearful that there might be another attack on the village, we decided that we should remain in the house, out of sight.

We positioned ourselves in the front bedroom and hallway near our second story windows overlooking the street, and kept our shutters closed while we looked out through the slats. It seemed that the other families in the immediate area were doing the same thing. Rumors began to circulate, and discussions took place through the shutter slats, from house to house, and it became evident that the planes attacked the bridge and fired on the German soldiers, killing several of them. After about fifteen or twenty minutes, as we were looking out into the street, we heard the sound of approaching motor vehicles, coming from the direction of the bridge and the Piazza. We pushed out on the shutters in order to get a better view and saw two military open bed trucks slowly moving along. As they approached our house our viewpoint was directly above the trucks and we were able to look down and see what was in the truck beds. Each truck contained the bodies of the soldiers who were killed at the bridge. The bodies, covered with blood, were placed in the trucks in random order and settled into grotesque positions like pieces of wood. I looked at the bodies as they went by and realized that this was the first time I had seen a person who died as a direct result of war and that I also could have been killed by the airplanes if they continued to fire their machine guns as they flew over the soccer field. I recall, from that fleeting moment, that I observed five bodies in each truck, and that the trucks were heading toward Borgo a Mozzano. I wondered who the men were, if their families were going to be notified of their deaths, and where they were going to be buried. Later, when we resumed our playing activities on the soccer field, I wondered if the British pilots noticed that children were playing soccer and whether they intentionally stopped firing their machine guns because we were kids. Early in the war people and children had viewed the British as enemies of Italy and viewed the Germans as friends. The attack by the British fighter planes on our village brought into focus how this opinion had changed. It appeared to me that the people now viewed the Germans as enemies and the British and the Americans as friends and liberators.

After the trucks passed by, people began to go out into the street trying to find out what happened. I got my bicycle and rode to the piazza where I saw some of my friends from the soccer game and we decided to ride down to the bridge. We found out that the attack specifically targeted the bridge and that several workers were also wounded. We saw pools of blood all over the ground. Several villagers mentioned that there were brass shell casings on the road and under the path that the airplanes had flown. We rode around and began collecting the empty shell casings which were ejected from the airplanes to keep as souvenirs. The bronze casings were from 20 millimeter machine guns and they were easy to spot. I kept one for many years and everytime I looked at the shell casing I remembered that warm afternoon when death had been so near to me.

Much of the discussion in Piazza centered around the attack, the location of the advancing Allied troops, and the future of our village. Some of the men thought that we were going to be in danger if we remained in the village, because it seemed as if the valley might become the setting for a major battle between the Germans and the Americans. A few people thought that we should leave the village, to go and hide in nearby mountain villages which were only accessible by walking up mule trails and narrow pathways.

When I returned home, my mother and father were discussing our options. My father felt that for now we were probably safe in our house and that we should remain in Diecimo, especially since we had the Red Cross sign on our house. I felt that the situation might be dangerous, especially since I had viewed the aerial attack and had seen the dead soldiers. This caused me to be somewhat fearful, but there was nothing that I could do. A few days after the attack, a few people from the village decided that it would be best to evacuate the area. They became *sfollati*, took whatever possessions they could carry, and made their way up the Pedogna Valley to try to locate relatives to house them for the time of the projected battle.

In Italy, General Sir Harold R.L.G. Alexander, Commander of Allied Armies in Italy, predicted that once Rome had fallen, the Germans probably would withdraw to the Pisa-Rimini or Gothic Line, imposing the maximum delay on the advance of the American forces by strong mobile rear guards and demolition. To execute the Allied intent of destroying hostile forces in Italy, future operations were divided into three phases:

1. Drive the enemy back to the Gothic Line, inflicting maximum losses in the process.
2. Penetrate the Gothic Line between Dicomano and Pistoia.
3. Exploit over the Apennines to the Po River Line and establish bridgeheads on that river.

During the two months following the fall of Rome on June 4, the Allied Armies in Italy were reduced by nine full infantry divisions and the equivalent of a tenth. The French

Expeditionary Force of four divisions and three groups of tabors (goumiers) and the VI U.S. Corps of three divisions, two infantry regiments, and three infantry battalion-size units together with a large number of field artillery, engineering and other supporting units were withdrawn to serve in France. The British 5th Division also left for service in the Middle East. This reduction of force left the Allied Armies in Italy with the difficult mission of holding the maximum German force and preventing them from being withdrawn for service on their Western front. Nevertheless the Allied Armies did not linger after the Germans left Rome but continued to advance northward rapidly in pursuit of the Tenth and Fourteenth German Armies. Rumors had circulated earlier in the year that the Allies were also planning a beach landing somewhere along the coast of Tuscany in the area south of Livorno. If the Allied landing were to take place it would be disastrous for our region, because the area leading into Lucca was flat with no major obstacles, and the advancing Allied army could reach our valley in no time and would be suddenly stopped by the German army that had prepared all the fortifications.

With the U.S. in the war, the War Department envisioned the organization and deployment of four black divisions, but three actually came into being: the 2nd Cavalry Division, the 93rd Infantry Division, and the 92nd Infantry Division. The 2nd Cavalry Division went to North Africa, was broken up and used in port operations. The 93rd Infantry Division went to the South Pacific deployed in regimental combat team strength in mopping up operations, principally on Bougainville. The 92nd Infantry Division went to Italy and fought as a division for more than nine months in extremely rugged terrain. Over 63 percent of the officers within the assigned and attached black soldiers were black, from 2nd Lieutenant to Colonel. Much of the time the 92nd Infantry Division operated over a broad front with a strength of about 25,000 troops, including approximately 10,000 attached troops, including a large contingent of British troops.

The 92nd was activated on October 15, 1942, at Fort McClellan, Alabama, then moved to Fort Huachuca, Arizona on May 5, 1943. It participated in Fourth Army Number 6 Louisiana Maneuvers from January 24 to April 5, 1944 and returned to Fort Huachuca on April 7, 1944. The soldiers departed Hampton Roads Port of Entry in early September 1944. After arriving in Italy, they were deployed in the North Appenines and the Po River Valley.

The typical organization of the 92nd consisted of the 365th, 370th and 371st Infantry Regiments; HHB Division Artillery; 597th, 598th, 599th, and 600th Field Artillery Battalions; 92nd Reconnaissance Troop; 317th Engineer Combat Battalion; 317th Medical Battalion; Headquarters Special Troops; Headquarters Company, 92nd Infantry Division; Military Police Platoon; 792nd Ordinance Light Maintenance Company; 92nd Quartermaster Company; and the 92nd Signal Company.

Their overseas wartime assignments were with the Fifth Army on November 4, 1944, IV Corps on December 25, 1944, and the Fifth Army on April 3, 1945. The Commanders were Major General Edward M. Almond in October 1942, and Brigadier General John E. Wood in August 1945. There were a total of 548 soldiers killed in action, 2,187 wounded in action, and 68 who died of wounds.

Diecimo had survived the war up to now. The Germans fortified the area but the people did not envision a major battle, thinking the Americans would arrive soon and life would go on as in the past. I didn't think that the Americans who would liberate Diecimo would be an all Black unit of the 92nd Infantry Division!

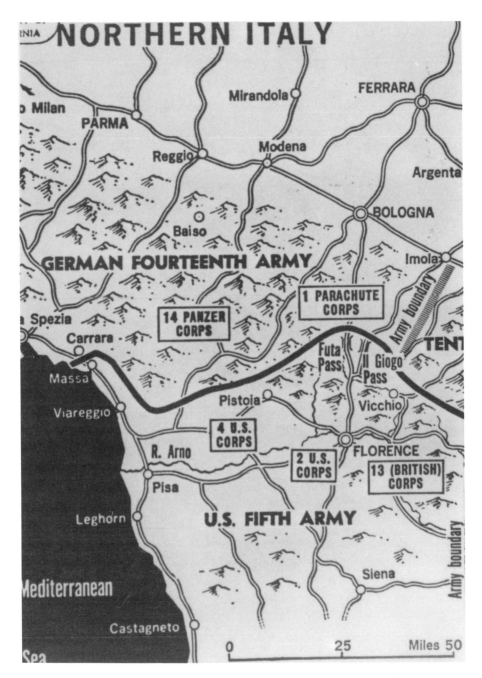

21.   Photo of a map showing the disposition of the German and
American forces.

22.   Lieutenant Harry Cox, 92nd Infantry Division, Italy, 1944.

9.
LO SFOLLAMENTO
(THE EVACUATION)

On July 13, 1944, my mother made plans to prepare my favorite pasta dish for my 14th birthday dinner. In Italy, even during the war, our main meal of the day, called *il pranzo*, took place at 12:30. During the summer of 1944 the food supply was scarce and we generally had to depend on locally grown fruits and vegetables for our daily food. I really don't know how my mother managed to prepare the *tordelli* for my birthday dinner, but she did. The pasta was rolled using a hand-cranked pasta machine, and was then cut into small squares which were filled with a very appetizing filling made of left-over chicken, dried bread, chopped Swiss chard, spices, eggs and grated cheese.

I could hardly wait for the *tordelli* to be served. As 12:30 approached, I could smell the tomato sauce simmering on the stove top. I went into the kitchen, sat at my usual place at the table, and was joined a few minutes later by my father. My mother removed the *tordelli* from the boiling water, placing them one by one in the serving bowl, covering them with sauce, then grated cheese. The bowl was then brought to the table, along with another bowl of cooked string beans and zucchini.

My mother said: "*Buon compleanno, Tullio!*" (Happy birthday, Tullio!)

The topic of conversation during the meal centered around the war and about the radio news reports that the Allied troops were having difficulty advancing up the Italian Peninsula. We were aware of the Allied Forces landing in

Normandy in June because occasionally someone was able to get a newspaper and would share the news with the people in the village. We could also tell that something was going to happen because from our kitchen window we had a direct view across the valley of the main roadway leading to the Brenner Pass, and we started to see a continuous column of German trucks and equipment heading north. Allied planes also flew regularly over our area, occasionally swooping down and opening fire on the trucks.

On July 13, after my birthday dinner, much against the advice of my parents, I decided to take a bike ride to the *piazza*. I hoped to see some of my friends, such as Dino, Umberto, and Piero who lived nearby. The public fountain which was on the shady side of the *piazza*, had a metal railing around it, and was a natural gathering place for people. When I arrived, Dino and Umberto were already there, seated on the railing, and after I pulled up on my bike and parked it, I started to tell them about my birthday dinner. I was interrupted by the sound of the motor of an approaching vehicle. Normally our first instinct was to hide, since it was common for the Germans to come around the villages for a *rastrellamento*, picking up able-bodied men and boys to take to northern Italy or Germany as workers. We were stuck on the one side of the *piazza* which did not have an exit so we had to remain by the fountain. The approaching vehicle turned out to be a German automobile containing four soldiers. I felt a stab of fear when it stopped in *piazza*. Two of the solders got out of the car, and walked toward the wall of a home that was usually reserved for the affixing of public notices. One of the men was carrying a large rolled up paper poster, which he started to place on the wall with glue. We watched as the poster unfolded and the soldier placed it on the wall, remaining as inconspicuous as possible. As soon as the soldiers were finished attaching the notice to the wall, they got in their automobile and left.

We immediately went to the wall and read the notice. The announcement was written in Italian, and stated that the people of Diecimo and all the villages in the entire valley were to be evacuated. The population was to be loaded on trains and shipped to northern Italy. The *sfollamento* (evacuation) was to begin on July 15, two days hence.

A few moments later, several adults came to read the notice, and gradually a large crowd gathered. The brewing topic of conversation was the *sfollamento*. Several of the people became very excited and some of the women began to cry. At first I really did not understand what impact a *sfollamento* would have on the village. As people began to talk, I realized that it meant that we all must leave our homes, and that we each could take only what we could carry. It meant that we would have to leave all of our belongings behind, and that we would be heading for an unknown destination in the north. As the day and evening progressed, there was a lot of discussion, and eventually, late in the evening, the parish priest, Don Udone Diodati, announced that there was going to be a meeting at the church to discuss the evacuation. My mother and I waited anxiously at home while my father attended the meeting.

When my father returned home, he informed us that we were going to have to leave Diecimo, but that the consensus was that the villagers did not want to be placed on a train to be transported to Northern Italy. The recommendation from the Pievano was for the people to take whatever they could carry and literally run away to the nearby mountains and valleys. He felt that people would be able to find shelter with families living in the various villages. This meant that we had to start walking up the Pedogna valley or the Valdottavo valley and find refuge in an inaccessible village for the duration of the war.

According to documents uncovered after the war, in the spring of 1944 the Nazi-Fascist authorities had prepared the following plan for the total evacuation of people and animals from the entire Province of Lucca:

1. After a state of emergency is declared the order to evacuate shall be communicated to the population by displaying a *manifesto* in all communities which will set a deadline for the evacuation to take place.

2. There shall be total evacuation, including *bestiame* (animals, such as cows, pigs, donkeys, pigs, horses).

3. People and *bestiame* will have to walk approximately 50 kilometers, toward Pistoia (up the Lima valley, in a north-easterly direction).

4. Secretaries of the *Fasci* (each village had a *Fascio*) shall nominate *capicolonna* (column leaders) for leading the people and the animals to their destinations.

5. The *Podestà* (adminstrative head of a community, such as a Mayor), *capi-frazioni* (heads of villages), and *capi-colonna* (column leaders) will be furnished with the proper documents which will allow them to requisition means of transportation for such an evacuation.

6. The itinerary for the evacuation will be communicated to the people after evacuation notices have been posted.

7. Police will be available in the evacuation and will help control the people.

(It is evident that this was to be a massive movement of refugees, considering that there were 35 *comuni* in the Province of Lucca with a total population of 359,276 people).

The following are the *comuni* in the Province of Lucca and the number of inhabitants as of the Spring of 1944:

Lucca	88,233	Molazzana	2,412
Altopascio	7,647	Montecarlo	4,298
Bagni di Lucca	12,064	Pescaglia	6,418
Borgo a Mozzano	7,860	Pietrasanta	21,382
Camaiore	22,291	Pieve Fosciana	2,911

Camporgiano	3,250	Porcari	5,840
Capannori	41,169	San Romano	2,187
Careggine	1,705	Seravezza	12,665
Castelnuovo G.	5,915	Sillano	1,902
Castiglione G.	3,318	Stazzema	7,957
Coreglia Ant.	5,716	Trassilico	1,722
Forte dei Marmi	6,213	Vagli Sotto	2,434
Gallicano	4,328	Viareggio	35,938
Giuncugnano	1,174	Villa Basilica	2,938
Massarosa	13,223	Minucciano	4,432
Villa Collemandina	1,970		

In the *Comune di Borgo a Mozzano* the following 16 *frazioni* were part of the *Comune*:

Valdottavo	Partigliano
Domazzano	Tempagnano
Oneta	Cune
Dezza	Diecimo
Cerreto	Gioviano
Anchiano	San Romano
Chifenti	Rocca
Pian Rocca	Corsagna

For Diecimo the *capo frazione* was to be Agostino Tolaini and Rinaldo Barsotti was named *capo ammasso* (head of the government pool of food resources).

Partisan activity in July 1944 interfered with the German plans for the area. The Allied Army had reached Pistoia and was in position to penetrate the Gothic Line from the valley of the Lima River. The defensive complex along the Apennines which was originally labeled the Gothic Line on April 24, was changed by the Germans on June 15 to the Green Line, but the Allied Army continued to use the term Gothic Line. The Germans discontinued the use of the term Gothic Line because they thought that they were going to have to abandon the front line and retreat to northern Italy. Since the name originated from the Goths when they defeated the Longobards in Italy many years before, they thought that the Americans would use the German retreat from the front line as a propaganda tool to discredit the Germans. German Field Marshal Kesserling abandoned the Pizzorne mountain range, then actuated a slow retreat up the Serchio River Valley, using retroguard actions against the Allied Army. Because of Kesserling's decision to go up the valley, Lucca was spared from major fighting. On the 3rd and 4th of September the Partisan group *Bonacchi* occupied Lucca. Colonel R.J. Sherman, commander of the 370th Combat Team, sent a patrol of 30 men under the command of Lt. Gandy, into Lucca on the morning of September 5th and linked forces with the Partisan group. Kesserling also gave up on the complete evacuation plan of the Province, because many people living in the Serchio River Valley had voluntarily left the area and were out of the way of any major battle.

We knew Rome was liberated on June 4, and we thought that it would not take long, possibly only a few weeks, for the Allies to advance northward and to occupy our area. Along with most of the inhabitants of the village my mother and father prepared to leave Diecimo, to look for shelter up the valley toward Pescaglia. Early the next morning we each pulled out a suitcase and packed our most needed belongings, basic underwear and clothes. I only had one pair of shoes, and one pair of wooden *zoccoli.* I planned to wear the *zoccoli,* and pack the shoes.

One of the critical considerations was food. The wheat harvest had taken place in June, and we had several sacks of the very valuable wheat. Our *contadino,* Angelo, came up with an idea. In his house, behind the wood burning bread oven, there was a room, which went up against the rock of the mountain. This was the room that I described earlier when we stayed with the Bertini grandparents in 1939. He thought that we could brick up the door leading into the room, and once the door was sealed, he felt that no one would be able detect the entrance and would not be aware that there was a room in that location. Angelo said that we could place our valuable belongings and sacks of wheat in the room, and our property would be safe from the German troops. We spent most of July 14 carrying materials, such as sheets, blankets, bicycles, sacks of grain, wine, silverware, crystal, and china dishes to the room. We had to be careful with our movements because we did not want other villagers to notice us taking our valuables into the house. Several immediate neighbors were also part of the project and placed their valuables in the room. Angelo prepared the mortar, and started to seal the doorway using some old bricks. Once the bricks were mortared in place, he then placed a thin coating of mortar on the exterior surface, texturing the surface like the adjoining wall. After the mortar had set for a few hours, he threw a lot of ashes from the fireplace against the wall to make the surface look old. It was a masterpiece! When one stepped back into the kitchen and looked at the darkened wall one would never know that there had been a doorway in that location!

We had resigned ourselves to leave the village on the following day. Unfortunately, another situation arose. Around 6 p.m., a group of about five or six German soldiers came to our house. They knocked at the front door, and said they wanted to examine the house. They entered, walked around in our living room, dining room and kitchen, then climbed the stairs to the upper floor and looked over the three bedrooms and bathroom, and then returned to the street level.

One of the soldiers said to us in broken Italian: "We like your home; we are going to take it over as our command post. We want you out of the house in one hour!"

We had made preparations to leave the following day, so we already had our suitcases packed, but the additional pressure of having to leave our home in one hour was very distressing for my mother. She was worried that we would never come back, and that we had to leave all our belongings and furniture in the house for the German soldiers.

We were able to make arrangements to spend the night with the Lazzari family across the street. Pia, the elderly spinster who lived on the top floor, had an extra bed for my mother and father. I spread out several pillows on the brick floor, and tried to get to sleep, but was unsuccessful. I was thinking about the next day, and our long walk up the Pedogna valley to find shelter. I also could hear the soldiers driving up and moving into our house. I peeked out the window several times to see what was happening. I still remember clearly that when we left our house we left the key in the front door. In Italy during that period of time it was still customary for people not to lock their doors and keys were always in the entry door locks. Eventually, when things became quiet in the street below, I fell asleep wondering if we would ever come back to our house.

The next morning, July 15, we got up early. We each had a suitcase to carry. In addition my mother had gathered some food, such as potatoes, fruit, and flour, and she had made parcels to carry the food. We each carried as much as we could, and walked out of the village, through Roncato (a group of about 10 houses which was beyond the church) heading up the valley toward Piegaio using the small back wood trails, until we reached the gravel road in Dezza.

Piegaio was about 8 kilometers away, up hill, with the road winding up the valley. Fortunately the sides of the road were lined with large mulberry trees (*gelso*) which provided shade from the warm July sun. We finally arrived in Piegaio after 1 p.m. Along the road we encountered many *Diecimini* (people from Diecimo) walking, carrying their possessions, trying to decide where to go, and seeking a place to stay. On the way we were joined by our tenant farmer Angelo and his family. Once we arrived in Piegaio, Angelo met an acquaintance who informed us that we probably would be able to find a place to stay in Convalle with a woman named Giustina.

He pointed up the mountain, and said: "There is Convalle. You will have to walk up the mule trail to get there. I think it will be a safe place to stay."

Angelo decided to go to a nearby village and stay with his cousin. He said good-bye and wished us *buona fortuna* (good luck).

We got our belongings together, and slowly began the ascent to Convalle. We arrived in the village in about 45 minutes, and asked a woman if she could give us directions to Giustina's house. She said it was not very far, and that she would take us there. Giustina was a widow who lived alone in a three story house on a hillside on the outskirts of the village. She said that we could have a bedroom and a kitchen which she did not use. She also said that she had another bedroom available, which could be used by Mariuccia, an elderly woman from Diecimo who had made the trip to Piegaio with us. I don't remember what financial arrangements we made with Giustina. We really did not have any money, so I never did find out if we paid rent, exchanged goods, or what. I imagine that, under the circumstances, people stayed in homes without having to pay rent, simply out of kindness. The bedroom had one large bed, large enough for my father, mother and me. The kitchen had a table, four chairs, a sink, no running water, a counter with two charcoal *fornelli* (burners), and a small fireplace. The kitchen was located on the second floor of the house and the bedroom on the third floor. On the evening of July 15, 1944 we settled into our new home. We were all exhausted from the long walk. We had some fruit, bread and *caffè e latte* for dinner, and then went to bed wondering what would be in store for us in Convalle.

Convalle was a small village, spread out along the side of a mountain. The mule trail from Piegaio led up to the center of the village into a small *piazza*. There were several houses facing the square including a small store and *appalto*. The mule trail, made of embedded rock and stones, continued in irregular patterns throughout the village leading to the various homes on the mountain side. The homes had a view of Piegaio and the small Pedogna River valley leading further up into the mountains. I estimate that the population was about 200 people who worked the terraced parcels of land and survived by harvesting the seasonal crops of potatoes, chestnuts, olives, fruits and vegetables.

Village life was pretty simple during July and August. I was able to make some new friends, especially with the Bernardi family next door. They had a son, about my age, named Alberto, and we became inseparable. Even though he had certain chores to help the family in their agricultural work, we found time to play. He had a small courtyard in front of his house and we used the area to play soccer. Unfortunately we did not have a ball, so we tied together several rags in the shape of a ball, and since we did not have shoes we played barefoot. Several other boys joined us in the game of *calcio* and we played for hours on end.

Alberto and I also pretended that we were masons, busily assembling miniature structures using small rocks and pieces of brick. Instead of using real cement, we used a wet mixture of ashes that had been used in the *bucato* (washing, laundry). People used a large terra-cotta container, shaped like a planter for small trees, approximately three to four feet high, and two to three feet in diameter, called a *conca*. The *conca* usually sat on a small pedestal, and had a drain hole in the bottom. The women loaded up the conca, starting from the bottom, with their dirty sheets and towels.

Once the *conca* was full, they placed a large piece of porous cloth, made of hemp or cotton on top, then spread on the top of the cloth about three to four inches of ashes gathered from wood burning fireplaces and bread ovens on top of the cloth. Then the women poured boiling water, which contained *lisciva* (lye) and was called *ranno*, over the ashes and let the *ranno* filter through the items to be washed. The boiling water process with the *ranno* was repeated several times until the water came through clean, signifying that the laundry was ready to be removed and rinsed in clear water.

The ash particles flowed through the load of laundry with the lye and actually cleaned the soiled articles; the chemical action was similar to using soap, which was not available during the war. Once the cleaning process was done, the top layer of wet ashes was removed and thrown out. The women then gathered up the wet sheets and towels, took them in baskets to a communal washing area with running water from a mountain stream and rinsed them out. Once rinsed, the sheets and towels were placed out on grass fields to dry. Alberto and I always looked forward to *bucato* days, because we then had our pretend cement, the wet ashes, already mixed and we could spend hours constructing our homes and villages. I remember that we each made a small trowel by flattening out a large tablespoon with a hammer, and shaping it like the trowel that masons used.

Our food supplies were scarce, so my mother, Mariuccia, and I walked down to Diecimo about once a week. When we had left Diecimo the fields were still loaded with vegetables and fruit, and as time passed, people went into the fields and took whatever they were able to carry. On our trips down the valley we left early in the morning and walked in the shade, along the gravel road. Once in Diecimo, we did not walk in the main street, but walked out in the fields, using the small paths called *viottoli* to bring us to the areas where fruit and vegetables were to be found. By doing this we avoided the Germans and were able to secure some food for the next week. We dug for potatoes, picking peaches, pears, zucchini, green beans, and onions. Once we had our cache of food in burlap sacks we made our way back up the valley to Convalle. The walk took about two hours each way, and in the summer heat it was very tiring. Occasionally we encountered other *sfollati* from Diecimo and inquired about friends and relatives to find out how they were getting along. We also asked about the Allies in order to find out if we were going to be liberated soon.

Sometime in mid-August, on one of the weekly food gathering trips to Diecimo, we encountered a German patrol of five soldiers. They stopped us and asked us what we were doing and where we were going. My mother told them that we were out looking for food. The leader of the patrol came over to me and looked me over. He asked my age. My mother quickly said that I was only 13 years old, that I was big for my age, and I had come along to help carry the food. The soldier said that I looked older than 13 and that the German army was picking up strong young men to work for them in northern Italy and Germany. My mother became very concerned at that time, because she thought that the soldiers might take me with them. She said that I was only a child, that I was too young to go with them, and she pleaded with them not to take me. The soldier thought for a minute, looked me over again, then told us to move along. During the time that my mother was talking with the soldier, I became very frightened. When we finally reached Convalle, my mother decided that I should not venture out of the village again.

Often when there were German patrols in Convalle, Alberto and I played in his house or Giustina's house in order not to be visible to the German soldiers. I remember that I had an inexpensive wristwatch that had stopped running. One day Alberto and I took the watch apart and attempted to fix it. We could not get the mechanical parts to work, but while we had the hands off and the face removed, I decided to try to repaint the face and numbers. Alberto had a small water color brush and using some old oil paint I painted the dial and numbers. I did not realize that oil paint took forever to dry and we were disappointed when the oil paint ran off the edge of the dial and made a big mess. We did not have many toys to play with in Convalle, so we often spent time drawing pictures of war-time activities on scrap paper, such as airplanes dropping bombs, soldiers shooting rifles, and anti-aircraft cannons shooting down planes.

Among my personal possessions at Convalle, I had the New York World's Fair ring that I had purchased in Brighton. The brass ring had so far survived the war, but I did not wear it because it would always leave a green band around my finger. Alberto enjoyed wearing my ring, and during one of our drawing sessions I gave him the ring as a present and as a symbol of my friendship. In return he gave me a *penna stilografica* (fountain pen) as a token of his friendship. I kept the pen for several years but eventually misplaced it.

One day, while were we playing in his courtyard, Alberto's younger brother came running towards us and told us that a German patrol was in the village searching for men and boys. Alberto was three years younger than I was and was of average size for an eleven year old boy, so he was fairly safe. I was fourteen and looked older, so I thought it best to go into Giustina's house and find a place to hide. According to the rumors, the Germans were searching each house in the village, and if they found men and older boys, they placed them under guard, took them down to Piegaio and eventually loaded the prisoners in trucks and drove them away. As we went into Giustina's house we tried to think of a good hiding place for me. After walking around in all the rooms and investigating several possibilities we decided that we could make a nice hiding place in Mariuccia's bed. The bed had a very thin mattress, about two inches in thickness. Instead of resting on a box spring, the mattress was laid on a large bag, in the shape of the bed, made of thick cloth, which was stuffed with dried corn husks. The corn husks were stuffed into the container through a long slit located in the center of the top surface running from the head to the foot of the bed. We discovered that we could push aside the corn husks from the center to each side, and that the narrow opening in the center of the pad would be able to accommodate me. I tried slipping into the opening and stretching out, with my arms down along the sides of my body. Then Alberto placed the mattress on top of me and my mother and Mariuccia replaced the sheets and blankets on the bed. They said that they could not tell that I was in the bed, it looked normal, and that they felt it would be a safe place to hide. They moved the sheets and blankets to one side, I slipped out and we decided that I should remain out of the bed, but to leave everything in piace so that if the German soldiers came to the house, I could immediately go into my hiding place. Alberto and I stayed inside all day, occasionally peeking out through the shutters, keeping an eye out for the German patrol. The Germans did not reach our home, since we were located on the outskirts and I did not have to use my hiding place on that day. We did keep things ready so that if the situation arose again, we would be prepared.

Toward the end of August and the beginning of September 1944, the grapes on the vines grew larger and started to ripen. Occasionally we had light rain showers which dampened the ground and allowed the *porcini* mushrooms in the chestnut tree groves to peek out of the soft ground and grow into tasty mushrooms. Alberto and I often ventured out into the canyons, partially hidden by the trees and brush to look for mushrooms. As we walked through the darkened groves of chestnut trees we had a commanding view of the valley and could observe the movement of the German troops on the road leading to Pescaglia.

Around the middle of September a group of soldiers started to work on the small bridge below us, which crossed the Pedogna river and led to the one-lane mountain road over Monte Prana connecting Piegaio to Camaiore and on to the west coast of Italy in the vicinity of Viareggio. The soldiers started to bore holes into the piers supporting the bridge, and we knew that they must be preparing to blow it up. The rumors around Convalle were that the Allied armies were close by and that the Germans were planning to retreat from the area. Occasionally during the day an Allied airplane, which people called *la cicogna* (the plane resembled a stork) flew overhead maintaining a low altitude. We were told that the plane was a reconnaissance plane surveying the valley for the Allied army artillery companies located on the other side of the mountains near Viareggio.

Shortly after we spotted the slow moving *cicogna* for the first time, we had a barrage of artillery fire which dropped shells on the main road up the valley and along some of the villages. In fact, Alberto and I were searching for mushrooms when the shelling began, and it was pretty frightening. We ran for shelter against the rocky surface of the mountain and as we settled in among the cave-like rocks we had a complete view of the valley and could see the incoming shells exploding on the road and up the slopes of the mountain. During the next two weeks in the evening and during the night we heard loud explosions from artillery fire and airplanes bombing the coastal cities of Pisa and La Spezia. We were certain that the Allies were getting close to us and that soon we would be liberated.

One night, around the 26 or 27 of September, artillery groups from the Viareggio and Carrara area again started to shell our region. The shelling began around midnight and continued non-stop until daylight. Around 12:30 we moved from our bedroom to the ground floor of the house and spent the night huddled under a stone stairway. I remember being terrified and hoping that an artillery shell would not hit the house. When the artillery fire stopped the next morning, there were many German vehicles in the valley below and we noticed that a group of German soldiers were gathered around the small bridge which had been prepared to receive explosives. We could see from our vantage point that soldiers were inserting the explosives in the holes they had bored in the bridge piers. Around two in the afternoon, most of the soldiers pulled away from the bridge and we knew that they were preparing to destroy it. In fact, shortly thereafter, the few soldiers that remained next to the bridge lit the fuses, then ran away rapidly, and the bridge blew up sending a huge column of smoke and debris into the air. After the smoke settled and drifted away we could see that the bridge was gone!

During the rest of the day German trucks, loaded with supplies and soldiers started to leave the area heading down the Pedogna valley through Piegaio. We knew that our liberation was near. All the people stayed in their homes, hidden from view, because they were afraid that during the last minutes of German occupation the soldiers might come into the village for a final *rastrellamento* or to shoot up the village and kill people as a reprisal for some of the partisan action that had been taking place in the nearby villages. By nightfall it seemed that all the German troops had left. There was a strange quietness in the air, no breeze, everything was calm and silent. We ventured out of the house and spent some time with the Bernardi family next door, trying to figure out what was happening. We eventually went to bed around midnight. We tried to go to sleep, but my father, my mother, and I, still sleeping in the same bed, talked most of the night about the possibility of seeing American soldiers, wondering when we might be liberated and when we would be able to return to Diecimo.

We got up early the next morning, September 29, 1944, and walked to the piazza in Convalle. There was a gathering of people and all the topics of conversation were related to the arrival of the Americans. They decided to send some people to the outskirts of the village to act as scouts for the incoming American troops.

Around two p.m., we heard shoutings: "*Gli Americani, gli Americani sono qui!*" (The Americans are here!)

We watched as a patrol of about 12 soldiers came into the village with their rifles in their hands, wearing steel helmets, dressed in dark green uniforms, led by the village scouts. When the soldiers saw the old people and children they began to smile and to shake hands with them; they patted the children on the head and gave them candy. My father, anxious as everyone else to meet the American soldiers, made his way to greet the soldiers and spoke to them in English. A funny thing happened: the soldiers did not respond in English, but in another strange language, similar to Italian. We could not understand them. We found out later that the soldiers were speaking Portuguese; they were Brazilian soldiers, part of the III company of the 6th regiment that was attached to the Fifth Army. We had been liberated by Brazilian, not American soldiers. But it didn't matter because we would soon be able to go home!

After the patrol of Brazilian soldiers surveyed the village of Convalle, they proceeded down the mule trail to Piegaio. Joined by other soldiers coming from the direction of Pescaglia they continued down the Pedogna valley toward Diecimo, eventually liberating Borgo a Mozzano and Bagni di Lucca. They occupied the Serchio Valley, and with the assistance of partisans and local people, cleared the flat land in Diecimo of the land mines which the Germans had placed in the valley. The railway station in Diecimo was a centrally located area, so the Brazilians set up their operations there, taking over many of the nearby homes to house the soldiers. A few days after we were liberated, rumors were circulating that people could return to their villages. We decided to pack our belongings and walk back to Diecimo. We got up early and said our good-byes to Giustina and the Bernardi family. I told Alberto that I would come back to see him some day. But it wasn't until nearly 50 years later, in 1993, that I met Alberto again in Convalle and during our brief reunion we talked about our experiences during the war. He remembered in detail some of our adventures and told me that he had kept the New York World's Fair ring for many years and was very upset when he lost it. When he grew up he became a *Carabiniere*, which is a policeman. He had just retired, and said that he enjoyed traveling around Italy in his camper. He became proficient at scuba diving and dove for sunken treasures.

We started our trip back to Diecimo by walking down the mule trail to Piegaio, then walking on the main gravel road leading to Diecimo. As we walked along we encountered many other people who were returning to Diecimo and other villages. Occasionally Allied Army jeeps and trucks came along carrying troops and materials. As the trucks went by, they raised large clouds of white dust from the road which covered us and the *gelso* trees. The soldiers riding in the trucks yelled and waved to us as they drove by. As we proceeded down the valley we saw the effects of the Allied aerial bombings and artillery fire. Many homes along the way had been partially destroyed and had large gaping holes in the walls and roofs exposing their interiors. Bomb and artillery shell craters were all along the road and in the fields. As we approached Diecimo, we walked along the road which led to the bridge crossing the Pedogna River. The bridge was no longer there; it had been blown up. Our *ponte* was gone! The U.S. Army Corps of Engineers had replaced it with a steel bridge crossing the Pedogna River at a lower level and closer to the main road leading into Diecimo. As we walked into the village and began heading toward our house we observed that a long line of traffic across the bridge was being controlled by a Military Police-man stationed at each end. We noticed that some of the homes right in Diecimo had been damaged by artillery fire or by bombs dropped from airplanes. We passed the piazza, and shortly after we spotted the front of our house; it seemed intact. Walking up to the front door, we saw that the key was still in the lock and the Red Cross sign was still affixed to the house. We turned the key, unlocked the door, then walked into the house, not knowing what to expect.

The house was empty, except for hay on the floor of the rooms; our furniture was gone, only a desk and a chair remained in one of the bedrooms. Our bathroom on the second story was filthy. The bathtub had a layer of dried human feces on the bottom; it looked as if the German soldiers had used the bath tub for a toilet. In the basement, there was evidence that an artillery shell had entered the rear door and exploded in the wall, sending shrapnel all over the room and causing some damage to the basement floor, walls, doors, and a utility table. The shell had entered through the glass door which had an exterior iron grate. The shell had bent the iron strap which was part of the grate, broken the glass, embedded itself in the interior wall and exploded, leaving a small crater in the wall. Fragments from the shell were all over the room and as I picked up a few pieces of steel I thought about what might have happened if we had been in the room when the shell exploded. (To this day the same grating is still on the glass-paneled door and one can still see where the artillery shell entered the door and bent the iron grate).

Our first task was to start cleaning the house. My father was still not very strong, so he could not do any major physical work. I helped to clear out all the hay. Mariuccia, who was still with us, and my mother swept the floors and cleaned out the bathroom. They used some old rags and mopped the tile floors throughout the house. We later found out that my mother's cousin, Cecco Castelli, had removed our furniture and transported it to Dezza by truck for safekeeping in a barn. In a few days we were able to have Angelo pick up the furniture and return it to our house. We were also anxious to see if our hidden room was still intact, so we went to Angelo's house as soon as they returned home. We all climbed the stairs leading to the second floor, walked into the old kitchen, and to our dismay we found that the wall which had been constructed to seal off the room had been torn apart. We lit a candle and entered the dark room. Most of the large items were still there, including our bicycles. The only things that were gone were the sacks of wheat and the bottles of olive oil which had been stored in the room. We were all very disturbed that the wheat was gone. This was to have been a major part of our food supply for the winter months, and we now had to think how we could manage without bread and pasta.

That night we were able to set up our beds and mattresses and go back into our own bedrooms. Mariuccia, the older woman who stayed with us in Convalle, had previously lived across the street from us in a house that belonged to Carola Luchi. Carola now needed the house for herself, so Mariuccia found herself with no place to live. She asked my mother if she could stay with us, and in exchange for room and board she would help out with the chores around the house. Mariuccia settled in the back bedroom and I returned to the bedroom in the front part of the house. Although our food had been stolen, we still felt very fortunate; we still were intact as a family, our home had not been destroyed, and we still had most of our belongings. We would survive now that the Allied soldiers had liberated us!

23. Fedra Lazzari, Tullio, and Ada Bertini posing in Borgo a Mozzano in December 1945.

24.   Ada Bertini and Giustina taken in Convalle. Giustina allowed us to stay in her house when the Bertini family evacuated from Diecimo.

25. Top: After the liberation, Summer 1945, some of the visiting teenagers. Tullio--far right, Ione--second from left.
26. Bottom: Istituto or Collegio Cavanis in Porcari.

10.
THE PARTISANS

On July 24, 1943, the King of Italy, Vittorio Emanuele III, accepted the resignation of Prime Minister and Secretary of State Benito Mussolini as head of the government and nominated *Maresciallo* d'Italia Pietro Badoglio as Head of State. The King declared that he was now in command of all the armed forces, and *Maresciallo* Badoglio stated he was assuming the leadership of the government. However the war continued with Italy still allied with the Germans.

When Italy capitulated on September 8, 1943, the surrender to the Allied Forces caused havoc in the country. There were numerous political factions that wanted to deal with the problems in Italy. There were the Fascists, the Anti-Fascists, the Communists, the German troops, Monarchists, and thousands of men from the various branches of the defunct Italian army who were stranded all over Italy, Albania, Yugoslavia and Russia.

The Italian state was in the midst of its most difficult crisis since its unification as a nation in the 1800's. Italy was divided into two parts: the central and northern regions occupied by the Germans, and the southern part being invaded by the Anglo-American forces. The administrative and bureaucratic structure collapsed, the economy was reduced to black market activities, the Italian armed forces were disbanded, allowing the Germans to intern 600,000 Italian soldiers in Germany. Another temporary Fascist government led by *Maresciallo* Graziani was formed in Milano in September 1943 after the *Duce* was liberated from Gran Sasso. At that time *La Resistenza* (the resistance) was formed in Italy as many people decided to resist and fight the Fascists and the Germans.

A nation that wishes to win independence must not limit itself to ordinary war methods. Mass insurrections, revolutionary wars, and guerrilla warfare are the only means with which a small populace can take over a large group, with which a weak army can confront a stronger and better organized army.

Karl Marx, *Lotta in Italia* 1849.

After the 8th of September, hearing about the fall of Fascism, the Italian people took to the streets to celebrate what they thought was their freedom. To their dismay they found the streets and piazzas full of *carabinieri* and Fascist troops. Some Anti-Fascists also surfaced and made plans to return Italy to a democracy. There were incidents where Italians resisted the Fascist and German troops, which resulted in killings and deportations to Germany. Groups gradually were formed within communities which became part of *La Resistenza*. The groups took on the name of *Partigiani* or Partisans. Throughout the Toscana region, near Diecimo, in the Garfagnana and in the Versilia areas there was considerable Partisan activity. Men took refuge in the mountains with the objective of fighting against the Fascists and the Germans with their own form of guerrilla warfare.

In Diecimo we heard rumors that Partisans were hiding up in the mountains. According to the rumors, some of the *Partigiani* were local men, and some were Italian soldiers who were stationed somewhere in Italy, and after the surrender had tried to make their way back home. When they arrived in their towns or villages, instead of living with their families and being in danger of being deported or placed in the Fascist Army, they chose to live in the mountains as Partisans. Those who were unable to travel back to their own towns or villages joined up with Partisan groups in other regions of Italy. The men wore a mixture of military clothing, some from the Italian Army, some from the German Army and some from the Allied Armies. They had an assorted combination of weapons and ammunition and during the night sneaked into villages to get food. Some of the local Anti-Fascists who had not been drafted into the Italian Army, either being too young or too old to serve, joined up with the Partisan forces in order to harass the Germans and to assist the advancing Allied Forces.

Around the time that Karl Marx wrote *Lotta in Italia* in 1849, when Italians were attempting to unify the country, an underground rebel group of men was formed to fight against the oppressors. Men gathered in groups in remote, hidden areas, such as in the *boschi* (woods, forests) to plan their activities. In order not to draw attention from the police forces the men pretended to be working in the woods making charcoal. In Italian the word for charcoal is *carbone*, which also means carbon. The men working and making charcoal were called *Carbonari*. The *Carbonari* in 1849 were Italians fighting for their freedom in Italy, while the *Partigiani* in 1943 and 1944 were Italian men fighting to be free from the Germans and Fascists.

Prior to the bringing of natural gas, propane gas and electricity into the communities, charcoal was the main source of fuel used to cook food in homes. As mentioned before, a group of *fornelli*, which held the ignited charcoal and supported pots and pans, was always built into the kitchens. People in the United States now barbecue with charcoal briquettes, which can be purchased in five or ten pound sacks. The charcoal is made of wood particles compressed into small cubes, slowly burned in an oxygen free environment, and thus converted into charcoal. In the early days of barbecue cooking, after World War II, Americans purchased charcoal in a different form. The charcoal was sold in the form of the original wood sticks from which the charcoal was made, namely, small branches of trees, which had been converted to black charcoal sticks.

Families in Diecimo were accustomed to making charcoal for their own use and also as a product which could be sold or traded for food. The process was not complicated and took place at a time when the *boschi* (woods) had to be cleaned up and the trees pruned, or when there was a large quantity of wood available in some of the inaccessible forests high up on the local mountains. Groups of village men hiked up into the woods and worked cooperatively to make the charcoal. They left their families behind and became *carbonari* for two or three weeks at a time each year. The men planned their meals and carried the minimum amount of food because they had to travel on foot up the narrow valleys, climbing the steep mountains to reach the *boschi*. The food products could not be perishable because there was no refrigeration or ice. They carried dry pasta, dry cheese, bread, eggs, fruit, onions, and sometimes pork products, such as *pancetta*, *salame* or sausage. They also had to carry their wood cutting tools, which were small and lightweight, because the wood that they had to cut consisted of small branches, trimmed from large trees and wild bushes. A common wood cutting tool was the *pennato*, shaped like the number seven, so that the interior part was the sharp cutting edge. The handle was affixed to the long leg of the *pennato* and had a large hook which was part of the handle. The men wore a metal hook on their belt so that the hook was positioned on their rear, and the *pennato* was carried on the hook, cutting edge facing up. The *pennato* could be reached easily and with one hand brought into use to trim branches from trees. The cutting process involved reaching up and hooking the top of the *pennato* in a downward sweeping motion to cut the branch. Small individually operated hand saws were also used to cut some of the larger branches. A camp site was chosen which was near a stream of water and which also had a flat area so that the men could stack the wood to make the charcoal. At times some of the men brought shotguns so they could hunt for birds or jack rabbits to augment their food supply.

Once the branches were trimmed and cut into small pieces two to three feet in length, they were stacked in the shape of a large *teepee* with a space at the bottom in which to start a fire. Once the wood was stacked to a height of about eight feet, the *teepee* was covered with dirt, so that there was no air flow from the bottom to the top. The center hole, resulting from grouping the wood to a point at the top, was sealed with a large piece of sod.

When the wood was completely covered the men started a fire in the bottom space and allowed the wood to burn slowly for a long period of time, up to a week or a week and a half. When one stack of wood was ignited, they then started building the next stack. The *Carbonari* remained in the area until the charcoal was done. If holes developed in the stack of wood, smoke would come out of the holes, causing a fast burning area. This was covered immediately with dirt, otherwise the wooden sticks would turn to ash instead of charcoal. When the charcoal was ready, the soil was carefully removed, uncovering the charcoal; then the charcoal sticks were packed into gunny sacks and readied for delivery to the village. The men carried the sacks to a central point which was accessible by a two wheeled wagon. When all the sacks were brought to the location, the charcoal was loaded on the *barroccio* (wagon) and pulled into the village. The *Carbonari* wore the same clothes during the charcoal making process and by the time they returned to the village they were a sight! Their clothes, their hands and their faces were covered with black charcoal dust.

According to folklore, the *Carbonari* invented a pasta dish for their meals while they were in the woods; it was called *spaghetti alla carbonara* (carbonara style). The dish is very popular in Italy and also in the United States. The *carbonari* cooked the pasta in boiling water, and when it was *al dente*, the pasta was drained and placed into a bowl or back into the drained pot. Next, several eggs were beaten and mixed in with the pasta along with grated dry cheese such as *parmigiano* or *pecorino*. At times they added cut up and fried *pancetta* for flavor.

Recipe for Spaghetti alla Carbonara

> 1 pound package of spaghetti
> 3 eggs
> 1 cup of grated parmesan or pecorino cheese
> ¼ pound of chopped pancetta or bacon,
>   fried until brown and crisp

Cook the spaghetti in boiling water until al dente, about 12 minutes. Drain the spaghetti, and place back into the large pot. Beat the three eggs with a whisk or fork. Pour the beaten eggs into the pasta and stir rapidly until the eggs cook from the residual heat. Add the grated cheese and pancetta, mix well, serve. A small amount of butter may be added to make the spaghetti a bit creamier.

When the Partisan groups were formed, the men went into hiding in the *boschi* where the charcoal was made. The areas were inaccessible and well hidden, and it was impossible to get there with motor vehicles. One had to hike in and be able to carry all the necessary supplies. Some of the Partisan groups were very well organized and some were not. The organized Partisans operated like military groups with men assuming leadership positions similar in rank to the positions they held in the Italian Army.

The Partisans also were able to get radio receivers and transmitters from the Americans by using civilians as couriers to smuggle the radio equipment across the German lines. By using battery-operated radio-transmitters, set up in remote areas or in houses, hidden from the Germans, the Partisans were able to send key information to the Allies about the location and movement of German troops. Frequently Allied airplanes flew at low altitudes over the valley at night and dropped packages to the Partisans, targeting a zone with a pre-arranged signal, such as a light or flare. Some of the less organized groups lived off the land and often raided villages during the night to secure food and provisions. They forcefully took what they wanted and at times were not liked by their fellow Italians. At times the Partisan groups harassed German troops and engaged in minor skirmishes. The German troops, angered by the encounters with the Partisans, often punished the nearby villagers by taking and shooting hostages.

As I mentioned in a separate chapter, the *sfollamento* of Diecimo and other villages in the vicinity of the Gothic Line took place around July 15, 1944. Once the people were gone, the German troops began to destroy bridges, roads, and houses and to place obstacles in the path that the Allied troops would have to take in order to advance to northern Italy. There were two major routes: one was along the coast through Pisa, Viareggio, Carrara and La Spezia, called the Versilia region; the other was the road from Lucca leading up the Serchio River Valley which eventually led to Modena and continued to the Brenner Pass. The road was called *Via del Brennero.* I previously described how during the early spring of 1944 the Germans came into the Serchio River Valley and started to fortify the area. In addition, the Germans began to pillage the area, helping themselves to food products that they wanted, confiscating all livestock and butchering it for their own use. The farmers in Diecimo tried to hide their cows, especially the milk producing ones, so they could continue to provide milk and cheese for their families.

On August 9, 1944, the 16th Panzergranadier auf Klarungs Abteilung SS arrived in Pietra Santa, on the coast near Carrara, Major Walter Reder in command. Reder was 29, an Austrian, and because he had a partial amputation of his left arm, he was called *il monco* (the stump) by the Italians. He arrived in Italy in May 1944 and was placed in charge of holding back the advancing American Army on the Cecina front (south of Livorno). He moved north to defend the Arno River around the 25th of July, where he remained until August 8. He had already established a reputation with the Italians: he was to be regarded as very dangerous and not at all sympathetic toward civilians. His orders: anyone caught helping Partisans would be shot on the spot.

During that time, as previously described, there were no official newspapers, so news traveled by word of mouth or was printed on sheets of paper that were passed among the people, like handbills. We heard that on August 12, just outside the walls of Lucca in Sant'Anna, over 500 civilians were shot and killed by German SS troops under the command of Major Reder. Apparently the Germans received information that some of the local residents were helping the Partisans by giving them food and shelter, and also that they were passing on information to the Allies describing the locations of German troops. After the war, official reports indicated that the SS troops came into Sant'Anna, herded all the residents into the village square, and began to machine gun the people, killing old men, women and children. A local priest, Don Innocenzo Lazzeri, 33 years old, Pievano of Farnocchia, whose village was burned a few days before, was present in Sant'Anna because he was trying to intercede with the Germans. After the first bursts of machine gun fire, he dashed among the fallen people attempting to rescue a wounded child. He was too late, the child was dead. In his anguish, he picked up the child and held the body high above his head, walking towards the Germans, imploring them to stop the massacre. The Germans paid no attention, but turned the machine gun on him, killing him instantly. The soldiers then turned the machine guns on the remaining crowd and killed another 131 bystanders. My uncle Nello, Pievano of Pieve di Compito, was a friend of Don Innocenzo Lazzeri, and after the war told me the story about the killing. After the war a monument was erected in memory of the 570 people who were murdered in Sant'Anna. All 570 names are engraved on the monument.

When my uncle told me the story of the massacre, I thought of the many times that my friends and I confronted German patrols in Diecimo and how lucky I was not to have been harmed. After hearing about the murders of the civilians at Sant'Anna I remembered the open military truck passing below my bedroom window containing the bodies of German soldiers gunned down by the British airplanes. I wondered to myself why nations continue to fight one another and why man can't grasp the futility of war.

Another priest, Don Aldo Mei, ordained at the same time as my uncle Nello in 1935, was Pievano of the village of Fiano. He was part of a local underground organization that was hiding Jews from the Germans. Don Aldo Mei often hiked up into the mountains near Fiano to administer Communion to the Partisans in hiding. During one of these trips he was asked if he would take an inoperative radio transmitter back with him. The transmitter was to be picked up by someone from the Partisan group near Lucca. Unfortunately, German soldiers, while searching the parish house for Jews in hiding, discovered the radio transmitter. Don Aldo Mei was taken to Lucca and kept imprisoned for two days. On August 4, 1944 at 10 p.m. he was brought to the Lucca wall at a spot near *Porta Elisa* (the Elisa Gate) and shot. He was accused of helping the Partisans, of being a spy, and of using the radio transmitter to send information to the Allied Army. My Uncle Nello lost another friend!

I was not aware of the persecution of Jews in Germany or in Italy, nor was I aware of the concentration camps in Germany. I don't remember any discussions about the Jews among my friends, or seeing newspaper articles about the Jews in Italy. Yet, under my very eyes, priests, nuns, and many Italians of goodwill were placing their lives on the line on behalf of Jews in Italy.

Many years later, I saw the Italian film, titled *The Garden of the Finzi-Continis* based on the book by Giorgio Bassani. The novel is a story of the love and blighted hopes of a young Jewish couple in Fascist Italy on the eve of World War II. The narrator finds himself attracted to the young daughter of the aristocratic Finzi-Contini in Ferrara, who are isolated behind their garden walls and do not see the dreadful future which awaits them. When I saw the movie and read the book, I realized that being a child in a small village spared me one truly horrible aspect of World War II.

After the war, my uncle Nello was honored by the Italian Government and given the title of *Cavaliere*.

Israel also gave him the following proclamation:

A forest of 3000 trees has been planted in Israel to honor the memory of Felicia Baumgarten-Campetti and to recognize the merits of the Reverend Don Nello Marcucci who has helped Jewish families in the time of German persecution.

According to records of the Archdiocese of Lucca, my uncle and three other priests, Don Paolo Ghiselli, Don Giuseppe Pellegrini and Don Narciso Fava helped the *Comitato di Liberazione* by sheltering refugees. From June

1944 to September 2, 1944, it was very dangerous to move about in the Compito area. The parish priests were instrumental in hiding people from both the Fascists and the Germans. My uncle Nello was able to hide people in his large parish house and to keep them out of sight while they awaited transportation to safety.

I remember that when we visited Uncle Nello it was an adventure for me to explore the church, the church bell tower and his enormous four story house. At ground level there was a large room with benches where my uncle showed films. There were also several small rooms dug into the mountain against which the house was built. Later in the war, when we visited my uncle to get olive oil, I was told to stay out of that area, but I had no way of knowing that the rooms contained people in hiding. After the war my uncle told us stories about hiding Jewish people and British airmen who escaped from a German prisoner of war camp.

The Partisans probably were responsible for some of the reprisals in the various villages not only by their actions against the Germans, but also by distributing flyers and placing placards on walls of buildings. I have translated below a handbill that the Partisans distributed to the Italian people and posted in Sant'Anna on July 29, 1944, approximately 10 days before the massacre.

PEOPLE OF VERSILIA!
After having turned Italy into a horrible battleground, the Nazis want to complete their opera of destruction by deporting all the men and boys to forced labor camps in Germany. Never satisfied, the Nazi are now persecuting women, children and the old, exploiting them with horrible demands.

People of Versilia, do not obey the Germans!
Women, children and old people, do not leave your homes. Offer passive resistance.

All men, arm yourselves with breech loading shotguns, if nothing else is available.

The Allies are only a few kilometers away, the Partisan troops are ready for action, and they will treat a reprisal with our own reprisal.

People of Versilia, arm yourselves!
Your liberty and salvation are in your own hands!

Death to the German oppressor!

Signed by the commander of the Partisan assault brigade Garibaldi 29 July 1944

The notice alerted the Germans to the possibility that the Italians might cause them trouble, and they prepared to deal with the situation. In order to prevent civilians from helping the Partisans, Major Reder started *rastrellamenti* (gathering up civilians by force), which in turn prompted the massacre at Sant'Anna and in neighboring villages. I often wonder if the Partisans, by their inflammatory tactics, were partially to blame for the killings. I also wonder whether some of the Partisans, especially those who were not organized, were simply opportunists who took advantage of their own people by demanding at gun point materials, food, clothing and valuables to further their own lives.

When the German soldiers came into our area to perform the construction work necessary for their battle plans, they imposed curfews, called *coprifuoco* in Italian.

The notices for the curfew were in Italian, printed and distributed by the local *comune* and posted on exterior walls of houses in the village. A curfew notice that was duplicated in an Italian book is translated below, and describes the policy. The hours of the curfew varied depending on the season of the year. During the winter the curfew started early, around 6 p.m.; in the summer, it was around 9 or 10 p.m. when it started to get dark.

COMUNE DI BORGO A MOZZANO
ORARIO DEL COPRIFUOCO

Il comando Militare Tedesco del Comune di Borgo a Mozzano comunica che con effetto immediato l'orario per il coprifuoco è fissato per le ore 22 precise.

Di consequenza l'orario per la chiusura dei locali publici (trattorie, bar, ecc.) viene stabilito per le ore 21,30.

Si rammenta che i tragressori saranno puniti severamente.

29 maggio, 1944
Il comando Tedesco

Translated into English:

CURFEW HOURS

The German Military Command of the Comune di Borgo a Mozzano communicates that in effect immediately the curfew hours are established to be 22 hours (10 p.m.) Consequently the closing time for public places, such as restaurants and bars, will be 21:30 (9:30 p.m.)

You are reminded that violators of the curfew will be punished severely.

(Signed) The German Command

In addition to the curfew, people in villages were not supposed to allow any light to eminate from their windows, so that Allied pilots flying over the area would not be able to see lights in villages which would provide possible targets for bombings. The villages, on the exterior, were supposed to be in complete darkness. At that time there was no electricity in the area, so the only light available in the homes was from candles, the fireplaces or the *carburo* lamps. Generally the windows in most houses were of wood frame construction with a hinged internal wooden panel, behind the glass, similar to a storm window, but on the inside. The panel then could be closed on top of the glass and seal out the light from the inside or the light coming in from the outside. With these conditions there was generally no problem keeping the village in complete darkness.

When I ventured out at night, after the curfew, especially when there was no moon, I had an eerie feeling walking the streets of Diecimo, because of the complete darkness and the silence in the village. One could hear the German patrols approaching because the soldiers traveled in pairs and the noise from their hobnailed boots reverberated along the deserted street. They patrolled the village from one end to the other, usually on a regular schedule, carrying loaded weapons. Because the evenings were long and boring I generally wanted to go out, to be with my friends, either at Piero's house or at Mauro's house, where Dino, Umberto, Mauro, Piero and I got together and played cards, either *scopa, briscola, tre sette,* or poker.

Usually after dinner, I carefully planned my outing, waiting until the German patrol passed. I walked along the sidewalk, close to the buildings, in the dark shadows, and hurriedly traveled the approximately 400 meters to the houses near the piazza. If I wore regular shoes, my footsteps made little or no sound, but if I wore *zoccoli,* (the wooden clogs), I took them off and walked barefoot. At times the German patrols toured the village with military vehicles. During the war, all automobile headlights were shielded by a black cover with a horizontal slit which directed a small beam of light to the ground. It was a strange sight: the slits looked like half-closed eyelids. As German patrol cars approached, we were warned by the sound of the motor because we could not see the headlights shining ahead on the street. Several times I was caught walking around when the patrol car came along. Fortunately, most people left keys in their front doors, so I was able to let myself in the front door of a house and hide until the patrol went by.

I remember one night in particular, because of what happened to me after I returned home. I went to Mauro's house where we played cards, ate *vinata*, (the chestnut flour and wine porridge), and before we knew it, the time was nearly 2 a.m. I decided that I had better go home! I knew that my parents were concerned about my whereabouts, because I was always fairly dependable and usually returned home before midnight. When I arrived home I was not surprised to see that both my mother and father were still up. My mother began to yell at me about being out so late and that they were worried that I was picked up by the Germans. My father did not say very much, but as he started to remove his leather belt from his pants and moved toward me, I dashed out of the kitchen and up the stairs to my bedroom, with my father and mother in pursuit. I figured that I was going to get a beating, so I ran behind my bed, crouched on the floor and made myself into a ball, exposing only my back to the eventual blows. When my father reached me, he had his belt in his right hand and raised it to strike me. I pleaded for him to stop, but to no avail. He raised and lowered the belt several times, striking me across the back. While the belting was going on, my mother kept shouting, telling me that it was wrong for me to stay out so late. To be very honest, the beating did not hurt. I realized that I was wrong, especially under the circumstances with the curfew and the German patrols. My parents were concerned that their only son was taken away by the Germans. Although my feelings were hurt and I did not speak to my parents for a few days, eventually things returned to normal and deep down inside I felt that my punishment was justified. The incident was never discussed with either my father or mother during their lifetimes.

In the Versilia region, near Viareggio, the partisans attempted to organize themselves, forming the Comitato di Liberazione Nazionale (CNL), a group which included Communists, Anti-Fascist forces, a few Socialists, Christian-Democrats, Liberals and Republicans, and many individuals not affiliated with a specific political party. A member of the partisan group named Manfredo Bertini (no relation to the author) assumed an active role in the Partisan activities. He was a Socialist who was vehemently opposed to the Fascists and the Germans. Because he thought that it was important to establish contact with the Anglo-American forces, he wanted to have someone cross the front lines to explain what the Partisans were doing, and to find out what they could be doing to help the Allies in the Versilia area. He selected another activist named Vera Vassale to undertake the task of crossing the front lines. She was a small woman who had polio as a child and because of her physical appearance and impaired walking he thought that no one would suspect her. On September 14, 1943, she left Viareggio, riding her bicycle, at times walking, and occasionally taking trains. She headed south, along the coast toward the front. On September 28 she reached the American troops. She spoke with an American colonel and explained to him the reason for her journey. The officer believed her story and took her to the O.S.S. (Office of Strategic Services) offices in Napoli. They informed her that she was to return to Viareggio after specific instructions and training on how to send and receive radio transmissions. On January 16, 1944 she was taken to Corsica by plane, and the next night she was taken back to mainland Italy by small boat and dropped off on the shore south of Livorno in German territory. As she made her way back to Viareggio she found the travel dangerous and difficult because she was carrying a small suitcase containing the radio transmitter. Eventually she made her way to a small village train station and boarded a train heading north. The train stopped at Cecina but was unable to continue because the train tracks north of the city were damaged by aerial bombardments. As the train pulled into the station at Cecina, Vera Vassale saw that the station was full of German soldiers who were searching all the passengers as they disembarked the train. She decided at that moment that she could not risk being searched carrying the radio transmitter so she disembarked on the opposite side of the train and ran for cover in the nearby fields. She went unnoticed and hid in the fields until darkness. Then she carefully started her journey walking toward Viareggio, avoiding main roads, and through sheer determination arrived in Viareggio on January 19, 1944 with her precious cargo. Officially, according to the American Army, she was an agent of the 2677 Regiment of the American O.S.S. Later she joined her partisan friends and formed the *Missione Rosa* group of Partisans.

In March 1944, Vassale established contact with the Allies with her *Radio Rosa* through the assistance of another partisan named Mario Robello. Manfredo Bertini, later referred to as *Maber*, organized the manpower to gather and bring the information to him for transmission to the Allies.

The radio transmitter was transferred in the latter part of June to a house in Camaiore, near the convent of the Friars. The activity of *Radio Rosa* was at a high level at that time because the Allies were advancing and they depended on information from the Partisans to plan their military action in Garfagnana and Versilia. On July 2, 1944, while Mario Robello was transmitting, German soldiers burst into the house where the transmission was taking place. According to reports after World War II, three women friends of the German soldiers turned in the location of the transmitter. In the confusion generated by the Germans attacking the house with machine guns, Robello threw four hand grenades into the oncoming German soldiers and was able to escape. The radio-transmitter was left behind and confiscated by the Germans. According to records kept by the partisans, *Radio Rosa* transmitted over 300 messages to the Allies which resulted in over 65 airdrops to Partisans of the region. The air drops consisted mainly of arms and ammunition for Partisan groups so they could continue to harass the Germans. After the war Vera Vassale received a gold medal for valor from the Italian Government and in a truly romantic ending married Mario Robello.

Manfredo Bertini continued his efforts to try to send information to the Allies. He was able to cross the front line with another Partisan and to give some direct information to the Americans about the Gothic Line. He re-crossed the front line, carrying another radio transmitter, returned safely to the Versilia area, and resumed the transmission of information to the Allied troops. In the process of returning, his left arm was severely wounded but he managed to escape and went into hiding with his Partisan friends. He had difficulty recovering from the wound because of a full scale infection and fellow-Partisans thought that he should have his arm amputated. He transmitted more than 100 messages on his *Missione Balilla* using one arm until his pain became unbearable. He could not face the removal of his arm; therefore on November 24, 1944, he left his hiding place, leaving his comrades in the radio-transmitter room, walked out into a nearby field and committed suicide by releasing the pin of a hand grenade under his chin. After the war the Italian government posthumously awarded him a Gold Medal for Valor. A book written by Liborio Guccione, *Missioni Rosa-Balilla Resistenza e Alleati*, published in 1987, describes in detail the Partisan activities in the Versilia region.

11.
LIBERATED
BY THE BUFFALO SOLDIERS

On June 6, 1944, the long awaited invasion of Europe was launched by the Allied Forces. Thousands of American soldiers stormed ashore on the Normandy beaches in France; thousands more landed in the following days and fought their way out of the beachhead.

On other battlefields, thousands of American soldiers sent the German and Italian forces reeling, first from North Africa and then Sicily. American General Mark Clark's Fifth Army, flushed from bloody victories at Anzio and Cassino and the triumphant conquest of Rome, was now poised along the south bank of the Arno River.

The 370th Infantry Regiment of the 92nd Infantry Division arrived in Italy in August 1944 and went into action with the 1st Armored Division on August 23, participating in the advance against minor German resistance across the Arno River and in the occupation of Lucca. Task Force 92, comprised of the 370 Infantry Regiment and members of the 1st Armored Division continued to advance on September 25 along the Serchio River Valley north of Pescia. On September 29 the task force gained control of Highway 12 along the Lima Creek and reached La Lima the next day. Task Force 92 assumed responsibility for the coast sector below Monte Cauala on the approach to Massa Carrara on October 5. The rest of the division arrived in October and the task force was dissolved on November 6.

The division continued to fight in the Monte Cauala area in October partially because supporting tanks and tank destroyers were unable to cross the rain-swollen streams. Finally, after capturing the mountain, the troops went towards the coast and were joined by the 371st Infantry Regiment. On December 23 the division in the Lucca area was reinforced by two brigades of the Indian 8th Division and the 337th and 339th Infantry Regiments of the 85th Infantry Division.

The German counterattack on Christmas Day 1944 against the division along the Serchio River and specifically in the village of Sommocolonia drove the American outposts back and precipitated a general withdrawal. Elements of the 8th Indian Division made their way through the retreating troops and made contact with the German forces causing them to pull back. The 365th and 366th Regiments made a limited attack to try to improve the positions in the Serchio River Valley and recovered Gallicano, Castelvecchio and Albiano on February 4, 1945. The entire division was reorganized in March 1945 for a major attack along the Ligurian Coast. In April, the division entered Massa, captured Aulla and reached Genova on April 27, 1945.

Again, Diecimo was liberated on September 26, 1944. We returned home from our hiding place in the mountains to find the village occupied by Brazilian soldiers who were attached to the Fifth Army. Within two weeks they moved out of the village and were replaced by Black soldiers from the 370th Infantry Regiment of the 92nd Infantry Division. Once we moved back to the village and into our home, we were part of the battle movements and lived in relative danger until the spring offensive in March and April 1945 caused the troops to move north.

During the German winter offensive in December 1944, the 92nd Infantry Division was augmented by the 8th Indian Division, regimental combat teams from the 34th and 85th Infantry, the 6th South African Armored Division and other reinforcements provided by General Mark Clark's 5th Army group. When reinforced by the 442nd Japanese-American and the 473rd Infantry Regiments, the 92nd Infantry Division conducted an offensive operation in the Spring of 1945 with outstanding success capturing Massa, Carrara, LaSpezia, Genova and Torino. During their Italian campaign they cleared 3,000 square miles of hostile forces and captured a total of 23,845 prisoners of war.

The Rome-Arno campaign began on June 22, 1944, following the collapse of the German resistance on the Winter Line, the Gustav Line, the Hitler Line and the cordon around the Anzio beach head, resulting in the fall of Rome. Field Marshal Albert Kesserling, the Supreme German Commander South West and the Commander-in-Chief Army Group C had at his disposal 25 German divisions and five Fascist Republican Italian Divisions. Twenty-one German divisions were assigned to the German Tenth Army commanded by General Vietinghoff and the Fourteenth Army commanded by Lt. General Lemelsen. Kesserling directed the Tenth and Fourteenth armies to pull back toward Northern Italy. After many rear guard and delaying actions all the way from Rome, Kesserling called a halt along the Arno River. Behind the positions were the rugged peaks of the North Apennines, reinforced by a series of fixed defenses, known as the Gothic Line. The Germans were determined to hold that line at all costs. Hitler personally directed that any general or staff officer who prepared withdrawal plans for evacuation of the Gothic Line would be executed. (*Buffalo Soldiers* by Thomas St. John Arnold OBE Colonel, U.S. Army retired.)

The *sfollati*, people who had evacuated from the coastal cities, stayed in the villages after the American troops arrived because they had no means of transportation back to their cities, and also because there was still danger of aerial bombardments by the Germans along the coast. After the war, a diary kept by an Italian actress named Maria Melato from Carrara, who was a *sfollata* at Foccette, near Barga, was published in Italian. She wrote the following about her experiences while working as a helper for the Black troops of the 92nd Infantry Division in a local villa that was used as a command post and whose kitchen was a mess hall for the soldiers. I translated the writing from Italian to English from the book *Val di Serchio e Versilia Linea Gotica* by Fabrizio Federighi.

There are many exquisite things that with an empty stomach I see passing my eyes: slices of fresh meat, huge loaves of white bread, rice pudding with pineapple, hot chocolate drink, and pastries. I see the cook frying innumerable slices of smoked pancetta, that they call bacon, whose aroma fills the entire kitchen and produces such an effect on me that it causes me to remember the times past when after a theatrical performance we went to fancy restaurants in the theater district. Or the delicious breakfasts that were served aboard ships in the morning when we ate eggs fried in lard. As the cook prepares the food, I sit in my usual corner in the kitchen, hoping to smell the frying bacon, happy when the impassive cook fries, fries and fries bacon.

We have become friends with these wonderful boys. The Lieutenant, a huge man, always smiling, ordered the cook to bring us food three times a day. It seems like a dream! Not all of their food appeals to our taste, but we eat. This is what is important. At every meal they give us as much coffee and milk as we wish. They also give us white bread, so good that it seems like cake. At breakfast they cover the bread with butter and jam. Even if we have nothing else, we must thank God.

The stores in our area are still closed, even in nearby villages it is impossible to buy anything. The only commerce is the exchange of goods. There are a few small stores where they are beginning to sell vegetables, squash, turnips and chestnuts. The weather is getting much colder. I observe the Negroes who fascinate me because they are so different than we are. They are all very young, tall, strong, not ugly in general, but personality-wise they seem strange, different from each other. Some are very sociable and ready to joke around, while others are reserved and never smile. I observe them, half hidden, seated in my corner, as they come and go. There is a lot of action in the kitchen because the cooks work all day and soldiers come in all day to get food.

It is hard to believe how much food is distributed. Trucks continuously drop off loads of cardboard boxes, strong as wooden ones, that contain smaller boxes full of tin cans with every possible type of food, such as meat, butter, cheese, bacon, jam, coffee, cookies, milk and cigarettes. I often wonder what is stored in those miraculous boxes, my mouth waters just thinking about it! The meals are ready at 8 in the morning and at 5 in the afternoon, but food is really available all day long. The cook is somewhat strange, talks very little, but is very generous and gives away a lot of food, and also drinks glassfuls of cognac that is swallowed as if water.

The food seems strange to me, often sugar, pepper and cinnamon are added as condiments. How much pepper! But we can eat nice slices of meat, eggs, and fruit cocktail with plenty of pineapple.

I'm ashamed when I come and go to the villa because people outside envy me that I'm able to live here, knowing the advantages that I have. They always try to send small children into the villa carrying empty tin cans which they hope will be filled with food by the generous cook.

Even the young ladies, the ones with short skirts and wearing lipstick, beg for chocolate and cigarettes. They don't ask for bread, they are friendly and are searching for other things from the soldiers. They laugh, they joke around, some are beautiful even though they are still children. The soldiers at times force themselves on the girls in brutal ways. They are young men, forceful men, away from their homeland, with animal instincts. Even if they have a dark skin and can't speak Italian, they are men and at times I think that the young girls forget who they are. These young soldiers are very happy. Last night, during a rest period, they played a harmonica and sang songs. They called us to come down and listen and have fun. Even I went down and sang "Lili Marlene." God knows how I detest this song, but I went along. While we listened to the more danceable music, a timid farm woman, sitting near me, did something that she never would have done in her life, she smoked a cigarette. She coughed a lot but she still smoked. She has one gravely ill son and one who is a prisoner in Germany. I did not know if I should laugh or cry. Why shouldn't we smoke now with all the cigarettes that are offered to us? I've seen a lot of 6 or 7 year old children smoking on the street, without even hiding. No one says anything to them, it seems normal. Evidently there is something that does not work in our brains. I know many timid women, scrupulous until yesterday, who now couple with the Negro soldiers without holding back or having any shame. I know one young lady, very intelligent, spinster, dressed in up-standing clothes, who began to dream about having an affair with a soldier before she dies. Everything that is happening around us is a folly, everything seems illogical, how will it end?

The excerpt translated into English reflects the confused feelings that people had during the period after the Germans left the area when they were occupied by the Black soldiers. Most Italians were never exposed to different cultures, and never saw people of color, unless they lived in Africa as the Fascists did when they tried to colonize Libya and Ethiopia. The presence of the American troops caused many to seek food and clothing from the soldiers. Young girls were especially attractive to the men because they had been without women for a long periods of time. It seemed that at times the Black troops were having such a good time that they forgot they were fighting a war.

After the first of the year, in January, February and March of 1945, things began to get back to normal. People began to resume their normal village lives. When the war in Europe ended in May, prisoners from Northern Italy and Germany began to return home; the *sfollati* returned to their homes on the coast, people began to work the land again, preparing the soil for the spring and summer crops. Many new political parties emerged, such as the Communists, the Christian Democrats, the Socialists, the Azione Party and many others as Italy began to recover from the war years.

The costs in lives was high, and the lists of killed, wounded, and missing in action were lengthy. Battle honors for combat units were numerous and impressive, and the names of individual heroes became household words in America.

But there were no battle honors for Black combat units or citations or awards for individual Black soldiers. Alas, even though America was at war since 1941, there were no

Black infantry units in action in Europe; as in other theaters, most Black soldiers were service troops.

On the morning of July 30, 1944, however, the first
American black infantry combat team to fight on the
European continent in World War II landed in Napoli,
Italy. These black soldiers, fit and ready to fight, belonged
to the 370th Combat Team, which was the advance detach-
ment of the 92nd Infantry (Buffalo) Division. This compact,
self-contained fighting force consisted of the 370th Infantry
Regiment, the 598th Field Artillery Battalion, and detach-
ments from the Division Combat Engineers, Medical,
Ordinance, Military Police, Quartermaster and Signal units,
and the 92nd Division Headquarters Company.

Its officers and enlisted men were believed to represent
the best cross-section of any Combat Team in the Division.
In the months following maneuvers, the 370th Combat
Team was completely re-organized. Officers and men felt to
be inept, poorly motivated, physically and/or mentally
deficient, or who were unable to pass basic tests, were
removed. They were replaced by better qualified and more
capable men, many of them volunteers. The pace and tempo
of training were increased, with emphasis on physical
conditioning, basic weapons proficiency, and improvement
of leadership and teamwork.

Colonel Raymond G. Sherman, commanding the 370th,
believed that his unit had high morale and great expecta-
tions for success in battle; it was secure in the knowledge
that it was well trained, in excellent physical condition and
that its personnel were hand picked.

> Rumors of the arrival of the Buffalo Soldiers had
> preceded them, and hundreds of Black soldiers,
> most of them service troops, were waiting at the
> docks in battered Napoli Harbor. As the thousands
> of black fighting men, in single file, debarked from

the crowded troopships, they presented an impressive and awe-inspiring spectacle. Armed with basic weapons and in full field battle dress, proudly wearing the circular shoulder patch with the black buffalo, they moved smartly and efficiently into their unit formations. As they marched away, every man in step, every weapon in place, chins up and eyes forward, a low rumbling babble of sound came from the troops on the dock, then swelled to a crescendo of thunderous cheering which continued until the last Buffalo unit had disappeared from sight. Many applications for transfer to the 92nd Division were processed after the arrival of the 370th Combat Team, and many new men participated in the combat operations which followed. From July 30 until August 23, the Buffalo soldiers were busy in orientation programs, assembling and cleaning weapons and other equipment, and in rigorous physical conditioning exercises. (*Buffalo Soldiers in Italy, Black Americans in World War II* by Hondon B. Hargrove, McFarland & Company, Publishers)

I described earlier how our village of Diecimo was first occupied by the Brazilian soldiers who were attached to the III Battalion, 6th Regiment. The Brazilian soldiers remained in Diecimo for approximately two weeks while members of the 370th Regimental Combat Team of the 92nd Infantry Buffalo Division continued up the east and west side of the valley. The American soldiers encountered some resistance but eventually worked their way up the Serchio River valley, north of Diecimo, to the vicinity of Barga. Some of the soldiers also continued up the Lima River valley, found little resistance and eventually linked up with Allied Forces near Pistoia and Florence.

When the Buffalo Soldiers replaced the Brazilians, they also set up the company headquarters at the railroad station, using large tents, the station building and the freight storage building. The soldiers also dug a large trench which was used as a bathroom facility (latrine) in a nearby field. The latrine trench was shielded from public view with tarps.

The entrance to the valley at Sesto di Moriano was narrow, but it gradually widened near Piaggione and Diecimo. The Germans concealed a strip of land mines in the flat area completely across the valley from the base of one mountain to the other, including the railroad tracks and the two main roads on the east and west sides of the river Serchio. Some village people were forced by the Germans to help them place the mines in the fields, so those same people were able to help the American soldiers remove the mines so that the entrance to the valley would be safe for the movement of troops. The land mines were made in the form of an 18 inch square wooden box, about 3 inches high. Square pieces of *tritolo* (dynamite) were placed inside the box with detonators placed at each corner. The mine was then placed in the ground and a wooden lid positioned over the top of the box with plungers at each corner that rested on the detonators. The wooden box was then covered with a thin layer of dirt to conceal the mine. If someone stepped on the box the detonators were set off, exploding the *tritolo*. The perilous process of disarming the mines first involved locating them, then carefully removing the wooden cover with the plungers that were set to trigger the detonator caps in the box, so that the box was safe to handle. The mines were located and disarmed within a few days of the arrival of the Brazilian soldiers.

The Germans retreated up the Serchio River valley toward Garfagnana in the vicinity of Gallicano and Barga, approximately 12 kilometers from Diecimo. Even though we were liberated, we could hear the artillery fire and occasional carbine and rifle fire in the distance, and we were aware that the German soldiers were not too far away.

Diecimo was evacuated in July, and by the time most people returned, around the end of September, most of the agricultural crops were gone, some were taken by the local people and some by the Germans. New crops were not planted because during the evacuation it was not possible to work in the fields. Grapes were still on the vines in the elevated areas and were available for the production of wine. The able bodied men, women and children picked the grapes, and, just as they did in previous years, went ahead and made the 1944 crop of wine. By October, the new wine was available and shared with the Black soldiers in the area in exchange for food.

Before the war, electricity in the area was generated by hydroelectric power in the Serchio River valley, between Gallicano and Castelnuovo, above Borgo a Mozzano, near Barga. Unfortunately the generating plant was blown up by the Germans when they retreated so no one had electrical power. People were left in the dark and tried to secure church candles and *carburo* (calcium carbide) for the carburo lamps in order to provide light for their homes. It was difficult to purchase candles and *carburo* so most people resorted to using American gasoline to light their homes. We filled a Coca Cola bottle with gasoline, immersed a narrow piece of cloth as a wick in the gasoline, and then lit the wick. The gasoline flame provided sufficient light for us but generated a lot of black smoke. By the end of the evening we all had a black lining around our nostrils from inhaling the smoke.

The U.S. Army food distribution, or *mess* line, was set up on the railway station platform, outside the waiting room. Soldiers went through the mess line for their meals, piling their food in their aluminum mess kits. I remember that when they were finished eating they dumped left-over food in a garbage can and rinsed their mess kits in two other cans that were filled with hot water. When meal time was over people came by to search the garbage can for food, taking the left-overs for themselves or for their pigs.

Various companies and platoons who were still engaged in minor skirmishes with the Germans were stationed up the valley, and as they occupied villages they would sometimes remain in the location. Supplies for the troops came by truck each day from the port of Livorno, which was located about 100 kilometers to the southwest. After the supplies were delivered to the railroad station, small trucks and jeeps from the front line areas came down to get the daily supply of food rations and ammunition.

When the 92nd Infantry Division soldiers arrived, my mother, father and I were able to speak English with them. I had not spoken English since my arrival in Italy in 1939, but I discovered that I understood the soldiers fairly well and was able to speak with them even though I had an Italian accent. After a few days of talking with the soldiers my English gradually improved. The soldiers were able to understand me and I helped them as an interpreter translating English to Italian and Italian to English as needed.

The schools were still closed, so most children had nothing to do except hang around the G.I.'s in the hope that they would be able to get some food, candy, or cigarettes. I was given an old knit G.I. cap and jacket which I liked to wear while I made myself available for work during the day. I helped unload the trucks, divided up the rations and ammunition for the various platoons, ran errands, and occasionally took short trips up the valley in a jeep or truck toward the front line to help deliver supplies. I was also allowed to go through the mess line after all the soldiers had eaten, so I had one good meal a day. In the evening, when I was finished for the day, the soldiers usually gave me food to take home, such as canned meat, a loaf of white bread, C-rations, candy and cigarettes for my father.

Most men in Diecimo enjoyed smoking cigarettes and cigars. Young boys also attempted to smoke behind the backs of their parents. The smokers were especially pleased by the arrival of the American soldiers because there were plenty of cigarettes available. In Italy tobacco products were sold only at the *appalti* (a government tobacco outlet), which in Diecimo was operated by Corinna and Olga Nardi. *Toscanelli* (Tuscan) cigars were popular with older men. The *Toscanelli* were short, dark cigars, slightly tapered, approximately 3/8 of an inch in diameter and slightly longer than a regular cigarette. When the men lit the cigars they sent out a horrible smell into the air. They also often kept the unlit cigars in their mouth and chewed on the end, similar to chewing tobacco. Cigarette smokers were limited to only a few brands of Italian cigarettes such as *Nazionali, Militi*, and *Serraglio*, and these were also rationed during the war. Men often purchased two or three cigarettes at a time, cut them in half, and smoked the short stubs almost to the end of the cigarette with the aid of a *bocchino* (cigarette holder).

My father really enjoyed smoking and was especially thrilled when the American soldiers arrived, because when we entertained the soldiers in our home they always provided packs of cigarettes. The most popular brands were Lucky Strike, Chesterfield, Phillip Morris, and Camel. Men in the village started picking up and saving the large cigarette butts that Americans threw away and used the left-over tobacco to roll their own cigarettes. My father also saved his cigarette butts and the ones that the G.I.'s left in our ash trays. When my father had a good collection, he sat himself down at the kitchen table, broke apart all the cigarette butts and blended himself a batch of cigarette tobacco. Often, as he ran his hands through the tobacco he would lower his head and inhale the smell of American tobacco and say, "*Che profumo!*" (What an aroma!)

Once he mixed the tobacco, he pulled out sheets of white typing paper and cut the paper into small strips the size of regular cigarette paper. He then used the paper to roll his own cigarettes which he would smoke when he ran out of American cigarettes. Occasionally I got cigarettes from the soldiers and gave some of them to my friend Mauro and to my father. I also tried to smoke, but to be honest, I never liked the taste of tobacco.

Many of the soldiers knew that my family spoke English, so in the evenings we very often had G.I. visitors come to our home in order to speak English with us, to socialize, and to drink wine with my dad. Many of the soldiers missed home cooking, especially greens; so my mother sometimes prepared an evening meal for the soldiers, who often brought some type of canned meat which my mother incorporated into a meal with potatoes, Swiss chard or *rapini* (turnip greens), and we would have a family style dinner. The soldiers said that the dinners reminded them of home and that they appreciated so much being able to forget about the war for a few hours.

There was considerable troop movement in our area during the months of October, November and December, 1944. The Allied Forces encountered strong opposition from the Germans in the area of Barga, and because of the cold rainy weather and the inaccessible mountainous terrain their advance was stalled. There were small skirmishes in the lower villages while the Germans controlled the mountain-top areas. The main road from Lucca to Barga went directly through our village and it narrowed considerably in Dieci-mo. Very often tanks traveled up the valley and when they encountered tanks coming the other way, there was very little room for them to pass each other on the narrow village streets.

The local people had to go to the municipal offices in Borgo a Mozzano to secure an Identity Card in order to travel around the area. There were several check points manned by Military Police who stopped all civilians who passed by. I still have my original Identity Card, which is duplicated below:

Certificato di Identità No. 10474
COMUNE DI BORGO A MOZZANO
PROVINCIA DI LUCCA
IL SINDACO
certifica che la persona raffigurata nella presente fotografia è
BERTINI TULLIO BRUNO
  di Nello e di Marcucci Ada
  Nato a Boston (U.S.A.) il 13 luglio 1930
  Stato civile: celibe, di nazionalità Italiana, professione: studente, residente a Borgo a Mozzano, Frazione Diecimo, Via Del Santo No. 81.

  CONNOTATI E CONTRASSEGNI SALIENTI

Statura:	*68 cm*	*Fronte:*	*giusta*
Corpo:	*snella*	*Occhi:*	*celesti*
Naso:	*regolare*	*Bocca:*	*regolare*
Colore:	*roseo*	*Capelli:*	*castagni*
Barba:	*rasa*	*Segni:*	

Borgo a Mozzano il 5 Dicembre 1944
    Il Sindaco
    Antonio Tonelli

I folded the I.D. paper and carried it in my pocket at all times, because several of my friends and I had bicycles and we liked to travel around the area to see what the soldiers were doing. We rode as far as Bagni di Lucca where we saw the results of the artillery fire that the Germans were directing toward the valley. The shelling caused much damage in the towns of Borgo a Mozzano, Chifenti and Bagni di Lucca, where we could see large gaping holes in many of the houses. All of the bridges that spanned the Serchio River were blown up and replaced by temporary bridges erected by the Corps of Engineers. The only bridge that was not blown up was the Ponte della Maddalena or Devil's Bridge. It was possibly spared because of its artistic value, or, more likely, because the bridge was very narrow and the Germans thought that military vehicles could not use it. Ironically, the bridge was just wide enough so that the U.S. Army jeeps were able to cross the bridge and to bring supplies and troops to the Bagni di Lucca area.

We were often stopped at control points by M.P.'s from the 92nd Infantry Division. At first they always checked our Identity Papers, but later, as we became friendly with the soldiers and because I spoke English with them, they always let us pass through. I became friendly with a couple of M.P.'s, Sergeant McNair and Second Lieutenant Johnson and invited them to come visit my home and to meet my parents. (I gave them our house number.) One evening they came by and enjoyed speaking English with us and especially enjoyed the wine that my father offered. Later on, during the winter, when they were assigned to another area, somewhere in Tuscany, they would return to visit us, together or individually when they had some time off. They drove into Diecimo in a jeep, which they backed down the steep path that led to the archway below the chapel next door to us to keep it hidden from road traffic. They always brought food, cigarettes and candy for us. Unfortunately, when they visited, I had to give up my bed and bedroom for them because they often stayed overnight. My mother tried to make them feel at home by including them at our dinner table and preparing potatoes, vegetables and eggs for them.

Sergeant McNair was from New York; before his unit shipped out to go to northern Italy, he gave me his address and telephone number. On our return trip to the United States, in February 1946, while we were staying with our friends, the Meconi family in the Bronx, I telephoned Sergeant McNair, who then came to visit us with his girlfriend. Sergeant McNair was a huge man, probably 6 feet 6 inches tall, and when he saw me he grabbed me and gave me a bear hug, saying how happy he was to see me. He brought me a present, of all things, a pack of Lucky Strike cigarettes enclosed in one of the plastic cases which were popular with G.I.'s that allowed one to store a package of book matches with the cigarettes. He remembered that I smoked cigarettes in Diecimo, (unknown to my parents), and thought it an appropriate gift for a 16 year old boy!

As we approached Christmas 1944 there was a discussion with some of our usual G.I. visitors about having a party on Christmas Eve. They asked my mother if she could prepare a dinner for them if they furnished most of the food. My mother, who at the time was 45 years old and fairly energetic, said she would be glad to prepare it. My mother invited my former tutor, who lived across the street, Fedra Lazzari, to have dinner with us, and to help out. Fedra tutored me for a while when the schools closed in 1943-44. She and her husband, a professor named Terzolani, were stationed in Ethiopia, in *Addis Ababa*, as school teachers. When her husband died in 1940, Fedra returned to live with her parents Niccola and Nello Lazzari, who owned the small store and bar next door to us. Mariuccia, who still lived with us, also helped with the food preparation.

We set up the table in our dining room for 12 people, 5 of us, and 7 G.I.'s. One of the soldiers said that he would bring some American records and a hand cranked record player so that they could dance to American music. I remember being excited about the party and that I helped out in setting the table. We had hidden our china, fancy glasses, and silverware in the walled-over room in Angelo's house so it was still available and this was our first opportunity to use it to entertain people. After we finished setting all the plates, glasses and silverware on the table, it looked like a table in a fancy restaurant.

Mariuccia made *ravioli*, and we also had green vegetables, and plenty of wine. The soldiers came to our house about 7 p.m. carrying the record player. As there was no electricity we ate by gasoline light. The soldiers were moved by the festive atmosphere and by the appearance of the dining room, commenting that being there with us was the next best thing to being home for Christmas. As we sat at the table and began to eat, the atmosphere became cordial and friendly, and we all seemed to forget about the war.

After the meal one of the soldiers set up the phonograph in the living room and started playing the American music. The soldiers asked my mother, Fedra and Mariuccia to dance. I don't remember the songs that were played, except that it seemed like swing orchestra music, such as the music of Glenn Miller or Tommy Dorsey. The soldiers also got together and sang Christmas carols for us before the end of the evening. In later years, I have often thought about that Christmas Eve party in Diecimo when the war brought the Black soldiers to Italy, how much we enjoyed their company, specifically their rendition of *Silent Night*, and how it seemed for a moment that we were back in America.

At approximately the same time that we were having our Christmas party, there were several troop activities taking place on the front line near Barga. On the morning of the 24th of December two companies moved out of Barga and into the tiny mountain village of Sommocolonia, in preparation for an attack on the German positions. Bebbio and Scarpello were each occupied by platoons from the 92nd Reconnaissance Troop. However, word finally came to the

370th Combat Team on the evening of the 24th of December that the proposed attack against the Germans was being postponed. Information that a German attack was to take place in the Serchio River Valley on the 27th of December prompted the reversal of plans. Captain Samuel Tucker of the Second Battalion, 366th, alleging deliberate delay in notifying his unit of the change of plans stated:

> I believe it was on the night of December 24 when Headquarters 370th Infantry ordered that the company in the vicinity of Sommocolonia under orders to attack would immediately retire from the assembly area and abandon the attack plans... Early that same day a Captain Schmidt... appeared in our sector and said to me that his mission was to develop some counterattack plans. I remember that our Section was ordered to pick up and distribute defensive materials. In retrospect, I can see that higher headquarters knew that what was about to happen and knew that it was imminent. We at Second Battalion Headquarters were told nothing. I believe that the failure to inform us was deliberate.

All front line units were notified during the night of the 24th of the change in plans. General Almond's Field Order Number 5 dated 25 December at 1600 exhorted the 92nd Infantry Division to: "reinforce, organize, occupy and hold present position at all costs. Intensive patrolling; make maximum improvement of existing defensive positions."

The night of December 25-26 was relatively quiet, although Sommocolonia received some artillery and mortar fire, and considerable long range machine gun fire fell on the east bank of the Serchio River. Just after midnight a message from IV Corps requested a follow-up of a report from a priest in Pierpoli that the enemy attack would come on December 27th. Early in the morning of the 26th the

Second Battalion was withdrawn back to high ground west of the Serchio and south of Gallicano with the mission of digging a main defensive position across the area. Around 5 o'clock in the morning fierce artillery fire, mortar fire and machine gun fire came directly from north of Sommocolonia aimed at the 92nd Infantry positions. German soldiers made their way down into Sommocolonia and engaged in hand-to-hand fighting against the U.S. troops who were aided by a group of Partisans and Austrian soldiers.

Late in the morning about 200 German soldiers from the Mittenwald Battalion poured down the valley causing the 92nd Infantry Division soldiers to withdraw to Coreglia. Bitter fighting continued in the area of Sommocolonia all day long and for several days thereafter. The ground troops were reinforced by planned air strikes by fighter bombers on Sommocolonia, Barga and Vergemoli.

1st Lt. John R. Fox of Boston, Massachusetts, an artillery observer with Cannon Company, 92nd Infantry Division was killed in action on December 26, 1944. He was posthumously awarded the Distinguished Service Cross. On Christmas Day, Lt. Fox volunteered to serve as an artillery forward observer in the village of Sommocolonia. He chose the second floor of a house as his observation post. The men of the 366th battallion were in a precarious position, having faced the Germans on a 30 mile front and were stretched thin. On the morning of December 26, Fox and his men woke up to find themselves overrun by German soldiers trying to break into the house where they set up the observation post. Fox got on his radio and called for artillery fire on the Germans soldiers nearby. He insisted that the fire control post fire the 105 mm guns directly into his post with the hope of killing all the German soldiers. During the barrage of artillery fire most of the Germans were killed but Lt. Fox was also killed. On January 13, 1997 President Bill Clinton presented the Medal of Honor to 1st

Lt. Vernon J. Baker for his valor in the Italian campaign as a member of the 92nd Infantry Division for his actions in the Versilia area. At the same time President Clinton also awarded the Medal of Honor posthumously to 1st Lt. John R. Fox and four other black heroes: PFC. Willy F. James Jr., Staff Sgt. Ruben Rivers, 1st Lt. Charles L. Thomas, and Pvt. George Watson.

In 1994 the village of Sommocolonia organized a 50th anniversary celebration to remember and honor the men who lost their lives during the battles of 1944. The village published a booklet titled *Per Ricordare Sommocolonia 26 Dicembre 1944* which describes the events that took place at Christmas 1944.

The 19th and 20th Indian Brigades (Gurkhas and Sikhs) of the 8th Indian Division were placed under the operational control of the 92nd Infantry Division and moved into the Serchio River Valley to support the 92nd Infantry Troops. I remember their arrival in Diecimo. We became accustomed to a lot of Sherman tank traffic and were surprised when smaller tanks with the British insignia came into the area carrying the tall, dark soldiers in British uniforms wearing turbans. The movement of the troops into the area took place on December 27 after more airplane attacks and artillery fire. Most of the people in Diecimo feared that the Germans were going to push the Allies back and that we were going to have to evacuate the village again. As the action was taking place near Barga and Gallicano, many people from the combat zone started to evacuate making their way down the valley, through Diecimo, heading for Lucca. They were walking, pulling carts, carrying their belongings, and telling us that the Germans were killing a lot of Americans and that we had better leave.

My father tried to speak with some of the Indian soldiers in order to find out what was happening. The soldiers were surprised to find someone who spoke English and became very friendly with us. They assured us that we were going to be safe, especially since they had arrived to help out the Black soldiers. Some of the Indians were stationed at the railway station, and as things at the front quieted down, they came to visit us in the evening because we spoke English and also were able provide them with wine. The soldiers really enjoyed the wine and were very generous with us, giving us food, cigarettes and candy. I had difficulty understanding the Indian soldiers because of their British accent.

Rumors began going around our village that the Indians liked to patrol during the night and were able to sneak up on the Germans and slit their throats with the large knives that they carried in special holders on their belts. They were menacing-looking men and most people were afraid of them, especially the women of Diecimo, who stayed out of sight while they were in the area. Eventually, before the end of December, the Germans were pushed back to their original position, behind Sommocolonia and the front line area became quiet again. The Indian troops left to rejoin their group, and the 92nd Infantry Division soldiers returned to Diecimo and remained for a while longer.

After Christmas we found out that the Germans were gradually moving out to the northeast toward Bologna, and as a result the American troops in our area were diminished in number. The weather was extremely cold and rainy during the months of January and February so that there was very little action at the front. It seemed that the soldiers of the 92nd Infantry Divison really suffered in the cold weather and always appreciated being inside the homes of the local people, sheltered from the cold damp climate.

The American Consulate for Tuscany was located in Firenze, approximately 60 kilometers from Lucca. Because of their war experiences, American citizens, including my parents, were eager to return to the United States. We contacted the Consulate by mail in order to find out when

we could return to the United States. We were told to go to
Firenze, appear in person at the Consulate, and fill out the
necessary papers to be able to return to the United States
along with the many other American citizens trapped in
Europe. We made plans to go to Firenze during the month
of February 1945, assuming that we could get a ride on one
of the many American vehicles in our area. There was no
public transportation from Lucca to Firenze because
railroad bridges were demolished by the retreating Germans. However, the American Fifth Army established a rest
camp for soldiers in Firenze so that occasionally soldiers in
our area were assigned to go there for a few days of rest
and recreation. The G.I.s were usually transported by truck
following the old highway repaired by the Fifth Army
Engineers. We received travel documents from the Consulate showing a specific date for our appointment with the
Consul and were advised to coordinate our transportation
with the local 92nd Infantry Division soldiers. Another
American woman from Diecimo, Virginia Maffei, was
scheduled to go to Firenze on the same day so that she
could make arrangements to return to the United States.

We spoke with the commander of the soldiers in Diecimo
and made arrangements to ride to Firenze on a army truck.
On a cold and rainy morning we walked to the railroad
station and waited for the truck to arrive and pick us up.
Around nine in the morning a large canvas covered Army
truck, with an open rear area and tailgate drove into the
station area The truck was full of G.I.s from the 92nd
Infantry Division going to the rest camp in Firenze, and
they were seated on the benches on both sides of the truck.
The tailgate was lowered so that we could climb in. My
father and I helped my mother and Virginia climb in, I
helped my father, then finally I climbed in. My mother and
Virginia were able to squeeze in with the soldiers on the

benches, while my father and I sat on the floor by the tailgate because there was no room on the benches.

The truck left the railroad station and headed toward Lucca following the route along the side of the mountains on the bumpy unpaved road. As we were driving along I could see the rain pouring down and my father and I tried to move further back into the truck so that we would not get wet. The G.I.s sitting toward the back on the benches wore raincoats and were protected from the splashes of muddy water from the road. Once we arrived in Lucca, the truck entered the *autostrada* (highway) and headed toward Firenze. As we drove along we passed Montecatini, Pescia, Pistoia, and Prato before entering Firenze. I saw several bombed towns with buildings torn apart by explosions. It was a very slow trip. By the time we arrived at the rest camp area, it was early afternoon. Once we got down from the truck, my father, mother, Virginia and I left the camp area to look for a bathroom. We went into a small *trattoria* (restaurant) to eat and asked to use the bathroom. There were still food shortages in Italy, so restaurants did not have much to offer. We each ordered a plate of pasta with tomato sauce and drank wine from the liter of wine that my father ordered. When we finished, we asked directions to the Consulate and also asked if they could recommend a nearby hotel or *pensione* (guest house).

Our appointment with the Consul was scheduled for that afternoon, around 4 p.m. Following the directions that were given to us by the owners of the restaurant we found an inexpensive hotel, where we were able to get a room with two small beds for the four of us. My mother and Virginia planned to sleep in in one bed, my father and I in the other. After we received our room assignment, we went to the hotel room and cleaned up a bit, then prepared ourselves for our appointment with the Consul.

We left the hotel, walked to the Consulate and arrived in time for our appointment. I don't remember if we actually spoke with the Consul or with a staff member, but I do remember that the man who met with us was very cordial and helpful and even gave me a package of Charms, the American fruit-flavored candy that was packaged in small cellophane-wrapped squares. We filled out all the necessary papers for our return to the United States and were assured that as soon as a ship was available we would be notified by mail. We were told that the waiting period for our departure might be as long as a year and that the ship would probably leave from Napoli. The gentleman also said it might be difficult to get a ride to Lucca and suggested that we should try to pick up a ride from an Army truck at the rest camp area where the trucks left to deliver soldiers back to their companies. We walked back to our hotel, very happy that we succeeded in preparing all the necessary documents for our return to the United States.

I had a pretty good night's sleep considering I shared the small twin bed with my father. To be more comfortable, we slept head to feet. The next morning, after getting dressed and using the bathroom facilities down the hall, we had our typical breakfast of *caffè e latte*. We then walked to the army rest camp entrance where we spoke with one of the M.P.s on duty, told him of our travel permit and asked if it would be possible for him to arrange a ride for us to Lucca. The M.P. said that he could not arrange a ride for us, but that we should stay outside of the gate and try to get a ride as the vehicles exited the area. At about 10 o'clock in the morning we placed ourselves outside the gate and tried to stop the military trucks as they exited. The weather was very cold and as the day progressed we discovered that all the truck drivers ignored us. We tried waving the travel permit paper in order to indicate that we had permission to travel, but no one stopped because we looked like typical Italians.

Finally at about 4 o'clock, a British open bed truck stopped. There were two soldiers in the cab. The driver rolled down the window, and asked in Italian:

"*Dove andare?*" (Where did we want to go?)

My father responded in English that we wanted to go to Lucca, that we had a travel permit, and that we were American citizens. The driver, surprised that we were Americans, said that he was going to Montecatini and that we were welcome to ride that far with them. My mother and Virginia were allowed to sit in the cab with the two soldiers, probably because they were women, while my father and I were told to ride in the back of the open bed truck. The soldiers had a blanket in the truck and they tossed it to us as we sat down with our backs to the cab window facing the rear of the truck. I don't remember what the temperature was on that February day, but I do remember that it was freezing cold and that we were very happy to have the blanket! As the truck made its way out of Firenze and headed toward Montecatini on the *autostrada*, I again had a good view of the damages to the city and the areas that we passed, but as the truck picked up speed the wind chill was almost unbearable and I lost all interest in sight-seeing.

We arrived in Montecatini at about 5:30 p.m., where the British soldiers dropped us off at an American troop post located in one of the large hotels. We walked into the hotel and as we encountered a couple of American soldiers we explained our dilemma. The soldiers were very friendly, especially after seeing how cold we were, so they took us into a mess hall and gave us cups of hot chocolate, white bread and butter. We were starved since we had not eaten since breakfast in Firenze. We were also told that we could not stay there for the night, even though we were American citizens, because the accommodations were for military personnel only. They also told us that all the hotels in

Montecatini were taken over by the military, so it would be difficult to find a room.

In 1934, my mother, father and I traveled to Italy for a few months during the summer. We spent most of the time in Diecimo with my grandparents, but we did have the opportunity to spend a few days in a hotel in Montecatini while my parents took the famous mineral water cure. My father remembered the hotel and the name of the people who either owned or managed the hotel. After we were fed and warmed up, we decided to take a walk to the hotel and see if by chance the people still lived there. When we arrived we discovered that the hotel was also occupied by the military, but the owners still lived there and were allowed to retain a few rooms for themselves. They remembered us from 1934 and were pleased to see us. We shared our war-time experiences in Diecimo and our trip to Firenze with them and explained our predicament. They were able to give us a bedroom for the night, but they said that the bedroom only had one bed. We accepted the offer and told them that we would be able to sleep in one bed for the night. Since we were all exhausted we decided to go to bed early. We had filled up with hot chocolate and bread at the American mess hall, so we did not need to have dinner. The sleeping arrangements were unusual to say the least. My mother and Virginia positioned their heads at one end of the bed, while my father and I positioned our heads at the other end of the bed. The room was not heated, so we slept in the bed with our clothes on, covering ourselves with the blankets that were provided.

Montecatini was famous before the war as Italy's most glamorous thermal spa, whose waters would cure whatever ailed you. It is still a luxurious resort today with trendy boutiques, cafes, and over 200 hotels. I'm sure that my memory of Montecatini is far different than most visitors to that lovely place.

Our biggest concern the next morning was to try to get a ride from Montecatini to Lucca and then to Diecimo. After having our *caffè e latte* and thanking our hosts for their hospitality, we walked to the road leading out of Monte-catini hoping to stop a military vehicle in order to get a ride. The weather was still cold, but the sun was shining which helped us to keep warm. We waited in vain for a few hours, as none of the jeeps or trucks passing by would stop for us. Finally, as the noon hour approached, my father spoke to a man going by with a horse-drawn wagon and asked where he was going. The man said that he was going to Pescia, which is between Montecatini and Lucca. My father asked the man if we could ride on the wagon and go as far as he was going. The man agreed and helped us climb aboard. The wagon was a flatbed two wheeled wagon with wooden planks running the length of the bed. As we climbed onto the wagon we arranged ourselves in such a way that the wagon was balanced front to rear so the weight did not place a strain on the horse. The trip to Pescia was extremely slow and bumpy, but eventually, around 4 o'clock we arrived. The man dropped us off near the main road leading to Lucca and suggested that we stand by the road and try to stop the army trucks as they were going by.

It became very frustrating for my father because none of the military trucks stopped. It seemed that the soldiers did not want to stop to pick up what appeared to be Italian civilians. We began to think that we would be stranded another night away from home, with little money for a hotel and food. Finally, just before darkness set in, at the point where we almost gave up hope, an American Army truck, driven by a Black Buffalo soldier, stopped. The driver got out, walked toward us, and asked if he could help. I recognized the soldier as one who visited our house. He said he stopped because he recognized us and he remembered that we spoke English. My father explained that we were in Firenze and that we were looking for a ride back to Diecimo. The soldier said that he was not scheduled to go up the Serchio River valley because he was reassigned to the coastal area near Viareggio. After speaking with us, and understanding our predicament, he said he would take us home because he remembered how kind we were when he visited our home. We gratefully accepted. My mother and Virginia rode in the cab, while my father and I rode in the canvas covered rear section of the truck.

When we arrived home we thanked the soldier and gave him several bottles of wine to take back to his outfit. The three day trip to Firenze was an adventure for me; even though the experience was difficult at times, it gave me the opportunity to see a portion of Firenze and also to see the effects of the war in the areas between Firenze and Lucca. The experience made me realize how helpful people can be in time of need, especially the United States Consulate staff, the hotel and restaurant people, the British soldiers, and the American Buffalo soldier who took us home.

12.
ITALY IN THE AFTERMATH

The Third Reich survived the death of its founder, Adolph Hitler, by seven days. Hitler took his life on April 30, 1945 and Grand Admiral Doenitz was appointed his successor. On May 4 the German High Command surrendered to General Montgomery all the German forces in northwest Germany, Denmark and Holland. The next day Kesserling's Army Group G north of the Alps surrendered. The German Armies in Italy surrendered unconditionally on April 29.

On May 7, Admiral Doenitz was informed by General Jodl that General Eisenhower demanded that the Germans surrender, otherwise the Allied front would be closed to German refugees. Admiral Doenitz communicated with General Jodl and gave him full powers to sign the document of unconditional surrender.

In a little red schoolhouse at Reims, where Eisenhower made his headquarters, Germany surrendered unconditionally at 2:41 on the morning of May 7, 1945. The capitulation was signed for the Allies by General Walter Bedell Smith, with General Ivan Susloparov affixing his signature as witness for Russia and General Francois Sevez for France. Admiral Friedeburge and General Jodl signed for Germany. Jodl asked permission to say a word and it was granted.

"With this signature the German people and the German Armed Forces are, for better or worse, delivered into the hands of the victors... In this hour I can only express the hope that the victor will treat them with generosity."

There was no response from the Allied side. The guns in Europe ceased firing and the bombs ceased dropping at midnight May 8-9, 1945, and a strange, but welcome silence settled over the Continent for the first time since September 1, 1939. (*The Rise and Fall of the Third Reich* by William L. Shirer).

The spring offensive in Italy began around the first of April. The 92nd Infantry Division was assigned to move up the coast toward Massa Carrara, La Spezia, Chiavari, Portofino and Genova. Prior to that time the American troops in Diecimo began to dismantle the facilities at the railroad station and some of the squads in the nearby villages were pulled out to join other forces pushing toward northern Italy. Many of our new friends came by our house to say goodbye although they couldn't tell us their destination. We could sense that something big was going to happen. The front line around Barga remained stationary throughout the winter months, since the cold and rainy weather made it difficult for any troop movement. We occasionally heard artillery fire in the distance and saw large numbers of aircraft flying toward northern Italy and Germany. After Christmas, during the month of January, a German airplane dropped several bombs in our area during the night. The bombs landed in the river bed and in some of the fields nearby. A few landed on some of the houses in the village. We had just gone to bed, after spending the evening with G.I.s in our home, when we heard airplanes overhead, and the whistling noise of bombs being dropped, followed by explosions. We looked out our rear window and saw the explosions along the river bed and we could only hope that the Germans would not come back and drop more bombs on the village. Fortunately no one was injured by the bombing.

The following day we discovered a live bomb directly behind our house, by the chapel of the *Madonna del Carmine*, but fortunately it did not explode. My mother was convinced that it was due to a miracle, that the *Madonna* had protected us! The bomb left a huge hole in the ground, and I peered over the edge, I saw part of the bomb protruding from the dirt that it moved in plunging into the soft ground. When the American soldiers learned of the unexploded bomb, they came to examine the hole, warning people not to go near it and placing a small barrier around it. Later a bomb removal squad came to disarm and remove the bomb. I have always felt that we were indeed lucky and that perhaps the *Madonna* really had protected us. Our kitchen and bedrooms were in direct line with the hole, and if the bomb had exploded we would have suffered major damage and serious injuries.

The next day, several friends and I walked out to the river to examine the bomb craters from the night bombing. The craters were very large, probably eight to ten feet in diameter and six to eight feet deep. We walked down into the various craters collecting shrapnel fragments as souvenirs to bring home to show our parents. I was amazed at the quantity of steel fragments around the craters. We all felt very lucky that we were not near one of these explosions, otherwise we would have certainly been killed by any of those jagged pieces of steel.

Shortly thereafter an incident happened in Borgo a Mozzano which affected me all my life. One afternoon my friends and I were in Piazza when someone came by on a bike saying there was a terrible truck accident in Borgo. We mounted our bikes and rode the 3 kilometers to Borgo a Mozzano as fast as we could. As we approached the slight uphill road leading to the railroad crossing, we saw a large number of people looking over the stone wall down into the rocky river bed. We leaned our bikes against the wall and looked over the edge. The sight of the wreckage startled us. There were about 15 to 20 people lying on the rocky surface below, some appeared dead, while others were bleeding and screaming for help. Lying partially on top of the people was an overturned U.S. Army truck.

What evidently happened was that the open bed truck, full of Italian people from the Barga area being transported away from the front lines, was traveling at a high speed. Tragically the G.I truck driver was not aware of the sharp 90 degree turn in the road. The truck continued straight ahead, hitting the low stone retaining wall and catapulting all the people down onto the rocks. The truck and driver continued down, falling on top of the people. Shortly after we arrived, U.S. Army vehicles drove up and the soldiers tried to sort out the wreckage and to help the people. I was especially shocked in seeing the horrible sight of the dead people while the injured ones kept screaming: "*Aiuto, aiuto...*," (Help, help...).

I felt helpless, as there was nothing I could do. I learned that as one lives in a war zone, one becomes accustomed to death and treats death indifferently, unless someone close dies. I saw the bodies of the German soldiers piled up in the two trucks after the airplane raid on the bridge at Diecimo and knew that one could die without any warning.

During the time that the U.S. soldiers were in Diecimo, they seemed eager to help the people by giving them food and clothing. Unfortunately there were also things going on that were not legal, namely the black market operation. Some American soldiers sold army clothing to Italians for money or in exchange for wine and *grappa*. Some of the items sold were army shirts, jackets, pants, leather boots, and woolen blankets. The Italians dealing in the black market then sold the items at inflated prices to other people. The winter months were cold and there was not enough wood for heating the homes, so the woolen garments and blankets were popular items. People used clothes dye to disguise the army clothing. Blankets were cut up and used to make jackets and overcoats. In addition, American cigarettes and pipe tobacco, very popular with Italian men, were easily available on the black market. There was a shortage of cash in Italy, so black market items were also traded for jewelry and food products. Some of the local villagers who dealt in black market products had to be very secretive about their deals, because the Military Police was always patrolling, on the look-out for soldiers and civilians who were involved with the black market.

One day, in the early spring, the Military Police conducted a raid on Diecimo. At around 10 o'clock in the morning several U. S. Army trucks and jeeps loaded with Military Police entered the *piazza* and methodically went to most of the homes in the village, including ours. They searched the houses and confiscated all the U.S. Army material they found. Fortunately, except for a few items, we did not have anything to hide. I had a well-worn military jacket and wool knit cap which were taken from me, and they also discovered a few cans of army food given to us by soldiers. The M.P.s let us keep the food, perhaps because we spoke English and we also told them that we were American citizens and needed the food. After the soldiers left, I walked to the piazza and to other areas of the village and was surprised at the large amount of clothing, boots and blankets recovered and loaded into trucks. Apparently G.I.s stole the clothing from supply depots and then went into different villages to sell them. I don't remember whether the Military Police arrested the Italians caught with Army materials. It seemed that they were only concerned with the recovery of the materials and that the raid was to serve as a warning to people that they should not engage in black market activities.

As we progressed into the spring and summer of 1945 the village people began to return to their normal activities. After the Germans surrendered in May, the Italian men in the Italian army or taken prisoners by the Germans began to return home and to recount their war stories. Some had been taken to German labor camps; some had escaped to France and Switzerland, while others had escaped from camps in Yugoslavia, remaining there until they could return home. The fate of the *Alpini* soldiers fighting on the Russian front remained a mystery, and no one ever heard from them again.

Most children were out of school during the previous year and a half with little to do except to assist their familes in working the fields and to socialize with their friends in the evenings. The governmental agencies planned to re-open the schools in the fall of 1945. There were still quite a few *sfollati* in Diecimo, but as reconstruction began in some of the coastal cities, such as Livorno and Pisa, they gradually began to return home. My friend Mauro, his mother and sisters remained until September, while his father returned to Livorno during the summer to resume his work. Mauro was a good friend, very sociable and we had a very enjoyable summer. I hated to see him leave.

The social activities in the summer varied depending on what was available in the village and what was within bicyling distance. After the rainy winter the Serchio river was flowing well that year and there were several spots that were deep enough to use for swimming. As the river wound its way through the valley it slowed down and formed itself into small ponds, several of which were about ten feet deep. One favorite spot was the one which paralleled the *scogliera*, which was an arrangement of rocks placed in such a way to form a breakwater to prevent the river from flooding the agricultural fields. It was possible to dive from the top of the *scogliera*, avoid a couple of sharp boulders in the river, and land in the deep cool water. Most kids found diving from the top of the barrier very challenging as they tried to avoid the rocks in the river below. We could see quite a few trout in the river but we did not have any fishing poles or lines to fish off the river bank.

Several men had secretly taken explosives when the German land mines were being disarmed and hid them from the Allies, planning to use them later on. The *tritolo*, or T.N.T., was used by many men for fishing in the rivers. This was illegal, but people used the method when they needed food. The men placed a fuse and detonator cap in a small block of T.N.T., lit the fuse and hurled it into the river. The T.N.T. sank to the bottom, then exploded under water, shooting a huge column of water in the air. The explosion sent shock waves through the water killing all the fish in the immediate area, and within a few minutes the dead fish rose to the surface of the water and floated down stream. As the dead fish floated to the surface, the children dove in and scooped them up. Unfortunately, the explosions killed all the fish, large and small, thus depleting the river of fish for the future. I never handlef the T.N.T. because I didn't have access to it and also because I felt that it was dangerous.

One of the boys who was about three years older than I was, named Gigi, lost his left hand when he was holding a handful of detonator caps. Gigi was trying to de-activate the caps by removing the small lid using a small cavity in a rock wall to pry the lid off. Unfortunately he was holding several caps in the same hand when one exploded, thus causing the others caps to explode, resulting in the loss of his entire hand to a point just above the wrist. My friend Angelo Catelani was standing near Gigi watching him, and to this day still remembers the shock and fear he felt as the caps

exploded. Gigi took off, running toward his house, screaming in pain, hoping to find someone to help him.

I was 15 years old in the summer of 1945 and began to
notice girls and to enjoy their company. Several girls in the
village were about my age, some of whom came to Diecimo
during the period of time that families were forced to leave
the big cities to escape coastal bombings.

Ione Menesini, from Lucca, was in Diecimo with her
mother and father. They lived in the *Piazza*, in a large three
story house belonging to the Menesini family for years.
There was also a trio of rich teenage girls from Viareggio
whom we called *le Tripoline* because they lived in Tripoli
before the war, who lived near Ione with their aunt and
uncle. Ione had four cousins, three of whom were close to
my age. We called them *le ragazze del Domini*, (the girls of
the Domini, which was their last name); their names were
Soave, Landa, Francesca, and Maria. There were also Mara
Coli, Ernestina Ambrogi, Alfea Agostinelli, and the Pierini
girls, Nora, Giuliana, Dora and Teresina. Late in the
evening, after dinner, the boys gathered in *piazza* and
started to walk in the street, walking the entire length of the
village; this was called *fare la passeggiata*. We walked toward
Zandori at the north end of the village, then back to the
piazza, continuing down *il Piastrone* and finally to the
wreckage of the bridge, destroyed the previous summer and
not yet rebuilt. The girls also went for a *passeggiata*, hoping
to meet up with the boys. As the evening progressed, we
eventually got together and visited near the bridge, talking
until after midnight.

During the summer of 1945 the theaters in Borgo a
Mozzano and Bagni di Lucca re-opened and started to show
old movies. We rode our bikes to the movies and at times,
if we were traveling in a group, some of the girls rode with
the boys on their bicycles, sitting across the metal bar on the
bicycle that connected the rear support to the front part of

the bike. Even though many of the local priests objected, the theaters showed the movies on Sunday afternoons. Dances were sometimes held in Borgo a Mozzano after the afternoon movies in the courtyard below the movie theater.

One Sunday afternoon Mauro, Umberto, Piero, Dino and I went to see a movie in Borgo a Mozzano. After the movie was over we stopped by the dance floor and watched the couples dancing. We talked about dancing and felt that it would be nice if we knew how to dance because it might be easier to meet girls. My friend Mauro was much more socially advanced than we were because of his experiences in Livorno. He smoked and also knew how to dance. After attending the movie with us, he went down to the dance floor and asked some of the girls to dance. We really envied him and wished we could do the same, but we had to be satisfied with merely watching and imagining what it would be like to dance while holding a girl in our arms.

A few days later, several boys asked Mauro if he could teach us how to dance and he agreed to to teach us. We started our lessons by dancing with Mauro as he took us through the basic dance steps without music, because there were no radios or phonographs. Since it was summer, we danced barefoot on the cool red brick floor in his house. I remember that at the end of our lessons the bottoms of my feet were red from the color wash that people painted on the brick floors. We wanted to keep our dancing activities a secret from our parents, because, according to the priest, dancing was a sin, and young people were not supposed to dance. After the dance lessons, on my way home, I stopped by the fountain in piazza to wash my feet. The thought of dancing with girls in the near future was very exciting and was the major topic of discussions with my friends. We started to plan for a dancing party but finding a location was a major problem.

Some of us had old 78 rpm records since before the war, featuring mostly Italian singers popular in the 1930's. In the past year some GIs had records featuring popular American dance bands, by Glenn Miller, Tommy Dorsey, Artie Shaw and Harry James and left them behind for us. A few families had radios, and we had a beautiful radio-phonograph combination. In preparation for our return to the United States and because of our lack of money, my father started to sell off some of our possessions. One of the first items to go was our radio-phonograph, which survived the war because it was hidden in the now famous walled-up room in the house of our tenant farmer. Ironically my father sold the radio to Paolo Menesini, the father of Ione, the girl to whom I was attracted. Because they moved the radio to their house in Lucca, it was not available for our party.

Ione convinced her mother to let us use her house for the dance and secured the help of the Domini girls to prepare the food for our dinner party. She thought that it might be nice to have *tordelli* for the main course. We all tried to get the necessary ingredients for the *tordelli* and made plans to bring the items to Ione for the preparation of the meal. Some people brought flour, some contributed bits of meat or chard, and I furnished some red wine for the dinner.

Meanwhile we were trying to locate a phonograph and records for the dance portion of the evening. I found out that the people who lived across the street from us, the Luchi family, had a hand cranked portable phonograph. I told them that my mother and father wanted to listen to some records and since we did not have our radio any more, I asked if they could lend us their phonograph for a few days. Elda Luchi, one of the daughters, said that it would be all right to borrow the phonograph, but not to damage it. I said that I would take full responsibility and I would be very careful. The dinner-dance would soon become a reality because we had now a phonograph!

About 20 came, and I was very pleased to be with Ione for the evening. Ione and the Domini girls set up a long table in the large *sala* in the front of the house which faced the *piazza*. Ione and her mother Paola did most of the cooking. The *tordelli* were served with a tasty tomato sauce accompanied by bread and vegetables. Even though we were teenagers, wine was served with dinner. As the dinner progressed and we drank more wine, we became relaxed and lost some of our inhibitions in preparation for the scary part of the evening, dancing with a girl, instead of Mauro.

After clearing the table and washing the dishes, we moved the table out of the way and set up the phonograph. Someone got a few American band records, which provided a variety of music for dancing. We each paired off with our favorite girl and began to dance. I explained to Ione that the only other person I ever danced with was my friend Mauro, and that I needed help. She was very understanding. We held on to each other until she began to guide me through simple fox-trot steps. I enjoyed dancing with her, holding her and moving to the rhythm of the music. Mauro had been a good teacher because all of the boys were doing well on the dance floor, either because of the lessons, or because of the wine, or a combination of both.

The music was quite danceable and we each took turns cranking the phonograph so that we would have continuous music during the evening. Although electricity was restored, people still used very low wattage bulbs. The atmosphere was pleasant, and the light low enough to give us privacy. Because of the ambience of the evening and the romantic low light level, the boys and girls occasionally paused at the end of a song and briefly kissed. While walking home well after midnight, I felt elated from the experience. I had a really great time with Ione, and felt that I was in love!

The following day I returned the phonograph to Elda and thanked her very much for the use. Elda mentioned she heard that some young people in Diecimo had a dance in one of the homes. She wondered if I was there and if I had used her phonograph. I assured her that the phonograph was only used in my home, listening to our records (a lie). I was amazed how swiftly gossip traveled. The next Sunday at Mass, the main topic of the sermon by *Pievano* Don Udone Diodati was dancing. He also heard that several boys and girls had danced together in one of the homes to recorded music, and was appalled at this activity he considered a mortal sin. He said that the boys and girls at the dance would have to confess their sins before receiving communion, saying how horrible it was for people to dance and that music and dancing would surely lead people to hell. I sat in the pew with my friends, glancing at each other sheepishly, but saying nothing. We suspected the priest knew who attended the party and that he would really lay into us in the confessional. I quickly decided not to confess because I did not consider it to be wrong; it was part of life, and I knew that dancing was a popular activity in the United States. Why should dancing be a sin in Italy and not in the United States?

As I grew older I had become aware of the opposite sex and began to like girls. Since we were in an agricultural village, we were accustomed to the sexual interchange between animals and we assumed that the same occurred between humans. There was no discussion about sex in the schools, and, of course, no discussion whatsoever from our parents. Books on sex were unknown; so, most of what we learned was by hearsay from the older boys--the experts!

When the German troops were in the area, there was talk that the Germans were having intercourse or making love with some of the women in the village. The term used was *fare l'amore*, and of course we knew what that meant.

We were often present when bulls were brought in to service cows in some of the barns, so we suspected that similar things went on with men and women in the homes or out in the fields during the summer. We also suspected which girls or women might be *doing it* with the soldiers, but we never did observe any of them in action.

When the American troops arrived, the same kind of interaction took place between the black soldiers and Italian women. We figured it was part of human nature, once again trying to guess who were *doing it*. We also noticed that when the military facilities set up at the railway station, several tents were erected in the freight yard as sleeping quarters. On several occasions, girls from other villages visited the soldiers. The women traveled in groups of two or three, but entered the tents individually while different soldiers went in and out of the tents. When the women emerged from the tents, after their activity, they always seemed flushed in the face. We always talked about the women and assumed that part of the love-making process involved getting overheated.

At times, soldiers unfamiliar with our village stopped by in their vehicles and asked us if there were girls to *fick-e-fick*, which at first was hard to understand. (I later found out that what I had interpreted as *fick-e-fick* was the American term *fuck-fuck*). It seemed that the soldiers assumed that we knew where the local women lived. Even though we suspected several in our village, we never gave specific directions to their houses.

At this time I was fairly well versed in the meanings of Italian *bad words* and at times, with my friends, used them in our conversations or stories. Since I left the United States when I was nine years old, I was not exposed to any *bad* American words in Massachusetts. When I eventually found out the meaning of the word *fuck*, so frequently used by soldiers, I did not think it proper to use it.

Another expression used by the soldiers was *son of a bitch*. I did not know the meaning of the phrase or what *bitch* meant. In fact, I mistook it for *beach*. After hearing the expression, I asked my mother the meaning in Italian:

"Mamma, what does the word *son* mean?"

"You know that word, Tullio, it means son, that you are the son of your father."

"What does *beach* mean?"

"Beach means a place near the shore of the ocean, where people go to swim and sun bathe."

"Then, what does *son of a beach* mean?"

"Tullio, *son of a beach* is a bad word and you should not use the expression, it is not nice!"

As I grew older, I wondered why *son of a beach* was such a bad word. Of course, somewhere along the line in my American education I found out that the word was not *beach* but *bitch* and then I knew why the term was a bad expression to use. When I hear the expression *son of a bitch* I think back to the day when I asked my mother about the *son of a beach* and how she managed to avoid the question and yet impressed on me that she did not want me to use vulgar language.

After the Allied troops left, people returned to their normal lives. There was an effort to re-establish the regional government in Lucca and the Comune of Borgo a Mozzano held elections for the first time, including the election of a Mayor. Antonio Tonelli, from Diecimo, was re-elected Mayor and he, along with the rest of the elected representatives, tried to re-establish governmental services for the people. There were still serious food shortages; meat, olive oil, bread and sugar were still not available, but a few seasonal vegetables and fruits gradually began to appear in the stores. People in Diecimo raised chickens and rabbits for their own consumption, but the butcher shop remained closed most of the time. People started to repair the damage to their homes caused by the artillery shells and bombs dropped in the area. Celestino Pierini and his sons

Beppe and Pier Luigi, the local stone masons, were busy with the repairs and managed to work even though it was difficult to secure cement.

The *contadini* began to plan their crops for the year, planting wheat and vegetable gardens in the spring. At that time the spading of the soil was done by hand because there were neither tractors nor animals to pull the plows. The type of shovel used to spade the ground was called a *vanga*. The *vanga* was a very large steel shovel about twice the size of a typical American shovel, shaped to a sharp point and more flat than curved. The *vanga* was affixed to a long wooden handle with a steel foot push rod emerging at right angles from the handle directly above the top of the metal blade. The steel rod could be positioned so that it was on the left side or the right side of the handle to facilitate the digging action. The proper action was to place the blade of the *vanga* so that it would cut approximately two inches of turf. Then one pushed on the steel push rod with his foot forcing the blade to go down to a depth of approximately a foot. The handle was then placed across the upper leg, directly above the knee, and with a rotating motion one lifted the clump of turf and flipped it over in front of an already established track. When the fields were ready for spading the men in the village rose at daybreak, ate their usual breakfasts of bread and *caffè e latte*, then set out for the fields carrying their *vanghe* on their shoulders and *fiaschi* of wine in their hands. When they reached the fields they started the process of turning over the turf. The fields were overgrown with left-over crops, weeds, or grass. The men started by establishing a *tacca*, which translated into English is a notch, nick or cut. The dirt removed from the *tacca* was scooped out and thrown further ahead, while the notch went across the width of the field to be spaded.

The men spaced themselves out across the field, perhaps 8 or 10 feet apart and started to dig. As the day progressed one could watch from a distance as the field turned from a rough green or yellow mess into an orderly arrangement of dark brown overturned clods of dirt. Most of the men worked at the same pace and the rhythm of the movement of the shovels was like a synchronized slow-moving dance. The men continued their work, taking time out for a mid-morning *spuntino*, or snack, and drinking an occasional sip of wine until mid-day. Then they went home for their noon meal and rested for a couple of hours. If the work was being done in the summer months, they returned to work later in the afternoon when the day became cooler and continued to work until dusk or until the fields were completely dug and ready to be raked.

I sometimes went along with the men and boys of our tenant farmers, the Giambastiani and the Piacentini families, and tried to help with the digging. At first I was enthusiastic about being able to help and enjoyed the work until I developed blisters on my hands and along my leg. I found the work very hard and thought to myself that I was not cut out to be a farmer. I will have to admit that the few agricultural skills that I learned in Diecimo did help me out in later life when working in my yard and garden.

The summer passed quickly as most of the people in the village tried to resume their normal routines. The train tracks and bridges were repaired so that by the early fall train service was re-established between the Serchio River Valley and Lucca. People began to harvest some of their crops and we enjoyed fresh fruit such as cherries, peaches, plums, and grapes. We also had plenty of vegetables and the corn crop looked promising. The chestnut trees provided an abundant crop so that we had *ballociori* and *mondine* in the months of October and November.

As I mentioned earlier, my parents were anxious to leave Italy and to get back to the United States. We were informed that we probably would be able to leave sometime during the winter, but we were not given a specific date. Due to the fact that my father did not have any money for our trip, he made plans to borrow money from my uncle Nello. Nello, as a parish priest, seemed to have more money than my uncle Dante, who was a *contadino*. The priests at that time supervised the agricultural property that belonged to the parish; therefore Nello was able to sell a large part of the olive oil which was produced by his *contadino*. In order to raise money for the trip my father also started to sell most of our household furnishings. Eventually, just before leaving, he sold the Boston bedroom set to Uncle Nello, along with the dining room set. We gave some of our kitchen furniture to Dante.

On September 14, 1945, the city of Lucca prepared to renew the annual celebration of the feast of *Santa Croce*, discontinued during the war. A reduced number of activities, including a shorter version of the religious procession that brought the *Volto Santo* through the streets of Lucca, were planned. The *Volto Santo* was a statue of Christ, carved from ebony, which was permanently displayed in the Cathedral of San Martino and was carried in a procession, called the *Luminaria*, from the church of San Frediano to the Cathedral through the streets of Lucca. The name *Luminaria* makes reference to the procession in which people walked a route through the darkened streets of Lucca carrying lighted candles. I did not go to Lucca very often, although it was only 16 kilometers away and I never saw any of the *Santa Croce* festivities.

Ione Menesini moved back to Lucca with her parents, in preparation for the re-opening of the schools. They lived in a flat above her father's tailor shop, *Sartoria Menesini*, on Corte Portici, near Piazza San Michele. The *Santa Croce* activities actually started the week before September 14 when the merchants of the city featured special food products which they sold from open air stands set up in

Piazza San Michele, such as the *buccellato di Lucca* (special cake from Lucca). Ione invited me to visit her during the time of *Santa Croce* and made arrangements for me to stay at her home overnight.

I rode my bicycle to Lucca, entered Porta Giannotti and easily located Ione's home. I was greeted by her mother, Paola, and was shown around the flat. I was told to sleep in the living room on the couch (right next to the radio-phonograph my father sold to them). In the afternoon, Ione and I went for a walk around Lucca, to Piazza San Michele, along Via Fillungo, around Piazza Napoleone, and we looked at some of the displays that vendors put up for the *Santa Croce festa*.

Ione's friend, Piera, owned a small hotel called *Albergo dell'Uovo*. Piera invited Ione and me for dinner at the restaurant. Around 7:30 we walked to the hotel and were served a very delicious dinner at a small table for two in the main dining room. We talked about the times in Diecimo and how much we enjoyed the summer. Ione made plans to attend school in Lucca at the end of September. I talked about my return to California instead of returning to Boston. After our meal we went to a movie. Some of the movie theaters in Lucca had re-opened and they usually showed old American movies dubbed in Italian. We walked to the theater, purchased our tickets and got good seats because the theater was not crowded. The movie was *Seventh Heaven* with Janet Gaynor and Charles Farrell. It was a love story and I thought Janet Gaynor was very pretty. Ione and I enjoyed it very much even though the film seemed to be more adult than one for teenagers.

After the theater, we walked slowly, our arms linked together (*a braccietto*), through the streets of Lucca, toward Corte Portici. We talked about our future and wondered what would become of us. Ione was looking forward to continuing school and said that she would like to become an elementary school teacher. I talked about America, telling her I was a bit scared about my future. I did not know what to expect in the United States, except that I would go to a high school in California.

We walked slowly across the deserted *piazza*, stopping in the shadows of the church of San Michele. Placing my hands on Ione's shoulders, I pulled her toward me. Looking into her eyes, I said:

"Ione, I am going to miss you. I like you very much."

I lowered my head and kissed her on the lips. It was a short, inexperienced kiss, but very memorable.

We hugged each other, and Ione said: "We had better go home; my mother will be worried about us."

We held hands as we continued the short walk to her house. We entered at the street level and climbed the stairs, walked by the darkened tailor shop, and proceeded up to the Menesini flat. Ione's mother was up, waiting for us in the kitchen. She asked about our evening together, and was pleased to hear that we had a good time. Ione walked me to the living room and brought me a blanket and a pillow for the couch. She leaned over, kissed me on the cheek, and said: *"Buona notte, Tullio."*

"Buona notte, Ione", I replied. When she left the room, I removed my shoes, pants and shirt, and settled down on the couch, covering myself with the blanket, and fell asleep, dreaming about Ione and *Seventh Heaven*.

I promised Ione that I would write letters and maintain our friendship, and I did write. As I got involved with work, the flow of letters eventually stopped. Later, when traveling to Italy with my wife and children, I renewed my friendship with Ione and her husband Renato, who now live in Rome, have two grown children, spend most of the summers and holidays in Diecimo in the family house that Ione inherited from her parents. We still write letters to one another and look forward to spending time together when we visit Italy.

13.
COMING HOME TO AMERICA

During the time that I lived in Diecimo I had several opportunities to think about death. I remember the trucks passing under my bedroom window with bodies of dead German soldiers killed by British fighter planes. I remember seeing the bodies of Italian civilians escaping the front and killed when catapulted over the road while riding in an American military truck. I also remember some of the village people who died, including my grandmother Teresa Bertini, who died in 1945. Older people died, but not much was said about the reason for their death, whether it was a heart attack or other illness. It seemed that people did not want to talk about sickness or death.

I remember the way that some of the old people in the village degenerated into sickly looking figures and eventually dying. It was a custom for older people to bring chairs out of their homes in the late afternoon or early evening during the summer months and to sit by the front door. As people passed by they stopped to say hello and to engage in conversations about the weather, about the war, and about village gossip.

I was curious about death and did not really know why people died, unless it was from an accident or by a gunshot or a bomb. I specifically remember a woman named Silvia, who often sat on a chair in front of her house in the afternoons and evenings during the summer. She always wore a scarf that partially covered the left side of her face. Instead of wearing the scarf like other women, across her forehead, and tied below the chin, she draped it so that the cloth went down from her head, at an angle, covering her left eye and her left cheek. One day, as I was passing by her house, she was conversing with another woman and her scarf slipped down, exposing the part of her face that was always covered. I noticed that below her left eye there was a gaping hole that went deep into her cheek, about an inch and a half in diameter, reddish-brown, and looked horrible and painful. I was shocked at the sight! At the time, I was not aware of many of the diseases in the world, and in asking around why Silvia had the hole in her face, I was told that she had *quel malaccio* (a bad illness, which I found out many years later meant cancer). As time passed, the hole got larger and Silvia no longer sat outside her home. After a period of time, I read her death announcement posted on one of the village walls, as was the custom.

When I returned to the United States, in February 1946, I realized we are not immortal. Life seemed to be a series of events: first we are born, then live our lives as best as possible, and then die. Most deaths are painful, especially for those having *quel malaccio!*

Around the end of November 1945, we received a letter from the United States Consulate in Firenze notifying us that the date of our departure from Italy had been set for approximately the 20th of January 1946. We were scheduled to leave from Napoli on a ship that would take us to New York. Now that we had the departure date, we made specific plans to vacate the house and travel to Napoli. At that time some of the train tracks were rebuilt, so it was possible to travel from Lucca to Pisa and then from Pisa to Roma by train. The Roma-Napoli railroad line was not yet completed, but we were assured that we probably could travel by bus from Roma to Napoli. During our final days in Diecimo my parents decided to lease our house to the local veterinarian, Dottore Donati.

The Christmas 1945 holidays were soon upon us and we were aware that these would be our last holidays in Italy. We made plans to leave Diecimo around the 14th of January because of the uncertainties about our trip to Napoli. A local boy from the adjoining village of Valdottavo, named Roberto, was also scheduled to return to the United States. His father lived in New York, and had requested, through the American Consulate, for his son to return to New York. My father said he was welcome to travel with us to Napoli, that we would look after him. Roberto was two years older than I and it seemed we might be good company for each other on the trip.

Prior to departure we planned our wardrobe carefully because we would each have only one large suitcase and one small accessory bag. My mother and father still had old clothes that fit them. I was a growing boy, so some exceptions were made. Mario Mechetti, the village tailor, was able to get a small amount of fabric which he used to make me a dark gray double-breasted suit for the trip. My mother took apart an old overcoat belonging to my father and made it into a short coat for me. The fabric was wool tweed and kept me very warm. We went to the home of a black market dealer in Dezza where we traded a half sack of wheat for the only pair of shoes he had in my size. The shoes seemed to be American, perhaps pilfered from Red Cross shipments of clothing and shoes, and were made of brown leather with a thick red rubber sole. Most Italians wore woolen undershirts during the winter and my mother forced me to wear them too, although they were hand knit with locally produced coarse wool and were not very soft or comfortable against my skin. Boys and men wore boxer-type cotton shorts. Generally I wore my underwear for three or four days, and I would change my underwear after my weekly bath. For this trip I packed a few sets of underwear and socks, my new suit, and a few shirts. I wore a pair of woolen pants made from an old pair of my father's, and I had one woolen sweater which I wore under my coat.

On our departure day, prior to going to Lucca to catch our train for Napoli, we went to Pieve di Compito to say good-bye to my grandmother Serafina and my uncle Nello. Pieve di Compito is about 26 kilometers from Diecimo and at that time could not be reached by bus or by train, so we made arrangements with Brunero Piacentini to take us there the morning of our departure in his old APE--a three-wheeled motorcycle propelled vehicle. The front part of the APE consisted of the front wheel and handlebars of a typical motorcycle and the driver sat on the motorcycle seat. The front was covered by a large windshield to protect the driver from the rain, and it also had a small seat beside the driver. The back part was like a small truck bed, with a canvas canopy, spanning the two rear wheels. My father sat alongside Brunero, while Roberto, my mother and I sat in the back portion of the APE along with our suitcases. We left Diecimo around nine in the morning on a cold rainy day and stopped by Pastino to say good-bye to my grandfather Davino, my uncle Dante, his wife Massima, and my two cousins Leonello and Dino. I said good-bye to my friends the day before and felt sad leaving Diecimo because it was my home for six and a half years. I did not know if I would ever return to Italy or see Ione again.

The APE was not very roomy and the roads were very bumpy making our trip to Pieve di Compito quite uncomfortable. After what seemed to be an eternity, we finally arrived in Pieve di Compito where we were treated to a farewell lunch and had a pleasant visit with my uncle and my grandmother. I am certain that my uncle Nello gave my father some additional Italian money for the trip, because they spent some time talking privately in my uncle's office.

In the late afternoon we left Pieve di Compito and continued our trip toward Lucca to the railroad station.

When we arrived I was really thankful we were able to get out of the tight quarters in the APE. We said good-bye to Brunero and made our way into the station. We took the train to Pisa, then waited for the night train to Roma, scheduled to leave at 11 p.m. We did not have seat reservations because at that time there were no reserved seats on trains and one hoped for the best. The train ride from Lucca to Pisa was short and fortunately the train was not very crowded. We arrived in Pisa around 8:30 and waited about two hours for the train to Roma.

The train originated in Milano, then went to Genova, and traveled down the coast to Pisa. By the time it pulled into the Pisa station, the train was jammed with people. We climbed aboard and were confronted with extremely crowded conditions. The seats were full and the aisles packed with people standing while holding their suitcases between their legs. My mother, who was a very small person, was able to squeeze in on a seat between two kind people who made room for her. Roberto, my father and I remained standing for the entire trip. Occasionally, we straddled our suitcase and sat on it for a while, but the seating was unsteady and it was easy to topple over. The train followed the coast down to Roma, stopping in Livorno, Grosseto, and other cities. As the first light of dawn emerged, we looked out the windows and saw that we were in the outskirts of Roma. I saw many homes and buildings destroyed by bombs and not yet reconstructed. When the train finally stopped in Roma, the people who stood all night carefully left the train. Once on the platform, they started to stretch and walk around to loosen their muscles. Our little group gathered in one place, took inventory of our suitcases and ourselves, and made preliminary plans to try to find transportation to Napoli. My father spoke with one of the employees at the railroad station, asking if he could direct us to a bus station so that we could find transportation to Napoli. The man said there were two buses that left Roma each day, one in the morning and one in the afternoon. He said that we should go to the bus station, located across the piazza from the railroad station, and if we were lucky we still might have time to catch the morning bus. We gathered our suitcases and quickly walked across the piazza to the bus station. When my father went in to inquire, he discovered that the morning bus had left, but there was another bus that would leave at four p.m. He purchased four tickets, assuring us each a seat on the four o'clock bus. Since there wasn't much to do in the area, and we did not have the proper winter clothes or shoes for the month of January, we thought it best to stay inside the bus station, protected from the cold weather outside. I had never been in Roma but was aware of the historical background of the city, having studied its ancient history in school and also knew about the recent king, Vittorio Emanuale III of the Savoia family. We also studied Fascism and saw pictures of the *Palazzo Venezia* with the balcony from which Benito Mussolini gave his speeches, and the Tomb of the Unknown Soldier directly across from the *Palazzo Venezia*. Though we were in Roma, we had no interest in seeing any of the sights. We were exhausted from the train ride and preoccupied with the necessity of getting to Napoli.

The bus was on schedule and shortly after four o'clock we began our journey south to Napoli. The ride was slow and in the countryside we continued to see the devastation from the war. Napoli was a very busy city because it was one of the major ports for the Allied armies and there were a lot of military people stationed there. We arrived late in the evening, around 9 p.m. After we got off the bus at the centrally located bus station, we inquired about finding an inexpensive *pensione* (boarding house) nearby. We were directed to one with a vacancy and made arrangements to rent one room until the departure date, January 20. The room had two small beds and we once again adapted to the situation. Roberto and I shared one bed, my mother and father the other. There was a wash stand in the room, with a wash basin and pitcher of water. The bathroom was down the hall and shared by all the people staying in the *pensione*. The room fee also included a breakfast of *caffè e latte*, *pranzo* (lunch) at 12:30, and *cena* (supper) at 8:00 p.m. That night we settled in our narrow beds and fell asleep without any problems. It had been a long day!

The next morning, we left the *pensione* and walked around the area to see if we could find the port and inquire about our departure. Fortunately it was a nice day and the sun was shining. We asked for directions and started to walk toward the port. We discovered that it was a long way from our *pensione*, but we did not have anything else to do, so we continued walking until we arrived at the port. My father made some inquiries and was able to speak with someone of authority who told him that our ship was going to be the *Gripsholm*, a Swedish ship, and that the departure was scheduled for January 20 in the early afternoon. The port official said that we should come back on the 19th to verify the departure time. We felt elated at the prospect of finally leaving Italy and returning to the United States. We still had a few days to spend in Napoli, so we made the best of the situation. While the weather was nice, we did a lot of walking around the port area. One afternoon we went to a movie theater and saw a movie with John Wayne and Marlene Dietrich titled *Seven Sinners* about the U.S. Navy in the South Seas. The film was dubbed in Italian. We enjoyed the movie, a pleasant diversion which took our minds off the the fact that we were alone in a big city.

On January 20, after our morning *caffè e latte* we gathered our suitcases and made arrangements to take a taxi cab to the dock. The taxi was very small, but we managed to squeeze inside. Our luggage pieces fit in the trunk, while the small bags were carried on our laps. Once we arrived at the dock we were left in an area close to the ship along with hundreds of other people standing in line with their suitcases. To me the ship appeared to be huge compared to the *Vulcania*, which was the ship that we took from New York to Italy in 1939. I later found out that the ship was the first large diesel driven trans-Atlantic liner and that the ship was used by the United States as a hospital ship to bring U.S. soldiers back to the United States after the end of the war in Europe. The passengers on this voyage were United States citizens trapped in Europe by the war and unable to return home. The payment for the trip was deferred until we got home and was to be paid to the State Department after we arrived in California.

After standing in line for what seemed to be hours, we were allowed to board the ship, and as we stopped at the boarding check-point we were given cabin assignments. The authorities had decided to allocate the first and second class cabins to women and female children. All the men and boys were placed in cabins in the third class, which were at or below the water level near the engines in the lower part of the ship. We were given identification slips which listed our name, cabin number, dining room number, seating time and table number. My father, Roberto, and I were assigned to the same cabin. The cabin had three beds, one lower bed on each side of the room, and one folding bed above one of the lower beds. Inside the cabin there was also a very small bathroom with a shower, toilet, wash basin with a mirror obove it, and a small amount of closet space. Of course there were no port holes in the cabin because we were at or below the water level. My father took one of the lower beds, I took the top folding bed, and Roberto took the other lower bed. By mid-afternoon we were settled in our cabin and as soon as we had everything stowed away, we went out to take an exploratory walk around the ship.

Even though we were assigned to the third class cabins we had access to the entire ship. We discovered the inside lounges with large comfortable chairs and couches, and we found and walked around the lounge areas on the perimeter of the ship, which were also furnished with tables and chairs and had a panoramic view of the ocean through large rectangular glass windows. The tables were starting to get filled, mostly by men, some of whom were already engaged in card games. We discovered a ship's store with displays of American candy bars, American cigarettes, Coca-Cola bottles, bags of Planters peanuts, and other assorted items. The items were protected by a metal security screen with a sign which indicated the store would open one hour after sailing and that the currency to be used on the ship was to be U.S. currency. My father had kept a few dollars from 1939, but the bulk of our money was in Italian lire, so eventually we would have to change the money so that we could make purchases in the store. The items of interest to me were candy bars and Coca-Cola; those of interest to my father were the cartons of American cigarettes.

Roberto and I left the comfort of the interior of the ship and walked outside on the deck by the life boats. It was cold and overcast on that January day in Napoli. We noticed that the dockside workers were making preparations for our departure, and we knew that soon we would be underway on our trip back to the United States. The *Gripsholm* was scheduled to go from Napoli to Marseilles to pick up other United States citizens who were being repatriated. We found out that the ship had started its journey in Greece, gone to Egypt and then to Napoli. Roberto and I remained on deck, watching all the preparations and remaining there as the ship pulled out of port. As I looked back toward Napoli with Mount Vesuvius in the background and as we made our way out to sea, I thought about the day that we left Boston in July 1939 aboard the *Vulcania*, how we managed to survive the war and now we were going home.

We re-entered the warmth of the lounges and walked around to explore the other compartments of the ship. I noticed that there were several teen-agers on the ship who spoke English. I said hello to a few boys and girls and began asking about their background and where they had boarded the ship. I found out that some of the teenagers had boarded the ship in Greece, and some had boarded in Alexandria, Egypt. Unfortunately Roberto did not speak a word of English, so he felt out of place. He decided to go out to the card playing lounge and hang around with the Italian speaking men. I remember that I met Dorothy Anas and her brother Vincent from Greece and Beverly Reed from Springdale, Arkansas, who was traveling with her mother and father and had boarded the ship in Alexandria. I also met several Italian young people who had boarded at Naples: they were Angelo Antonacci, Tosca Pampaleoni, and Lucy Pellegrini.

My father, my mother and I were assigned to have our meals at the second seating time, and the time for our first dinner was 8:00 p.m. We were assigned a table against the side of the ship, with a port hole by our table. I was surprised by the elegance of the dining room. The tables were set with white tablecloths and napkins, silverware, attractive glassware, and there were menus placed by each setting. After having survived the war years, and not having had much food for the past three or four years, we were amazed at the offerings on the menu. There was a soup listing, two or three main course choices, two desserts, one of which was ice cream, and coffee, tea or cocoa. Our waiter was a Swedish man in his thirties who spoke English very well. I don't remember the food that I ordered that first night, but I do remember that it was good and plentiful. I specifically remember that I ordered ice cream for dessert. The waiter catered to me that evening and for the rest of the trip. He always brought me a second dish of ice cream, because he said that he enjoyed seeing me eat all the food that was given to me, and how much I savored the ice cream. The next morning we were given a complete breakfast menu, with choices of bread, butter, jam, juices, fruit, cereal, eggs and bacon, and coffee, tea or hot chocolate. I could not believe the amount of food that was available, but during the trip we still followed the Italian custom for breakfast: bread and jam with our *caffè e latte*.

We arrived in Marseilles the next day for a short stop. A small group of passengers boarded the ship and as soon as they were boarded we pulled out to sea. We were finally on our way to the United States! According to the daily newsletter published by the ship we were scheduled to travel down near the Spanish coast to the Straits of Gibraltar and then across the Atlantic Ocean to New York. Included among the French people who boarded the *Gripsholm* were a few teenagers, including a cute girl named Brigitte. The English speaking teenagers aboard the ship formed an enjoyable social group which usually gathered around the lounges during the daytime and in the evenings. One day, as we were exploring the large ship, we took the elevator down to one of the lower decks to the swimming pool. As the elevator door opened we found ourselves on the deck of the indoor swimming pool. Although it was winter, the water was heated, so we swam several times while we were traveling in the Atlantic waters, which were very rough during the month of January. The ship bobbed up and down, and as the water level in the pool followed the movement of the ship, water overflowed onto the deck on one end, while becoming shallow on the other end.

Since we had a mixed crowd we had to be prudent about wearing the proper swimming attire, because most of us did not come equipped with bathing suits. The boys improvised by wearing underwear that did not have the typical buttons or openings down the front, while the girls were able to use one piece knitted woolen bathing suits furnished by the ship. While in Italy I had done a lot of swimming in the Serchio River but only knew one type of swimming stroke, the breast stroke. I enjoyed swimming, but I had never swum in a pool or in salt water. After swimming in the pool for a short time I discovered that I did not enjoy the salt water entering my mouth, nose and eyes. I did notice that I was able to float on the surface of the water much better than in fresh water. We had a lot of fun swimming in the pool and as the trip progressed the group became very friendly with one other and smaller groups were formed, based on the boy-girl interaction. I liked to be around Beverly Reed and Dorothy Anas because they were charming and friendly. Beverly was about my age, while Dorothy was 18 years old.

After we were underway, the ship's store opened for business. I did not have any money for personal expenses, but I convinced my father to give me a few dollars so that I could purchase some of the candy bars and bottles of Coca-Cola that were for sale. During the war in Italy the supply of sugar was limited and rationed so that chocolate candy and the hard candy known as *caramelle* were not available in stores. After the American soldiers arrived, they gave away chocolate bars to the children and for the first time in years I was able to treat my sweet tooth. When I saw all the types of candy bars in the ship store, I could not believe my eyes. It reminded me of the days when I went to the Saturday movies in Brighton. There were Baby Ruth's, O'Henry's, Hershey bars, Wrigley chewing gum on display and they were only 5 cents apiece! It is difficult to remember how many candy bars I bought each day, but it was quite a few. I probably gained ten pounds or more during the trip, because of all the candy, the good food, and the ice cream that our Swedish waiter served me.

Our group of teenagers became friendly with the crew and one of the crew members arranged for us to use a separate small lounge room for some of our evening activities. The room was close to the ship's store and was not used by the other passengers. In the evenings we purchased Cokes and snacks which we carried into the lounge room. There were comfortable chairs, card tables, and couches where we could sit, share stories about the war, and develop the boy-girl relationships. We occasionally played card games and also found the game *spin the bottle* most enjoyable. Time passed quickly and because most of us had been confined in small European villages during the war, without proper food, life on the *Gripsholm* was like Heaven. Secretly I was hoping the trip would never end.

As previously mentioned, the Atlantic Ocean was very turbulent during our trip. The up and down movement of the ship caused many of the passengers to become seasick. The seasick passengers remained in their rooms, attempting to sleep and trying not to throw up. My mother, father and I were fortunate in that we did not become seasick but went about our activities without any problems. Unfortunately it was not very pleasant to be in the sleeping quarters of the ship, because many of the men had vomited, and even though they cleaned up their mess, the smell became unbearable in some areas. I found relief by spending my time out on the decks breathing the fresh sea air. There were many chairs on the decks, and our group of teenagers gathered, snuggling on the deck chairs covered by the warm wool blankets. With the excuse of trying to keep warm, we snuggled under the blankets with our favorite girls.

At meal time, the dining room was often partially unoccupied because of the seasick people. It was interesting to observe the up and down movement of the ship through the port holes or the large windows. As I looked out toward the front of the ship I could see the bow of the ship bob up so that only sky was visible and then as the bow descended, we only saw the ocean. It was this up and down movement that affected many people. I also discovered why the tables in the dining room had small raised edges around the perimeter: they prevented the dishes and silverware from falling off the table as the ship moved up and down or rolled from side to side. During some of the more turbulent days I observed the table settings on vacant tables actually shifting from one side to the other as the ship bobbed up and down.

We were scheduled to land in New York on February 1, 1946. On the last night out we were given a set of immigration papers to fill out on which all the questions were in English. My mother took charge of the process and managed quite well. At one point she was given a bit of help from Dorothy Anas, the girl from Greece, who spoke and wrote English very well. We had our passports in order and as a result we did not expect any problems in New York. We had made tentative plans to have the Meconi family meet us when we arrived. Esther and Egidio Meconi lived in the Bronx, and were natives of Diecimo who had emigrated to the United States about the same time as my mother and father. They had three daughters, Frances, Egle and Jo. Esther and Egidio owned a moving company called the Santiago Moving and Storage Company in the Bronx. My parents had written a letter to them from Italy when we found out our departure date and tentative arrival date. We were to telephone them as soon as we landed and they said that they would drive to the dock area to pick us up.

On February 1, in the late afternoon, the M/S *Gripsholm*, loaded with returning United States citizens from Europe, sailed past the Statue of Liberty heading for a dock in the Port of New York. As I stood on the deck, leaning on the railing, alongside my mother and father, in the cold February weather, with rain sweeping across my face, I gazed at the imposing view of the Statue of Liberty and felt that she was staring directly at me. Although I had seen pictures of the statue in books I was surprised at how tall it actually was. My mother saw me staring and said in Italian:

"Tullio, your father and I first saw the Statue of Liberty in 1920 on arriving in New York. Remember what you are observing now: it's as if she is welcoming us back to America. I have a feeling that things will be all right."

However, I felt a bit apprehensive about my arrival in New York; in fact I was afraid of what might lie ahead. I was fifteen and a half years old, had missed nearly three years of school, spoke English inadequately, and all my worldly possessions were in one suitcase.

As the *Gripsholm* maneuvered into the dock area with the aid of a tug boat, we got our suitcases together and prepared to disembark. While waiting in line at the gangplank my father said to me in English:

"Tullio, when I first came to the United States in 1908 I was almost your age, I was 14 years old. I lived with friends from Italy and was able to get a job as a dishwasher in a restaurant. I gradually started to work in the cooking section of the kitchen and eventually became a cook. It was not easy for young people then, and it won't be easy now. We are going to California and we will have to work hard to survive. America is a great country, and there is opportunity for everyone, especially if we work hard."

We took our turn at the gangplank and walked down to the dock area. We scarcely noticed that it was raining and cold because we were back in the United States of America! We walked along the dock, following directions given by a uniformed immigration official. I remember stepping in water puddles along the way, feeling the cold water splashing on my shoes and feet. We were led into a large assembly hall where our documents were checked at the door;

then we were allowed to go into the hall to wait along with the other passengers, to gather our belongings and to leave the building for an unknown world.

My father located a telephone and called the Meconi family notifying them that we had arrived and that we were ready to be picked up. I encountered some of my new friends from the ship and said good-bye again. On the ship, before arriving in New York, we had exchanged addresses and promised to write. As we said good-bye again we wished each other good luck in the future.

In what seemed to be a short period of time, Egidio Meconi arrived with his wife Esther. After we hugged and greeted one other we left the hall heading for their automobile. We loaded our suitcases in the trunk and the three of us sat together in the back seat. As Egidio left the dock area and started to drive towards the Bronx, I was able to see the New York skyline, all the lights, and all the traffic. I was fascinated by the number and size of the cars on the road. I thought to myself "Boy, it sure would be nice to be able to drive an American car !"

We stayed in the Bronx for about a week and a half. During that time my father contacted the John Hancock Insurance Company in Boston where he was able to collect a sizeable check from his annuity program which had accumulated during the years that the payments had not been sent to Italy because of the war. We had the opportunity to meet and visit with the rest of the Meconi family. Their daughters, Frances, Egle and Jo had visited us in Boston during the 1930's, so we were acquainted with them from that time. We also had the opportunity to meet their husbands. Egle had married Thor Peckel, a man of Norwegian descent, and Jo had married Robert Arminio, a high school teacher and football coach. It's funny how I remember certain small incidents. Thor wanted me to taste a piece of dark, smelly Norwegian cheese. I did not want to taste it, but he kept urging me, making me feel uncomfortable. Coach Arminio was a friendly man who talked about high school sports and gave me a new leather volleyball to take home. When I arrived in California I inflated the ball and used it as a soccer ball because I did not know about the game of volleyball. After talking with the coach I was eager to get to California and start high school so that I could participate in sports.

We left New York by boarding an overnight train for Chicago at Grand Central Station. We had contacted Harry and Julia Moroni in Chicago by telephone and they had asked us to stay with them for a few days. Julia was my mother's first cousin who had married Harry Moroni, a man from Chiesina, a town near Lucca, who had emigrated to the United States. Harry had started out in Chicago, like my father, as a dishwasher, then he became a cook and chef, and eventually opened his own restaurant in Chicago, the *Corona Cafè*. Harry was a successful businessman whose two sons were also working in his restaurant. They lived in a lovely, large home in the suburbs of Chicago where we stayed with them for four or five days. Julia took me to see my first American movie in a local theater, *Unconquered*, with Gary Cooper and Paulette Goddard, which I thought was an exciting adventure film.

We were driven to the train station by Harry in his 1942 Buick to catch the evening train to Oakland, California, a journey of three days. The train ride from New York to Chicago had been pleasant and short. During the overnight trip we were able to sleep in the nice, over-stuffed reclining chairs. The train from Chicago, bound for the West Coast, was a different story. The seats were wooden slat benches and were very uncomfortable to sit on. We were able to get up and walk around during the day, to have our meals in the dining car, but at night we had to remain in our seats. I remember trying to sleep sitting up and finding the experience very uncomfortable. My father had problems with his feet because his ankles swelled up during the night and he could barely walk when he woke up in the morning.

Before we left Chicago we telephoned my mother's aunt Marianna Guadagni who lived in South San Francisco and gave her our approximate arrival time and the train number. She said that she would meet us at the Oakland train station. When we arrived in Oakland, around mid-morning, we were greeted by Aunt Marianna and her son-in-law, Leo Scardigli, who drove his 1937 Chevrolet sedan to pick us up. We loaded up the trunk of the car with our suitcases and climbed into the back seat of the car to make the trip from Oakland to South San Francisco. I had seen pictures of San Francisco, but was not aware of the geographic location of Oakland, the Bay Bridge, the Golden Gate Bridge, or of South San Francisco. I thought that perhaps it was a part of San Francisco, like South Boston.

As we were driven across the Bay Bridge, heading toward San Francisco, I was astonished by the view of the city, the Bay, Alcatraz Island, and the Golden Gate Bridge. As we arrived on the San Francisco side of the bridge and headed south on the Bayshore highway, I then realized that South San Francisco was a separate city. When we arrived in South San Francisco we turned right off the Bayshore highway and headed up a street called Grand Avenue. I noticed several bars and restaurants in the first few blocks and an Italian clothing store named Santini and Roccucci. We drove by the City Hall and as I looked up toward the mountain, behind the City Hall, I saw huge white letters that spelled out SOUTH SAN FRANCISCO THE INDUS-TRIAL CITY. Shortly after that we arrived at our destination, Marianna Guadagni's house, on the corner of Grand and Magnolia Avenues. This was mid-February, 1946.

A few months later I was able to secure my first job as a dishwasher at the *Skyway Cafè* at Mills Field which later

became San Francisco International Airport. I earned $1.00
per hour working the swing shift on Sunday afternoons from
3 to 11 p.m. By the time I started my job I had already
enrolled in the second semester of the tenth grade at South
San Francisco High School. After I completed my first
Sunday work shift, I took the Greyhound bus from Mills
Field to Grand Avenue and then walked about one mile to
my aunt's house. As I was walking along, I thought about
what my father had said to me when we arrived in New
York. Indeed America was a land of opportunity! I had a
job, I was attending school, I was earning $8.00 per week,
and if I worked hard enough I could follow in my father's
footsteps and become a cook.

Tullio Bertini with former Buffalo Soldier, 2LT Harry Cox, at the home
of Tullio in Millbrae, CA, looking over a relief map showing the
location of the Gothic Line.

Epilogue

Nello Bertini, my father, got his first job in California as a cook in a restaurant in Marin County called *The Buckeye* in March 1946, shortly after we arrived. We continued to live with my Aunt Marianna and her daughter Edith in South San Francisco on Grand Avenue. My father stayed at the restaurant during his work week and came home by bus on his days off. His schedule was demanding and he found it quite difficult. Fortunately, about a month after he started at *The Buckeye*, he got a job on the night shift at the *Skyway Cafè* at Mills Field. He also got a dishwashing job for me on Sunday afternoons 3 to 11 p.m. I was a good worker and expanded my job to Saturdays and Sundays, working weekdays during the summer, and eventually becoming a bus boy. Later, my father found a better daytime job with the United Air Lines kitchen during the time that the airline began to establish in-flight meals.

In the fall of 1946, we purchased a two bedroom home built by Ferruccio Corruccini at 310 West Orange Avenue in South San Francisco. My father had enough money for the down payment, got a mortgage, and once again we moved into an empty house. At that time my father was earning about $10.00 an hour as a cook.

My father became acquainted with Lyle Johnson in South San Francisco, who was planning to open a new restaurant, named *Lyle's*, on El Camino Real. My father agreed to work with Lyle as the chef. However, he suffered another heart attack and died on August 14, 1947; he was 53 years old.

Ada Marcucci Bertini, my mother, was 48 years old when my father died. She was emotionally distraught and felt abandoned in this large country. Her mother and father were in Italy, along with her two brothers, Nello and Dante. Her only link to Italy was her Aunt Marianna and family in South San Francisco. Fortunately my father had purchased two small life insurance policies through United Airlines in the amount of $16,000, which she used to pay off our mortgage, and, after funeral expenses, she was left with about $6,000.00 which she placed in a savings account. Later, she also paid off the balance due on our trip to the Federal Government. While I worked and attended school, she worked as a seamstress for the *Wardrobe Cleaners* in South San Francisco.

On August 7, 1955, I married Jeanne Daly, from Altamont, California, whom I met at San Francisco State College during the summer of 1954. Jeanne was an elementary school teacher in Millbrae, having received her teaching credential from San José State College in 1953. Shortly after our marriage, my mother returned to Italy to live with her mother in Pieve di Compito. In 1958, she moved to her native village of Diecimo, living in the same house we left in 1946. She remained there, except for a few trips to California to spend time with her two grandchildren, Robert, born in 1965, and Bill, born in 1968. As she got older, she found it more and more difficult to travel; as a result, she made her last trip to the United States in 1976. One or more members of our family visited her nearly every year until her death in April 1991 at the age of 91.

INDEX

DANTE UNIVERSITY PRESS, Inc.
17 Station Street Box 843
Brookline Village, MA 02147
Tel (617) 734-2045; Fax (617) 734-2046;
Web Page: danteuniversity.org

BOOKS OF ITALIAN AMERICAN INTEREST

AMERICA'S ITALIAN FOUNDING FATHERS by Adolph Caso includes works by Beccaria and Mazzei. Cloth, ill., ISBN 0-8283-1640-4, $25.95.

DANTE IN THE 20TH CENTURY by Adolph Caso et al includes articles by several American and European scholars on Dante. Ill., ISBN 0-9378-3216-2, $25.95.

ISSUES IN FOREIGN LANGUAGE AND BILINGUAL EDUCATION by Adolph Caso recounts the plight of limited English-speaking students and their struggle to introduce the Italian language into our public schools. ISBN 0-8283-1721-6, $11.95.

LIVES OF ITALIAN AMERICANS--They Too Made This Country Great by Adolph Caso has 50 biographies of those who contributed in the formation of the U.S. Cloth, ill., ISBN 0-8283-1699-6, $15.95.

MASS MEDIA VS. THE ITALIAN AMERICANS by Adolph Caso explores, critically, the image of Italian Americans. Paper, ill., ISBN 0-8283-1831-X, $11.95.

ODE TO AMERICA'S INDEPENDENCE by Vittorio Alfieri is the first such composition written on the emerging nation, in Italian and English by Adolph Caso. Paper, ISBN 0-8283-1667-8, $11.95.

ON CRIMES AND PUNISHMENTS by Cesare Beccaria influenced Jefferson, Adams, Washington and many more. To a great degree, America owes its present form of government on this book. Int. by Adolph Caso, paper, ISBN 0-8283-1800-X, $5.95.

PAGES AND WINDOWS by Adolph Caso, is a macro package for writers, editors and publishers using WordPerfect 5.1. Paper, ISBN 0-828301989-8, $19.95.

ROMEO AND JULIET--Original Text of Masuccio, Da Porto, Bandello, and Shakespeare. Edited and with an Introduction of

Adolph Caso. "A rose by any other name would smell as sweet." Cloth, ISBN 0-937832-4, $19.95.

STRAW OBELISK The by Adolph Caso: effects of World War II on a southern Italian village. Cloth, Ill. 0-8283-2005-5, $24.95. (See review below.) *

TO AMERICA AND AROUND THE WORLD--The Logs of Columbus and Magellan by Christopher Columbus and Antonio Pigafetta contains the first reports on the first voyage to America and the first voyage around the world, edited and with an introduction by Adolph Caso. Cloth, ill., ISBN 0-8283-1992-8, $25.95.

TUSKEGEE AIRMEN--The Men Who Changed A Nation. Charles E. Francis. 4th Edition--Revised, UpDated and Enlarged by Colonel Adolph Caso. Long before the Civil Rights movement, the Tuskegee Airmen were already living and fighting for equality. As a result, by integrating the Armed Forces, they integrated the whole nation. Their combat feats over the Italian peninsula have become legendary. This volume of over 500 pages contains about 100 photos, an appendix full of documents, and an Index of 25 pages. ISBN 0-8283-2029-2, hard cover, $29.95.

WATER AND LIFE by Adolph Caso contains poems in the original English and Italian. Paper, ISBN 0-8283-1682-1, $11.95.

YOUNG ROCKY--A True Story of Attilio (Rocky) Castellani by Kinney-Caso tells the life story of a great boxer. Paper, ill., ISBN 0-8283-1802-2, $11.95.

WE, THE PEOPLE--Formative Documents of America's Democracy by Adolph Caso contains document and lengthy commentary on the formation of America's Democracy. Cloth, Ill. ISBN 0-8283-2006-3, $22.95.

DANCE OF THE TWELVE APOSTLES by P.J. Carisella reveals Italy's biggest sabotage of a German plan to destroy Rome. Cloth, ill., ISBN 0-8283-1935-9, $19.95.

FROGMEN--FIRST BATTLES by William Schofield and P. J. Carisella tell an authenticated story of the birth and deployment of underwater guerrilla warfare by the Italians of the World War II. Cloth, ill., ISBN 0-8283-1998-7, $19.95.

INFERNO by Dante Alighieri, by Nicholas Kilmer, illustrated by Benjamin Martinez, is rendered into modern English with a separate illustration for each canto. Cloth, ISBN 0-9378-3228-6,

$19.50.

IMPERIAL GINA--The Very Un-Authorized Biography of Gina Lollobrigida by Luis Canales tells the story of this great Italian woman and actress. Cloth, ill., ISBN 0-8283-1932-4, $19.95.

ITALIAN CONVERSATION by Adele Gorjanc offers easy to follow lessons. Paper, ISBN 0-8283-1670-8, $11.95.

ROGUE ANGEL--A Novel of Fra Filippo Lippi by Carol Damioli traces the tumultuous life of this Renaissance man who was both a great artist and womanizer. Cloth, ill., ISBN 0-9378-3233-2, $21.95.

TALES OF MADNESS by Luigi Pirandello, translated with an introduction by Giovanni Bussino, includes of the best of Pirandello's short stories dealing with the theme of human madness. Cloth, ISBN 0-9378-3226-X, $17.95.

TALES OF SUICIDE by Luigi Pirandello, translated with an introduction by Giovanni Bussino, includes some of the best of Pirandello's short stories dealing with suicide. Paper, ISBN 0-9378-3231-6, $14.95.

TRAPPED IN TUSCANY by Tullio Bertini, tells his story, from his birth in Boston, to his move to pre-World War II Italy to his return to California. A must for every Italian American. Paper, illustrated, ISBN 0-9378-32359, 19.95.

* Caso, Adolph. *The Straw Obelisk. (Review)*

This strange, antiwar novel is set in post-World War II Italy where Samuele, a young soldier ill with consumption, returns to his village much changed by the horrors he witnessed in battle. Always hot tempered, he is now more accepting of human foibles. This contrasts sharply with the often harsh traditions of the village. A young married woman pays with her life for a momentary indiscretion, and many feel her murder justified. Not Samuele, who tracks down the killer, who happens to be her husband and his friend. The obelisk of the title is a tall, intricately detailed structure that must be transported using dangerous maneuvers, but Samuele uses his waning strength to lead the effort in bringing this symbol of love and peace to the town square. Although not poetic, the writing is competent and does evoke the reality of village life. For the fiction collections of large public libraries. *Library Journal* May 1995

At your local stores, or directly from the Dante University of America Press:

Visa-Master Card orders only: 1-800-359-7031, Or, send check or money order to above address. (**Postage and Handling: $5 first book, $1 each additional**).